Secessionism and Terr

This book examines secessionist terrorism in a comparative context across Europe and Eurasia.

The volume seeks to uncover comparative linkages between terrorism and secessionism; specifically examining terrorist organizations that also have a political goal of independence. It examines a wide range of case studies, including the IRA in Northern Ireland, ETA in the Basque Country, FLNC in Corsica and ARD in Brittany, KLA in Kosovo, PKK and TAK in Turkish Kurdistan, and IK in Chechnya. In doing so, the book shows the linkages in terrorist tactics and demands, as well as when and how ceasefires come into place. Ultimately, none of the terrorist organizations studied here has obtained their maximalist goal of gaining independence, but each has caused significant bloodshed, and has contributed to the debate on the future of governance in Europe and Eurasia. The major strength of this format is to glean wider lessons on ethno-nationalism, as well as the causes and outcomes of terrorist actions. Each case study also updates the literature on the individual cases to provide the most recent account of events in these countries.

This book will be of much interest to students of terrorism and political violence, ethnic conflict, nationalism, European politics and International Relations in general.

Glen M.E. Duerr is Associate Professor of International Studies, Cedarville University, USA, and is author of *Secessionism and the European Union* (2015).

Political Violence
Series Editor: John G. Horgan
Georgia State University, USA
Founding Editor: David Rapoport

This book series contains sober, thoughtful, and authoritative academic accounts of terrorism and political violence. Its aim is to produce a useful taxonomy of terror and violence through comparative and historical analysis in both national and international spheres. Each book discusses origins, organizational dynamics and outcomes of particular forms and expressions of political violence.

Victims of Terrorism
A comparative and interdisciplinary study
Edited by Orla Lynch and Javier Argomaniz

Lone-Actor Terrorists
A behavioural analysis
Paul Gill

Evolutionary Psychology and Terrorism
Edited by Max Taylor, Jason Roach and Ken Pease

Understanding Apocalyptic Terrorism
Countering the radical mindset
Frances L. Flannery

Understanding Terrorism Innovation and Learning
Al-Qaeda and beyond
Edited by Magnus Ranstorp and Magnus Normark

Terrorist Histories
Individuals and political violence since the 19th Century
Caoimhe Nic Dháibhéid

Secessionism and Terrorism
Bombs, Blood, and Independence in Europe and Eurasia
Edited by Glen M.E. Duerr

For more information about this series, please visit: www.routledge.com/Political-Violence/book-series/SE0196

Secessionism and Terrorism

Bombs, Blood, and Independence in Europe and Eurasia

Edited by Glen M.E. Duerr

LONDON AND NEW YORK

First published 2019
by Routledge

2 Park Square, Milton Park, Abingdon, Oxfordshire OX14 4RN
52 Vanderbilt Avenue, New York, NY 10017

Routledge is an imprint of the Taylor & Francis Group, an informa business

First issued in paperback 2020

British Library Cataloguing-in-Publication Data
A catalogue record for this book is available from the British Library

Library of Congress Cataloging-in-Publication Data
A catalog record has been requested for this book

ISBN: 978-1-138-59551-4 (hbk)
ISBN: 978-0-367-66599-9 (pbk)

Typeset in Times New Roman
by Wearset Ltd, Boldon, Tyne and Wear

For my parents, Michael and Jane Duerr

Contents

Illustrations

Figures

Tables

Contributors

Glen M.E. Duerr is Associate Professor of International Studies at Cedarville University. Born in the United Kingdom, he moved to Canada as a teenager where he obtained a B.A. from the University of Western Ontario and a M.A. from the University of Windsor, he then moved to the United States where he completed his Ph.D. from Kent State University. He is the author of the 2015 book, *Secessionism and the European Union: The Future of Flanders, Scotland, and Catalonia.*

John Sutcliffe is an Associate Professor of Political Science at the University of Windsor, Ontario, Canada where he is also Department Chair. His research interests include municipal politics in Scotland and Ontario, as well as the politics of the U.S.-Canada border.

Geoffrey Alchin is currently a research assistant at the University of Windsor. He has recently completed his Master of Arts degree in Political Science at the University of Windsor. In addition, he has also co-authored two papers for the Fraser Institute on British Columbia's upcoming electoral reform referendum.

Britt Cartrite (Ph.D., University of Colorado Boulder, 2003) is Professor of Political Science and Associate Provost at Alma College. Dr. Cartrite's research explores regionalism in Western Europe broadly, and his most recent publication, with Dan Miodownik, is "Determinants of Regional Political Distinctiveness," *Nationalism and Ethnic Politics* (2016).

Liam Anderson is currently a Professor of Political Science at Wright State University, where he teaches classes in Comparative Politics and International Relations. His research interests focus on issues of constitutional design, particularly the use of ethnic autonomy arrangements in divided societies.

Elena Pokalova is an Associate Professor of International Security Studies at the National Defense University, Washington DC. Dr. Pokalova has a vast record of publications, including her book *Chechnya's Terrorist Network: The Evolution of Terrorism in Russia's North Caucasus*. Her articles have appeared in such journals as *Terrorism and Political Violence*, *Critical*

Studies on Terrorism, *Studies in Conflict and Terrorism*, and the *Journal of Balkan and Near Eastern Studies*.

Vaughn Shannon is an associate professor of political science at Wright State University's School of Public and International Affairs. Dr. Shannon earned his Ph.D. at Ohio State University, with emphasis on international security, political psychology, and Middle East politics. Dr. Shannon has authored three books, including co-editing *Psychology and Constructivism in International Relations: An Ideational Alliance* (Michigan, 2011), and published several peer-review articles on international relations and the Middle East.

Acknowledgments

This book is a compilation of the work of many people. To start, the contributors have each given graciously of their time and expertise to create a volume that is expansive in scope, and presents information and answers on a range of diverse cases throughout Europe and Eurasia. Each contributor also has a family, and a support system through which the completion of their respective chapters was made possible. To all of these people, I offer my heartfelt thanks.

On a personal level, I would like to first thank my family. My wife, Rebecca, has, as always, provided steadfast support for my academic endeavors. She is deserving of special recognition here for being the rock upon which our family moves forward. My children, Declan, Harper, and Camille, provided a constant source of enjoyment in the midst of researching, studying, and writing about a troubling subject matter like terrorism. I am also thankful for my in-laws, Dr. Hugh and Connie Miller, for helping Rebecca and I with our young children, and for lovingly supporting us all the time. I would finally like to thank my parents, Michael and Jane Duerr, without whom the ideas for this book would never have germinated. It is with immense gratitude that I dedicate this book to them.

I am thankful to the students at Cedarville University representing a campus branch of the American Enterprise Institute for supporting a presentation by three of the authors (myself, Liam Anderson, and Vaughn Shannon) on March 2, 2017. The panel discussion was attended by over 125 students, faculty and staff members, as well as guests; their thoughtful questions helped to mold and refine this project. I am also thankful for a discussion in Washington D.C. on the substantive chapters of the book. My students Molly Bolender, Mae Dewhurst, Esther Holm, Amanda Kwak, and Sarah (Schopps) Rea all had the opportunity to read sections of the book, and provided valuable feedback on each of the chapters. Throughout the course of writing, compiling, and editing this project, several talented Research Assistants have been essential to the completion of this book. They are Michael Wilt, Sarah (Schopps) Rea, Jacob Mach, Marcus Waterman, Lauren Payne, Spencer Woody, and Kelly Parliament, all exceptional students (and former students) in the Department of History and Government at Cedarville University.

Additionally, I would like to personally thank a number of other students who took most, if not all, of the following courses with me: International Relations,

Comparative Politics, History and Politics of Western Europe, History and Politics of Russia and Eastern Europe, and International and Domestic Terrorism. Their work in these classes, as well as their astute questions, means that they contributed to this book. They are: Molly Bolender, Annie (Evans) Bruza, Jacob Calloway, Emily Guilliams, Jake Hibbitt, Esther Holm, Amanda Kwak, Vincenzo Morrone, Rebekah Noyes, Marshall Pickering, Briana Sadowski, Jesse Thompson, Christian Townsend, and Ben Warder. For anyone I may have missed, I sincerely apologize.

I am thankful for the support of numerous colleagues in my department. In particular, Frank Jenista, Patrick Oliver, and Mark Caleb Smith took a major interest in this project, and helped me with pertinent, political, diplomatic, and security questions. I would also like to express my appreciation to the administration at Cedarville University for providing a grant and a course release to complete this project.

Finally, I would like to thank the courteous and professional staff members and editors at Routledge (and various subsidiaries) for their work on this manuscript. Andrew Humprhys, Alan Jarvis, Pip Clubbs, and Bethany Lund Yates were all exceptionally helpful throughout the process. I would also like to thank Eilidh McGregor for her outstanding work editing all of these chapters in meticulous detail.

With the help of these many people, I humbly offer this volume as a contribution to the academic literature, and to the motivations and outcomes of terrorism. They have all helped me to put together a volume that hopefully can provide background, some answers, and analysis to this horrific subject that bestows so much damage upon people and their families. However, for all of the faults and shortcomings of this volume, I alone accept the limitations.

SDG
Glen M.E. Duerr
New York, NY, USA
March 26, 2018

1 Introduction: secessionism and terrorism

Glen M.E. Duerr

On February 7, 1991, three mortar bombs were launched by the Provisional Irish Republican Army (PIRA) at the rear of 10 Downing Street, the Official Residence of the British Prime Minister. The target of the attack was John Major, the new Conservative Party Prime Minister who had recently taken over from Prime Minister Margaret Thatcher. At the time of the attack, Major was in 10 Downing Street meeting with his cabinet to discuss the Gulf War. There were no fatalities, but three people were injured as a consequence of this attack.

My father, Michael Duerr, was working in his office at Teleglobe in central London (Stag Place by Victoria Station), just a few hundred yards away from 10 Downing Street at the time of the attack, and heard the mortars detonate. Both my mother (Jane Duerr) and father, who, at times, worked in central London from the late-1970s to the mid-1990s, faced numerous situations when their trains were delayed and their workplaces closed because of bombings or bomb threats. For example, very soon after the 10 Downing Street attack, there were PIRA attacks launched at the Victoria and Paddington Stations, just 11 days after the attempt on John Major. The Victoria Station attack resulted in the death of one person, 38 injuries, thousands of pounds sterling of damage, and major delays for commuters in the City of London. In terms of fatalities and injuries, the Victoria Station attack was the worst bombing on London since the 1983 Harrods attack. Throughout the year 1991, the PIRA initiated numerous attacks, especially around Greater London. All of these terrorist attacks occurred within a period known as the Time of Troubles, which began in 1968, and ended with the Good Friday Agreement in 1998. These attacks, and the discussions at the dinner table, resulted in a lifelong quest to consider what happened, and to gain greater insight into the root causes of terrorism.

This volume investigates secessionist terrorism across major cases in Europe and Eurasia. A common element in all of these cases is (in some cases, was) that there is an asymmetric power struggle between the supporters of independence or, at the least, of greater autonomy, who represent a subnational unit and the central government. Sometimes the rebels, or people representing a subnational unit, engage in armed conflict, which can lead to protracted conflicts (Hironaka 2005). However, in many areas, the rebels do not have the ability to fight against the central government, and thus opt for terrorist tactics as a means of agitating for independence. Secession is the "formal withdrawal from a central authority by a member unit" (Wood 1981, 110), which also includes a component of international recognition (Bartkus 1999). Secession is a rare event in world politics, especially in mature democratic countries (Dion 1996). Moreover, secessionist movements do not typically garner much sympathy among the international community, especially when terrorism is used. In the end, secession is only viewed as a legitimate force in hindsight (Buchheit 1978).

Another point of commonality, political violence erupted in each of the cases at some point over contestation within the society, sometimes cultural (Ross 2007). Terrorism often arises given the asymmetric nature of each conflict, wherein one side is much more powerful than the other; in most examples, the government is the strong "legitimate" holder of power, although others may consider this power to be illegitimate and resort to violence as a means of reacting against state power. Thus, terrorism may seem to be a natural outcome—perceived repression on the part of separatists leads to a violent response, but not through military means because of the gulf in power capabilities. Yet, as the chapters in this volume will highlight, terrorist action looks very different across lots of cases. And, in some cases, terrorism is viewed as repulsive even among groups who have a deep desire for sovereignty and recognition in the international community.

Obviously, there is a centuries-long historical backdrop to the Time of the Troubles in Northern Ireland and the terrorist actions of the Irish Republican Army (IRA), but as I later learned, my experience in my childhood home in the southeast of England was not an isolated one. As in the United Kingdom (UK), people living in similar situations in Spain and France had been impacted by the terrorist violence committed by Euskadi Ta Askatasuna (ETA), an ethnonationalist[1] terrorist organization in the Basque Country. Elsewhere in France, terrorist organizations had waged similar campaigns in Corsica and Brittany. The province of Kosovo in the old Yugoslavia faced a prolonged period of violent conflict related to terrorist activities. Parts of Turkey were frequent targets of the Partiya Karkerên Kurdistanê (PKK), known in English as the Kurdistan Workers' Party, and the Teyrêbazên Azadiya Kurdistan (TAK), Kurdistan Freedom Hawks. Finally, in Russia, Chechen terrorists have likewise committed acts of terror. The situations across each of these cases are clearly different, and judgments should be reserved until learning of the idiosyncrasies and issues within each one. Nevertheless, the comparison raises two important, academic questions: What are the connections and linkages between secessionism and terrorism? How can governments best employ counterterrorism measures through policing and military measures, but also through policy changes?

Because of these similar situations across a broad range of cases in Europe and Eurasia, this volume assesses a range of different cases. Chapter 2 focuses on the IRA in Northern Ireland (UK) and is written by John Sutcliffe and Geoffrey Alchin. Britt Cartrite authors Chapter 3 on ETA in the Basque Country within Spain and, to a lesser extent, France. The dual cases of Front de Libération

Nationale Corse (FLNC), the National Liberation Front of Corsica, in Corsica and Armée Révolutionnaire Bretonne (ARB), the Breton Revolutionary Army in Brittany (France) written by Liam Anderson is the subject of Chapter 4. In Chapter 5, Elena Pokalova describes the case of the Kosovo Liberation Army (KLA) in Kosovo within the wider Yugoslav conflict. In the context of Turkish Kurdistan, the PKK and TAK are the central groups examined by Vaughn Shannon in Chapter 6. Liam Anderson discusses Имарат Кавказ Imarat Kavkaz (IK) in Chechnya (Russia) in Chapter 7. The chapters are ordered as such to reflect geography—moving from west to east across Europe in a reasonably fluid motion, albeit like that of a wave cresting and moving across the continent. Finally, the volume concludes with my own chapter on why terrorism emerged as a norm in some separatist regions, but not in others. The chapter specifically examines the cases of the Front du Libération du Québec (FLQ) in Quebec, Scottish National Liberation Army (SNLA) in Scotland, and Terra Lluire (TL) in Catalonia.

In many ways, the linkages between secessionism and terrorism become apparent in these chapters. Terrorism is possible in any place where a power asymmetry exists between distinct groups. It is important to note that many supporters of independence also try to work within existing democratic structures where possible to obtain their maximalist goal: secession.

The substantive case study chapters contained in this book are all directed by the following format: (1) present a general overview of the case, (2) provide a history of political grievances in the specific region as to why a secessionist movement exists including theoretical dimensions to the discussion, (3) present a rebuttal from the viewpoint of the government; again, including theoretical dimensions, (4) provide an overview of major terrorist attacks carried out by the terrorist organization being studied, (5) explain how the government responded to these terrorist attacks, (6) describe any changes that have occurred with regards to the structure of the state, or any government agencies, as a means of undercutting support for secessionism or the terrorist organization, and (7) conclusions relevant to each of the cases.

Each of the contributors was given freedom within this structure to make arguments suitable to their own substantive areas of interest. For example, different authors prefer slightly distinctions in terminology such as secessionist terrorism, nationalist terrorism, or ethno-nationalism. Where it makes sense, uniformity is imposed. A second example is the extent to which each scholar interacted with the academic literature. In some cases, their argument fit a particular strain of thought within a wider debate; others chose to limit the theoretical discussion to increase the details of the case. The Breton and Corsican cases cover a range of different theoretical possibilities; Northern Ireland is perhaps most strongly tied to the notion of consociationalism, which is why the authors focused on the topic of institutional structure based in tandem with religious affiliation. Some of the cases are also highly contested, so the authors often chose a more moderate approach by discussing a range of different theoretical perspectives, or focusing on one specific aspect of the case. Again, where the situation makes sense, a level of uniformity is otherwise imposed. Interestingly, this project has many similarities to the cases that all revolve around ethno-nationalist terrorism, even though there are divergent authors writing in a volume that is centrally orchestrated.

For this major reason, there is diversity in the theoretical and methodological approaches to these chapters. However, this broad approach best helps the reader understand the myriad different views on terrorism, and how terrorist groups can be defeated, while simultaneously also seeking to treat the people in these regions well so that they are better governed. Each chapter is relatively uniform stretching between 8,000 and 12,000 words. The exception here is Chapter 4 on Corsican and Breton nationalism. The reason for this chapter—in excess of 13,500 words—is that it effectively covers two cases within one state.

Each of the contributors is considered an expert in his or her area of specialty. Four of the six contributors were born—and raised—in Europe or Russia; the other two have spent copious amounts of time in their regions of interest, including dissertation research and other fieldwork. All of the contributors now live in North America, a purposeful point in the selection process to more objectively and dispassionately view the events of terrorism in Europe and Eurasia from some distance.

Some of the cases such as the IRA or ETA are well-known, and a vast literature exists on these groups. Other groups, especially in Brittany, Corsica, and Kosovo are typically less well-known. Some groups still operate in the present and are relevant to ongoing policy discussions such as the PKK in Turkey; others have recently disbanded such as ETA in the Basque Country of Spain. The key component in this volume is to find common linkages across these different cases, so that lessons may be learned as a means of more competent counterterrorism and for better governing people.

Ethno-nationalist/secessionist terrorism in the academic literature

The academic literature on terrorism is vast. Since 9/11, renewed interest in the field has led to the publication of thousands of works related to terrorism. The field has a significant history that encompasses dozens of cases across the world (Laqueur and Alexander 1978; Laqueur 1987). Some works on terrorism specifically examine groups with an in-depth discussion of cultural and political elements, which is particularly useful in assessing different cases (Crenshaw 1981; Pape 2005). Literature on ethno-nationalist, or secessionist terrorism is also extensive but usually revolves around single cases, like those discussed within this volume, or cases like the Tamil Tigers in Sri Lanka and the Uighurs in China, among others (Tambiah 1997; Wayland 2004). Some scholars have examined the overlap between nationalism and terrorism broadly (Volkan 1998). In both fields, terrorism and nationalism, there are myriad different working definitions and viewpoints on how to best understand these subjects. Lack of consensus on the definitions of terrorism and nationalism make defining a particular viewpoint challenging.

The political scientist, David Rapoport's, four "waves" thesis is long-standing as a framework on terrorist time periods (Rapoport 2013). The first wave, Anarchist, started in the 1880s through the 1920s. For example, terrorist acts on Tsar Nicholas II of Russia, and the assassination of Archduke Franz Ferdinand—a catalyst for World War I—in 1914. The second wave, Anti-colonial terrorism, started in the 1920s and lasted through the 1960s. The overarching goal was to liberate colonial societies and gain de jure statehood, replete with entrance into major international organizations such as the United Nations. The third wave, The New Left Wing, began in the 1960s and ended in the 1990s. Conflicts like Vietnam and the Palestinian/Israel struggle fit into this category. The fourth wave, The Religious Wave, started in the 1990s and runs through the present. Religious terrorism is predominantly Islamist in nature given the Iranian Revolution of 1979, and the Soviet invasion of Afghanistan (Rapoport 2013).

Rapoport also denoted three types of "traditional terrorism": left, right, and ethno-separatist. In this volume, the focus is on ethno-separatist terrorism, but this type may be interconnected with leftist or rightist terrorism depending on the case. Additionally, the focus of all of the chapters is the democratic state in the west. Paul Wilkinson's (1986) book entitled, *Terrorism and the Liberal State*, presents an overview of the impacts of terrorism on liberal states in the world. Many of the cases of ethno-nationalist terrorism described in this volume occur in liberal states, especially the cases within the UK, France, and Spain. The challenges of maintaining a mature, robust democracy in the face of terrorist violence are myriad. Yet, the occurrence of terrorism within these states speaks to contestation, abhorrent as it may be, to the contestation framework of the state. It is argued that some form of autonomy or federal structure may well work, it is argued, as a mechanism to offset violence. However, the academic literature is split in terms of an outcome, and shows that granting autonomy in some cases leads to a reduction in violence, and in other cases to independence for the group, thus exacerbating similar claims for more power (Bird *et al.* 2010).

This volume concentrates largely on secessionist terrorism, also known as ethno-nationalist terrorism. However, given the array of different actors and terrorist groups operating throughout Europe and Eurasia, there is crossover with other forms of terrorism. Some groups, for example, have Marxist or broadly leftist leanings. The Breton Revolutionary Army/Breton Liberation Front (ARB/FLB) in Brittany was strongly tied to a Marxist ideology (see Chapter 4). Some level of Marxist connection is evident in several of the cases, especially when an economic grievance is present. However, this depends on elites in the society as this connection is not true in all subnational units, even when economic deprivation is a central factor in the grievances of the group.

Separatism is defined by one of the contributors to this volume, Elena Pokalova (2010, 430), as "a self-determination movement on the basis of an ethno-nationalist identity that encompasses claims ranging from increased cultural and political rights to struggles for territorial independence." In tandem with this definition, secession is defined as "the formal withdrawal from a central authority by a member unit" (Dion 1996). Other scholars add an important element to a definition of secession—international recognition. Thus, a definition of secession includes the "formal withdrawal from an established, internationally recognized state by a constituent unit to create a new, sovereign state" (Bartkus 1999, 3), or "a demand for formal withdrawal from a central political authority by a member unit or units on the basis of a claim to independent sovereign status" (Wood 1981, 110). All of the chapters contained herein grapple with terrorism starting with this baseline definition surrounding ethno-nationalist/separatist terrorism.

In general, secession is a rare event in world politics. Secession is even more rare in well-established democratic states (Dion 1996). In fact, the last case of secession in the West was the Republic of Ireland from the UK in 1921, and even then, the Irish Free State, as it was known, remained a dominion of the British Empire until severing ties through a constitution in 1937, and decoupling from the monarchy in 1948. Secession is typically viewed as illegitimate and anathema to existing state structures; secession is only really viewed as legitimate in hindsight (Buchheit 1978).

None of the terrorist organizations in this book has proven successful in achieving their political goals. However, many of the governments have devolved powers to more local levels as a means of pacifying overt demands for independence. Northern Ireland is still part of the UK, but now enjoys some devolved powers in a representative assembly. The Basque Country is still an autonomous community in Spain (some of the historic Basque territory also overlaps into Navarre)—part of the traditional Basque area also encompasses a small part of southwestern France. Brittany and Corsica are regions in France, although they both managed to avoid being amalgamated into a larger region in the 2016 administrative reorganization. Kurdistan is still fully enveloped within Turkey; some ethnic Kurdish kin also reside in neighboring Syria, Iraq, and Iran. Finally, Chechnya remains one of Russia's 83 subnational units, albeit with the status of Crimea and Sevastopol being under the control of Moscow despite the objection of the international community.

The possible exception is the Kosovo Liberation Army that mobilized into a political force, and now governs the territory of Kosovo. Although Kosovo enjoys widespread international recognition, its territorial status is still widely contested—Kosovo is not a member of the United Nations (UN) or the European Union (EU). Again, Moscow's opinion diverges widely from the rest of the international community. The difference, however, is that Russia has some support as dozens of countries still do not recognize Pristina (Kosovo's capital) as an international capital; in Crimea, the opposition to Russian annexation is virtually uniform in the international community.

All of the regions/subnational units studied in this volume have histories as independent units, replete with cultural and often linguistic distinctions. In some cases, these territorial distinctions are long-standing, going back centuries.

Coupled with these independent histories are parallel histories of assimilation within larger states wherein culture and language, where applicable, have been subjugated.

In some senses, secession should be crudely defined as a binary: secession or no secession. Either the event occurs, or it does not. This volume, however, delves deeper into the subject by examining how governments have responded to terrorist organizations by providing some measures of autonomy. A discussion of autonomy provides an extra level of depth to secession because it highlights a continuum of powers that the state can offer to subnational units. Of course, autonomy is difficult to measure, but policy changes can be listed so as to display levels of autonomy by comparison with other cases.

Terrorism, as noted earlier, is defined in numerous different ways, and almost every government and every scholar have a slightly different definition. Nonetheless, some common elements are present in numerous definitions of terrorism. First, there is a violent act. This violent act might include assassinations, bombings, using a vehicle as a weapon etc. The violent act may be very crude, such as a knife attack, or can be very sophisticated, as in hijacking an airliner that is subsequently crashed into a major building. Second, the attack is carried out by a possible range of actors. This may include individuals, covert government agents, or non-state actors including several cells of terrorists. Thus, terrorist attacks may be carried out by "lone wolf" terrorists, but also by highly coordinated cells of extremely motivated people. Formal government agents seeking to do damage to a target may even sponsor terrorist attacks. Third, the attack has the potential to inflict pain on a civilian target even though some forms of terrorism target a political elite, such as an assassination, or an assassination attempt. As noted in the first paragraph of this book, the attack on 10 Downing Street had a particular political target, but it could have killed or injured civilians who happened to be in the vicinity of the bomb—in this sense, terrorism is indiscriminate in its definition. Fourth, terrorism thrives off of the element of surprise. Clandestine methods are used to attack a target, which may surprise a person, or a large group of people. These methods may include bombs at transportation hubs located in garbage cans, or detonated via a suicide vest. In the case of 9/11, a hijacked airliner was crashed into high profile targets in the United States; virtually the whole world was caught off guard by the boldness and severity of the attacks in 2001. Fifth, there is a psychological element that is designed to impact the population with a general view towards creating fear. This fear may cause many to question the current government, or public policy ideas. These questions may then lead to pressure on the government to initiate changes in the society. Finally, and in tandem with the third point, there is a desire to change public policy. The terrorists seek to change an existing political relationship, which may even include gaining independence. In the case of this volume, the maximalist goal of the terrorist organizations is the creation of a new state replete with de jure international recognition at the UN. Many scholars, policymakers, governments, and organizations will add various other elements to a definition of terrorism, especially when a legal element is involved in prosecuting terrorists. However, in general, these six elements exist in every minimalist definition of terrorism.

Plan of this book

The structure of this book, as alluded to earlier in this introduction, is as follows. Chapters 2 through 4 discuss cases in Western Europe: Chapter 2 examines the case of the IRA in Northern Ireland, Chapter 3 investigates ETA in the Basque Country, and Chapter 4 describes the cases of Breton and Corsican secessionist terrorism in France. Chapters 5 through 7 move to cases within Eastern Europe and Eurasia: Chapter 5 reveals some interesting components of terrorism as the KLA was eventually brought into the legitimate structures of the state in the case of Kosovo despite once being labelled as a terrorist organization. Chapter 6 presents a discussion of Kurdish separatist terrorism in Turkey, and Chapter 7 discusses Chechen terrorism within Russia. Finally, Chapter 8 presents a foil of the other chapters examining cases like Scotland, Catalonia, and Quebec—regions in which terrorist organizations disbanded early and effectively ceded ground to legitimate, independence-seeking political parties within their respective subnational regions.

John Sutcliffe and Geoffrey Alchin's chapter on the IRA in Northern Ireland describes the intricate religious balance in the territory, over which significant political and economic grievances also exist. Drawing on significant Protestant and Roman Catholic history in the region, their chapter describes in detail how grievances festered, ultimately leading to the creation of the IRA. Significant legislation and mediation has taken place, ultimately resulting in a case that is much more peaceful now than in the 1990s. Political issues are not fully settled in Northern Ireland, but the situation is more hopeful now than in previous decades. The signing of the Good Friday Agreement in 1998 and the formal creation of a Northern Irish Assembly in 2006 are two events that have helped facilitate peace (Hancock *et al.* 2010).

Britt Cartrite's chapter on ETA in the Basque Country (which is mainly located in Spain but also straddling to France), discusses one of the most well-known cases of separatist terrorism (Duerr 2017). After providing a rich overview of the linguistic distinction of the Basques, Cartrite provides a discussion of Castilian Spain as an expansive empire. Homogeneity of Spanish, both as a people and a language, in the Franco dictatorship contributed to the rise of ethnic animosity throughout Spain, which resulted in violence in the Basque case. The Spanish government did much to frame ETA as a Basque problem, and, through cooperation with the French government, managed to imprison numerous high-level members of ETA. Like the Northern Ireland case, ETA has now disbanded, and the region is much more peaceful than in previous decades.

Liam Anderson's first chapter on Corsica and Brittany provides a lucid overview of the French state and the lengths to which Paris has attempted to create a uniform French polity. Anderson weaves a fascinating narrative as to the historical cultural and political distinctions of the Corsican and Breton peoples, and how, over time, the French state has limited the autonomy of these groups. Terrorist attacks were sporadic in both regions, but a deep desire for greater linguistic protections was at the forefront of demands made to the French government.

Elena Pokalova's chapter on the KLA in Kosovo is most intriguing because the international community ended up supporting the aspirations of the KLA, given the violence in Yugoslavia, especially given the perception that Serb nationalist forces were to blame for the violence. The KLA case is unique in world affairs because outside actors came to sympathize with Kosovo in the broader context of the Yugoslav conflicts that entrenched the country in fissiparous ethnic conflict for significant portions of the 1990s. Kosovo now enjoys widespread international recognition and membership in major cultural and sporting bodies, but does not have formal membership in the UN.

Vaughan Shannon presents an intriguing overview of the PKK and the TAK in Kurdish parts of Turkey by showing the historical causes of the conflict. Shannon also discusses the Kurdish issue in the wider Middle Eastern theatre, especially in cases of present conflict as in Iraq, Iran, and Syria, all of which contain significant Kurdish populations. The spillover concern in this case is a reason why Ankara so vehemently opposes Iraqi Kurdish independence, even though the region falls outside of Turkey's borders.

Liam Anderson's chapter on Chechen terrorism paints a picture of brutal terrorist attacks followed up harshly by repressions from the Russian government. Terrorist actions provoked a response that ultimately culminated in two civil wars from 1994 to 1996, and then again from 2000 to ~2009. Although the violence has been quelled, and repressive order implemented by Putin's ally, Ramzan Kadyrov, Chechen separatists have aided ISIS in Syria, leading Russia to fight this battle in a foreign theatre.

My chapter seeks to present a distinction between cases. Primarily examining the cases of Scotland, Quebec, and Catalonia, there are places where secessionist terrorism sprang up and then died out quite quickly, or much earlier than the other cases. A central question is examined: where political violence becomes a familiar situation as noted in the above cases, why did terrorist action peter out, especially after the first (and only) fatality in these regions? Additionally, other peaceful secessionist cases such as Greenland, Flanders, and Veneto are discussed to further tease out distinctions across cases. The goals of ISIS are also discussed as a means of differently viewing how a terrorist organization may seek to claim territory in atypical parts of the world. Political violence is certainly not a "natural" state, yet terrorist activities even occur in some of the most peaceful examples.

Finally, conclusions are drawn in Chapter 9, replete with a comparison of all cases. Most noteworthy are the six "core lessons" that connect all of the chapters. Overall, the book's main arguments examine the reasons why secessionist movements emerge. In many respects, it is a compilation of historical independence, culture, sometimes language, sometimes religion, and often economics, that drives people to support independence where limitations exist on their ability to govern themselves and/or anger at the central government is present. Terrorism generally emerges on the part of a few people who feel a sense of relative deprivation who then seek a violent remedy to the previously described scenario. Whether or not a part of the public supports, or at least sympathizes with, their actions helps to dictate whether the terrorist organization continues. Some groups, however, never really emerge by committing widespread acts of terrorism, and others sometimes fizzle out through a political agreement, or because of a loss of support. Terrorism can come to an end if the central government provides democratic outlets for secessionist expression, and devolves specific powers to subnational units. Secessionist terrorism is a force that has disrupted lives throughout Europe and Eurasia. This book will help to draw conclusions about the nature, actions, and outcomes of this variety of terrorism.

Note

1 The terms of ethno-nationalist terrorism, secessionist terrorism, are used interchangeably throughout this chapter. Although there are slightly different connotations, both infer a desire to gain independence or autonomy through violent, terrorist tactics.

References

Bartkus, Viva Ona. *The Dynamics of Secession*. Cambridge, UK: Cambridge University Press, 1999.

Bird, Richard M., Francois Villancourt, and Édison Roy-César. "Is Decentralization 'Glue' or 'Solvent' for National Unity?" *International Center for Public Policy*, Andrew Young School of Policy Studies, Georgia State University, 2010.

Buchheit, Lee C. *Secession: The legitimacy of self-determination*. New Haven, CT: Yale University Press, 1978.

Crenshaw, Martha. "The causes of terrorism." *Comparative politics* 13, no. 4 (1981): 379–399.

Dion, Stephane. "Why is secession difficult in well-established democracies? Lessons from Quebec." *British Journal of Political Science* 26, no. 2 (1996): 269–283.

Duerr, Glen. "Independence through terrorism? The linkages between secessionism and terrorism in the Basque Country," in Romaniuk, S.N., Grice, F., Irrera, D., and Webb, S. (Eds.) *The Palgrave Handbook of Global Counterterrorism Policy*. New York: Palgrave Macmillan, forthcoming (March 2017), chapter 20.

Hancock, Landon E., Joshua N. Weiss, and Glen M.E. Duerr. "Prospect theory and the framing of the Good Friday Agreement." *Conflict Resolution Quarterly* 28, no. 2 (2010): 183–203.

Hironaka, Ann. Neverending Wars: *The international community, weak states, and the perpetuation of civil war*. Harvard University Press, 2005.

Laqueur, Walter. *The age of terrorism*. Boston, MA: Little, Brown, 1987.

Laqueur, Walter, and Yonah Alexander, eds. *The terrorism reader: A historical anthology*. Philadelphia: Temple University Press, 1978.

Pape, Robert. *Dying to win: The strategic logic of suicide terrorism*. New York: Random House, 2005.

Pokalova, Elena. "Framing separatism as terrorism: Lessons from Kosovo." *Studies in Conflict & Terrorism* 33, no. 5 (2010): 429–447.

Rapoport, D.C. "The four waves of modern terrorism" In Horgan, J.G. and Braddock, K. (eds.) *Terrorism Studies*, pp. 63–82. London: Routledge, 2013

Ross, Marc Howard. *Cultural contestation in ethnic conflict*. Cambridge: Cambridge University Press, 2007.

Tambiah, Stanley J. *Leveling crowds: ethnonationalist conflicts and collective violence in South Asia*. Berkeley, CA: University of California Press, 1997.

Volkan, Vamik D. *Bloodlines: From ethnic pride to ethnic terrorism*. Basic Books, 1998.

Wilkinson, Paul. *Terrorism and the liberal state*. Vol. 2. London: Macmillan, 1986.

Wayland, Sarah. "Ethnonationalist networks and transnational opportunities: the Sri Lankan Tamil diaspora." *Review of International Studies* 30, no. 3 (2004): 405–426.

Wood, John R. "Secession: A comparative analytical framework." *Canadian journal of political science* 14, no. 01 (1981): 107–134.

2 Terrorism from the Troubles to Good Friday: the IRA in Northern Ireland and the British Isles

John Sutcliffe and Geoffrey Alchin

Introduction

Northern Ireland is a component part of the United Kingdom of Great Britain and Northern Ireland. Currently home to around two million residents, Northern Ireland was established in 1921 by an act of the British Parliament. This resulted in the partition of the island of Ireland into two separate units: the Irish Free State in the south, which in 1937 became the Republic of Ireland, and Northern Ireland in the north, which remained, and indeed remains, part of the United Kingdom. This partition roughly reflected religious divisions on the ground as the majority of the population in what would become the Republic were Catholic while the majority in Northern Ireland were Protestant and strongly supported the continuation of the link with the United Kingdom. Significantly, however, Northern Ireland contains a sizeable Catholic minority, many of whom expressed open dissatisfaction with the new constitutional arrangement.[1]

The use of violence, particularly acts of terror, and attempts to resolve this violence through various peace proposals, are recurring features in the life of Northern Ireland. Violence was evident in the formation of Northern Ireland. Partition followed the 1919 to 1921 Anglo-Irish War, itself the result of an armed uprising by Irish nationalists against British rule in Ireland. At this time, there was a clear link between violence and secession as the nationalists sought the goal of an independent state and used violent means to secure this end. Violence continued after the creation of the Republic of Ireland with varying degrees of intensity, but with the focus of the violence and political conflict revolving around the status of Northern Ireland. On one side of the conflict were nationalists (or republicans in the lexicon of Northern Ireland). Within this group, there was a willingness to use violence, along with other means, to secure secession from the United Kingdom, but not to form a separate state. Instead, their central goal was to join with the Republic of Ireland so that the entire island would be united within one state. On the other side of the conflict were unionists (also referred to as loyalists) who argued and fought for the maintenance of the status quo where Northern Ireland would remain part of the United Kingdom.

As with other cases examined in this book, therefore, violence in Northern Ireland has been very much tied to the issues of territoriality and political control. It has been used as one tool, alongside participation in the political system, by actors on both sides to secure their desired goals with respect to political control over the territory. Also as in other cases, the violence in Northern Ireland generated repeated peace initiatives. Unlike some of these other cases, these initiatives have ultimately borne fruit and, with the acceptance and implementation of the 1998 Good Friday Agreement, the result has been a sometimes uneasy peace in the region. The 2016 referendum in which a majority in the United Kingdom voted to leave the European Union—for Brexit—is the most recent threat to the peace.

The Northern Ireland case is much studied both in isolation and in comparative context. This study of the conflict and the peace process has not led to an agreement within the scholarly community. As will be examined in the chapter, there is disagreement with respect to the causes of the conflict. There has also been considerable academic disagreement about the peace process.[2] A central point of contention here concerns the extent to which the institutional structures, put in place by the Good Friday Agreement, serve to foster peace through power-sharing or whether they cement inter-group division.[3] A related question concerns whether peace can be achieved through a top-down (elite-driven) process or whether it will ultimately depend on social transformation in the competing communities.[4]

History

As with almost every secessionist or nationalist conflict, the history of the conflict in Northern Ireland is highly contested with distinct narratives emphasized by the different parties to the conflict and with the stories and symbolism of these narratives themselves becoming a catalyst for conflict.[5]

The roots of the modern conflict stretch back at least to the sixteenth century when England secured full control over the island of Ireland. This was also the start of the sectarian divisions in Ireland as the succeeding years saw the arrival of Protestant settlers from both England and Scotland who supplanted Catholic landowners. The 1801 Act of Union brought Ireland fully into what, as a result of the act, was the United Kingdom of Great Britain and Ireland. Under the terms of this act, the pre-existing Irish Parliament was abolished and responsibility for government in Ireland was transferred to parliament and government in London.[6] The elected members that were transferred from the Irish Parliament to the House of Commons represented towns, cities, counties, and boroughs. On the surface, this process appeared to provide favorable democratic representation to the citizens of Ireland. However, the Irish delegates were still mostly from the Anglo-Irish upper class. Similar to their actions in the former Irish Parliament, these delegates tended to focus their attention on the interests of the mostly Protestant upper class and ignore the issues facing the mostly Catholic lower class. Many felt that Ireland had no voice in London.[7]

This period therefore saw the formation of groups seeking to secure some form of home rule for Ireland or outright independence. In the 1850s, for example, a group called the Fenian formed in New York City and focused on liberating Ireland from British control.[8] Two individuals, James Stephens and John O'Mahony, were especially instrumental in its creation.[9] By 1858, the two men separated, with O'Mahony staying in New York to create a new organization that would fund and arm a revolt in Ireland and Stephens heading back to Ireland to create the Irish Republican Brotherhood (IRB). The IRB spread through Ireland fueled by American money and numerous Irish-Americans heading to Ireland to join the IRB.[10] In 1866, supporters of the IRB's cause in the United States attempted an invasion of Canada in an attempt to trigger an Anglo-American conflict.[11] This attempt was unsuccessful, but it created new momentum for Irish independence.[12]

The late 1800s also witnessed attempts to introduce home rule for Ireland. This was evident in the formation of the Irish Parliamentary Party (IPP) under the leadership of Charles Stewart Parnell and in the ultimately defeated home rule bills introduced by William Gladstone in 1886 and 1893. In spite of these failures the campaign for Irish home rule continued with particular pressure coming from the Irish Parliamentary Party under the leadership of James Redmond. In 1912 it was successful in getting a new Home Rule Bill introduced at Westminster.[13] A Conservative Member of Parliament from Dublin, Sir Edward Carson, led the opposition to this Bill and the concept of Home Rule. Carson's stance on this issue allowed him to recruit over 100,000 men, called the Ulster Volunteers, to help him resist Home Rule.[14] In response to this, the IRB approached Eoin MacNeill, Vice-President of the Gaelic League, to create a similar volunteer force to counter the Ulster Volunteers. The Irish Volunteers were founded in 1913 in Dublin's Rotunda.[15] The Irish Volunteers were not the only active armed force in Ireland at the time. In late 1913, the Irish Citizen Army was also founded. It was created to protect striking workers during the Dublin lockout and quickly became a trade union militia.[16]

When the British entered World War I in 1914, Irish nationalists—now dominated by a new political organization, Sinn Féin, which sought to end British rule in Ireland[17]—saw an opportunity for an armed uprising. By 1916, while the British forces were preoccupied with the war, the Irish Volunteers and the Irish Citizen Army, along with various other nationalist groups, became involved in an armed rebellion, later called the Easter Rising, against British forces. By 1917, the Irish Volunteers and the Irish Citizen Army merged to create the Irish Republican Army (IRA).[18] The IRA became involved with occupying British forces in 1919, sparking the Anglo-Irish war.

The war began with the creation of an Irish Parliament, the Dail Eireann, considered illegal by Westminster. This new Parliament, controlled by Sinn Féin, proclaimed an independent Ireland and declared war on the British Empire.[19] During this conflict, the IRA targeted British police and military personnel in Ireland.[20] The war came to an end in 1921 with the signing of a truce between the IRA and the British government. The treaty, called the Anglo-Irish Treaty, laid out four terms that both Ireland and Britain would recognize. First, two parliaments would be created in Ireland. One of those parliaments would be in the southern part of the island and the other would be in the northern part of the island. This created the Irish Free State in the south and Northern Ireland in the north. Second, the Irish Free State would have Dominion status under the Empire.[21] The Irish Free State would continue to have Dominion status until the introduction of the *Republic of Ireland Act* in 1948. This *Act* removed all powers of the monarch.[22] Third, the southern government would have the right to maintain its own armed forces. And lastly, all individuals in the south would be required to acknowledge the authority of the English crown.[23]

In March 1922, the IRA split into two factions, one comprising individuals who supported the Anglo-Irish Treaty and the other individuals opposed to it. The anti-Treaty IRA called up arms against the newly created Irish Free State military and a civil war ensued.[24] After immense losses for the anti-Treaty IRA, both parties agreed to a ceasefire in 1923, ending the civil war. The IRA, however, continued to use physical force against the British with a particular emphasis on opposition to the existence of Northern Ireland, its place in the United Kingdom and its unionist-dominated political system. In 1956, for example, the IRA commenced a border campaign, which they called "Operation Harvest." During this campaign, the IRA concentrated all of its attacks in the border counties. These attacks were focused on bridges, customs posts, and police stations. This campaign ended in 1962, leading to an arms dump and an end to the IRA's terror operations.[25] It did not, however, end demands for a change in the constitutional status of Northern Ireland nor to the existence of individuals and groups willing to use violent means to achieve that goal. A new group formed to fill the physical force void left by the "Official" IRA; the Provisional IRA.

The rise of the Provisional IRA is associated with the period referred to as the Troubles.[26] The Troubles began with a 1968 civil rights march of Catholics protesting against discrimination at the hands of the Protestant-controlled parliament in Northern Ireland.[27] This protest became increasingly violent, which in turn led to first the deployment of British troops in Northern Ireland and later the suspension of the Northern Ireland parliament and the imposition of direct rule from London. In this context, the IRA assumed the role of nationalist defender against the British.[28] In 1972, support for the IRA rose in response to British troops shooting and killing 13 civilians during a march in the City of Derry. This event was referred to as Bloody Sunday.[29] The events of Bloody Sunday led the British Government to suspend Stormont, giving London direct rule over Northern Ireland through a Secretary of State.[30] There followed an approximately 30-year period of conflict marked by terror tactics used by the IRA within Northern Ireland and reaching into the British mainland, a series of military and political responses by the British government, as well as violence and terrorism perpetrated by unionist paramilitary organizations seeking the maintenance of Northern Ireland's status as part of the United Kingdom. The Troubles also saw the rise to prominence of hardline political parties on both sides of the divide: Sinn Féin, the political wing of the IRA, became increasingly powerful starting in the 1980s and the Democratic Unionists slowly emerged, starting in the 1970s, as a major voice of the Protestant community alongside the Ulster Unionists.

The IRA's conflict with the British state, as is examined in more detail below, extended until the 1998 Good Friday Agreement and ultimately until 2005 when the IRA announced the end of its armed campaign and the final decommissioning of its weapons.[31] Although violence on a lower scale continues to the present day as various splinter groups, including for example the Real IRA, have expressed their opposition to the Good Friday Agreement and to the IRA ceasefire, peace has held in Northern Ireland.

Terrorist attacks by the IRA

The Irish Republican Army is considered a secessionist terrorist organization.[32] Throughout its existence, it used violence to achieve its goal of securing the removal of Northern Ireland from the United Kingdom and its union with the Republic of Ireland.[33] These terrorist attacks targeted the institutions of the state in Northern Ireland (such as the Royal Ulster Constabulary and the British army), but also government and civilian targets in both Northern Ireland and mainland Britain. They were matched by terrorist acts, mostly aimed at Catholic civilians, carried out by unionist paramilitary organizations such as the Ulster Defence Association (UDA) and Ulster Volunteer Force. In total, it is estimated that over 3,000 people were killed in the Northern Ireland conflict with tens of thousands more wounded.[34]

During the course of its bombing campaign, the IRA carried out 488 attacks in Britain from 1973 to 1997, resulting in the deaths of 115 people.[35] The first attacks occurred in 1973 when the IRA detonated book bombs at the Old Bailey, the Central Criminal Court for England and Wales, and the Northern Ireland Information Office.[36] Later that year, they targeted Victoria station, Kings Cross station, and Euston station in London.[37]

The IRA increased the number of attacks in 1974. Their first attack occurred at the Palace of Westminster. Later that year, the IRA successfully detonated a bomb at the Tower of London.[38] Following this attack, the IRA detonated a bomb at a pub in Guildford.[39] A month later, the IRA attacked another pub in Woolwich. The IRA also focused their attention on the City of Birmingham. On November 5, the IRA attacked the Conservative Party's Headquarters.[40] Sixteen days later, the IRA attacked two pubs in the city center.[41] The IRA continued their attack on England into December. In London, three locations were attacked: Victoria Station, Piccadilly Circus, and a General Post Office telephone exchange. The City of Bristol was also subjected to IRA terrorism when a bomb exploded on the busy Park Street.[42] The late 1970s witnessed a decline, but not an end, of IRA attacks in Britain. In these years, bombs were detonated in Liverpool, Bristol, and Dover among other places.[43]

The IRA revived their bombing campaign in England in 1981 by attacking the Chelsea Barracks and Oxford Street in London.[44] By 1982, the IRA was fully immersed in a bombing campaign in London. The first attack was at a Changing of the Guards Ceremony at Hyde Park. Later that same year, the IRA placed a bomb under a bandstand in Regents Park.[45] In 1983, the IRA placed a bomb outside Harrods, London's most prestigious department store.[46]

Perhaps the most notorious of the IRA's terrorist attacks in Britain occurred in September 1984 when they attempted to kill Prime Minister Margaret Thatcher and members of her Conservative Government at a Conservative Party conference at the Grand Hotel in Brighton.[47] All cabinet members survived the blast, but others were not as fortunate.[48] The attacks continued into the 1990s when there were periodic attacks on public places in major English cities including London, Manchester, and Liverpool. Not only did the IRA orchestrate attacks in England, but they also attacked locations in Northern Ireland.

As with the attacks in mainland Britain, the IRA's attacks were not only directed at military and government targets, the so-called occupying forces, but also at civilians, in this case residents in Protestant areas. The first attack in Northern Ireland occurred in 1972 at a restaurant in Belfast's city center.[49] Later that same year, the IRA detonated more than 20 bombs throughout the City of Belfast. This event was called Bloody Friday, and it was the IRA's deadliest attack in Northern Ireland.[50] Bombings of both civilian and military targets continued throughout the 1970s and 1980s. In 1976, for example, the IRA killed 10 Protestant civilians in South Armagh. In 1979, the IRA detonated two bombs at Narrow Water near Warrenpoint.[51] In November 1987, the IRA detonated a bomb in the town of Enniskillen. This attack was known as the Remembrance Day Massacre.[52] Terrorist attacks by the IRA continued into the 1990s including the 1993 bombing on the Shankill Road in Belfast (a predominantly unionist area of the city).[53]

The British government's response to conflict in Northern Ireland

Throughout the conflict, the British government employed various tactics aimed at diminishing or eliminating the threats posed by the IRA as well as bringing peace to the region.[54] These tactics ranged from the use of military and police forces to combat terrorist threats to political measures aimed at resolving the issues underlying the disputes. These types of measures were evident in the period prior to the creation of Northern Ireland as, for example, in 1919 when the British government sent the army to Ireland following the uprising that ultimately led to the Anglo-Irish War,[55] and the subsequent negotiation of the 1921 Anglo-Irish Treaty.

A similar mixture of measures was used by multiple British governments in the disputes over the situation in Northern Ireland and particularly since the start of the Troubles. In 1969, as noted above, the British government triggered emergency power legislation, including internment without trial for terrorists and suspected terrorists, and deployed troops with the goal of maintaining order in Northern Ireland.[56] This military deployment certainly did not secure its immediate goal of containing violence in the region. Indeed, the military presence combined with several controversial incidents involving the British military, including the events of Bloody Sunday, resulted in increased support for the Provisional IRA.[57] The British response to the IRA's increased terror activity was the deployment of more troops, as well as the creation of the Ulster Defence Regiment within the army, in an attempt to neutralize the threats posed by the IRA.

The British government used other tactics, including legislative measures, to contain the terrorist threat in Northern Ireland. In 1971, for example, the Conservative government passed the *Immigration Act* that attempted to address the potential for violence in Britain. This *Act* introduced controls for travelers entering Britain from Ireland with the specific goal of limiting the movement of IRA operatives and preventing them from operating in mainland Britain.[58] As is indicated by the number of terrorist actions that took place on the mainland, these efforts did not stop the IRA. Other legislative measures included the *Prevention of Terrorism Act* (PTA), passed in 1974 following IRA attacks on Birmingham.[59] The goal of the PTA was to impact the activities of the IRA in Britain. To achieve this, the PTA introduced three new powers. The first allowed the British government to label the IRA as a terrorist organization.[60] The second power was the ability to issue exclusion orders. The British government would have the power to send individuals involved in the IRA back to Northern Ireland.[61] These individuals would then be immediately re-arrested and jailed. However, this second power created problems for Northern Ireland. According to Merlyn Rees, the Northern Ireland Secretary of State at the time, this created a strain on an under-equipped prison system in Northern Ireland. Lastly, the PTA introduced the power of arrest and detention. This allowed the police in Britain to detain individuals suspected of being members of the IRA for seven days. The PTA resulted in over 950 arrests.[62]

Alongside the military and police response to the IRA, the British government also engaged in a series of attempts to develop a lasting peace in Northern Ireland and thus bring about an end to the terrorist violence. At different times, these peace negotiations involved Sinn Féin (the political wing of the IRA), the Irish government, the U.S. government, and the leadership of the IRA itself.[63] In 1972, for example, a delegation from the IRA that included Martin McGuiness (who would later become Deputy First Minister of Northern Ireland) entered into secret talks with the British Home Secretary, William Whitelaw. Although a truce was agreed at these talks, it was short-lived.[64] The international dimension to the conflict was evident in 1985 when the British and Irish governments signed the Anglo-Irish Agreement that set out terms for a peace agreement for Northern Ireland that would include a devolved government for Northern Ireland and a potential advisory role for the Republic of Ireland's government in Northern Ireland in the form of an Anglo-Irish Intergovernmental Conference.[65]

These dynamics appeared again in the Good Friday Agreement; the peace treaty that ultimately led to the declaration of a ceasefire by the IRA and which established the framework for what has brought a more or less lasting peace in Northern Ireland. As with previous peace negotiations, the Good Friday Agreement was not the result of only negotiations between the IRA and the British government. Instead, the negotiations involved a wide range of actors that was party to, and affected by, the conflict. This was evident in March 1991 when the

British government announced the opening of peace talks. The announcement pointed to a three-component approach, with each component involving a fundamental set of relationships. The first involved negotiations among the political parties within Northern Ireland—between the Protestant, or unionist parties, and the major Catholic, or republican, party.[66] The second component concerned negotiations within the island of Ireland and the relationship between Northern Ireland and the Republic of Ireland, and the third involved negotiations between the British and Irish governments. Each component of the negotiations involved different issues, had different dynamics, and proceeded at different speeds. On various occasions, talks between unionist and republican parties stalled because one or more of the parties rejected ideas proposed by the other side or accused the other of negotiating in bad faith.[67]

The sets of negotiations occurred along parallel tracks. Thus, at the same time as the difficult and frequently stalled negotiations between unionist and republican parties were occurring, the British and Irish government continued their negotiations. These discussions led to the 1993 Downing Street Declaration that itself became a central part of the Good Friday Agreement. The Downing Street Declaration jointly issued by the then British and Irish leaders, John Major and Albert Reynolds, affirmed "the right of self-determination on the basis of consent freely and concurrently given, North and South, to bring about a united Ireland if that is their wish." The British government was therefore indicating its willingness to accept a united Ireland if this was the will of the people. By the same token, the Irish government accepted that the people of Northern Ireland could not be forced into a new constitutional arrangement with the Republic. Finally, the Downing Street Declaration, stated that "political parties tied to terrorist groups (specifically Sinn Féin) could participate in peace talks if they abandoned violence and sought an agreement through peaceful means." More specifically, it stated that

> democratically mandated parties which establish a commitment to exclusively peaceful methods and … have shown that they abide by the democratic process, are feel to participate … in democratic policies and to join in dialogue … between the Governments and the political parties on the way ahead.

This was, at least in part, responsible for the IRA declaring a ceasefire in August 1994.[68]

These principles were reiterated in the 1995 *Framework Documents* produced by the British and Irish governments. The first document, drafted by the British government, was called *A Framework for Accountable Government in Northern Ireland* and it proposed a devolved government in Northern Ireland. The second document, created by the British and Irish governments, was called *A New Framework for Agreement* and it proposed a Northern Ireland–Southern Ireland cross-border body and East–West (London–Dublin) intergovernmental cooperation. The 1998 Good Friday Agreement contained many of the principles outlined in these *Framework Documents* and the earlier Downing Street Declaration. The Good Friday Agreement contained seven components, each based around a commitment to a non-violent future that enabled and would be based on reconciliation. The first was the creation of a devolved legislative assembly in Northern Ireland that consisted of 108 members.[69] The second component created the Northern Ireland–Southern Ireland Ministerial Council, which was tasked with consulting government leaders in Northern Ireland and the Republic of Ireland and helping them reach an agreement on common policies. It consisted of members from both the Northern Ireland Assembly and the government in Ireland.[70] The third component replaced the intergovernmental arrangements made in the Anglo-Irish Agreement with a new administration that would be under the control of a British–Irish Intergovernmental Conference. The fourth component created the British–Irish Council, which was made up of representatives from the British and Irish governments and the devolved governments in the UK.[71] A confederal aspect was created to link the Northern Ireland Assembly and the Irish government to the British–Irish Council. This link would be used to facilitate bilateral or multilateral agreements.[72] The fifth and sixth components involved the creation of a civic forum for voluntary groups and a micro agenda for areas including policing, the disbanding and disarmament of paramilitary groups, human rights, and the promotion of equal economic and social development.[73]

Among the many things that the Good Friday Agreement did to create peace in Northern Ireland, was the elimination of the hard border between Northern Ireland and the Republic. A second, and perhaps the most important component of the agreement according to the IRA and Sinn Féin, was the British government's commitment to revoke its right to Northern Ireland under Section 75 of the *Government of Ireland Act* of 1920 and to accept that Northern Ireland can join the Republic if this is the majority will of citizens in both Northern Ireland and the Republic of Ireland. Another important aspect of the deal for republicans was the release of prisoners who were arrested by the British government for their involvement in paramilitary groups. An important aspect of the deal for the British government was the Irish government's agreement to hold a referendum to drop its territorial claim to Northern Ireland. Central to the whole agreement was the acceptance that Northern Ireland would remain part of the United Kingdom until such time as majorities existed in both Northern Ireland and the Republic that supported constitutional change. This referendum was held, and the territorial claim dropped as a result, on May 22, 1998. A referendum was held in Northern Ireland on the same day and produced a more than 70 percent majority in favor of the peace agreement.[74]

The establishment of the Good Friday Agreement was difficult and generated controversy in both major communities in Northern Ireland. Its implementation has also not been without difficulty and, as is examined below, there have been several occasions when the new political institutions created in Northern Ireland have had to be suspended as a result of disagreements between the political parties. Nevertheless, the Good Friday Agreement did ultimately result in the

IRA decommissioning its weapons and established, an albeit uneasy, peace in the region.[75]

Understanding the conflict

The conflict in Northern Ireland has attracted considerable academic interest, debate, and disagreement. One explanation for this disagreement is the complexity of the conflict and the interconnection of several issues dividing the communities in Northern Ireland as well as the clear external dimension to the conflict with prominent roles played by foreign governments and citizens (see below).

One strand of thought draws attention to the role of the British government and British responsibility for the conflict. This is sometimes referred to as the colonial explanation.[76] In this perspective, the central British view is that Northern Ireland is part of the United Kingdom and must remain part of the state. To ensure this, successive British governments have committed thousands of troops to Northern Ireland to defend the territorial integrity of Britain's "last colony."[77] Although the British government claims to have no economic or strategic interest in Northern Ireland, its loss to the state would be humiliating for any government and it is this that explains their continued presence. This view, which often echoes arguments made by the IRA itself and its supporters, is that British rule in Northern Ireland led to numerous crimes against the Irish people, including the introduction of anti-Catholic laws, widespread discrimination, and the violent repression of Irish citizens by British troops. In what some scholars call the last all Irish election in 1918, a majority of Irish citizens voted for the nationalist party, Sinn Féin, indicating that they wanted to see a united Ireland.[78] However, against their will, the British partitioned the island, creating Northern Ireland and the discrimination against its Catholic minority that followed.

This view, however, has difficulty accounting for British governments' frequent public declarations that it was willing to accept and support a change to Northern Ireland's constitutional status. The economic and security burden of maintaining Northern Ireland as part of the United Kingdom, combined with the limited mainland public interest in the conflict, led various British governments to indicate their willingness to accept a united Ireland if this was the expressed will of a majority of the population in Northern Ireland.[79] This was later re-emphasized in the 1993 Downing Street Declaration and became a central feature of the Good Friday Agreement.

Irrespective of the extent to which the British government is seen as bearing responsibility for the conflict in Northern Ireland, it is necessary to point to the internal Northern Ireland dimension to the conflict. Within Northern Ireland there are two communities containing individuals with diametrically opposed views on the territory's future. One group, the loyalists/unionists, defend the constitutional status quo and want Northern Ireland to remain part of the United Kingdom. The other group, the republicans/nationalists, desire secession from the United Kingdom and to join the Republic of Ireland. This division is variously defined as being ethnic, nationalist, ethno-nationalist, economic, or religious/sectarian. It is perhaps not possible to isolate the relative importance of the factors that divide the two communities. Multiple factors are involved in explaining identity and in self-identification of identity,[80] and these factors are complex, interrelated, and mutually reinforcing.[81] Religion, for example, is clearly evident in the divisions within Northern Ireland.[82] The Protestant majority overwhelmingly define themselves as unionists while the Catholic minority are equally as likely to define themselves as nationalists. Yet, as McGarry and O'Leary identify, to a large extent religion is simply a label attached to the different groups rather than being in itself fundamental to the conflict.[83] In a sense, religion is the basis of ethnic identity in Northern Ireland.

The divisions within Northern Ireland also overlap with, and are reinforced by, the political structure. Traditionally, the Northern Ireland political system disfavored Catholics. In the 1920s, proportional representation was removed as the electoral system. In its place was a system of gerrymandering that allowed Protestant unionists to control the government. In this context, the Catholic minority came to be represented by "their" political parties, while rival parties represented the Protestant majority. The result was a system where political parties exist on both sides of the divide that "claim to represent 'their' community, advocate for its perceived interests and make exclusive appeals for its support."[84] Although cross-ethnic, or non-denominational, parties do exist, the major political parties draw their support almost exclusively from one of the two communities. The two main parties on the unionist side are the Democratic Unionist Party and the Ulster Unionist Party, while the two parties on the republican side are the Social Democratic and Labour Party and Sinn Féin.

The political structure therefore maps on to the divided communities in Northern Ireland and possibly helps to cement and accentuate these divisions. It is sometimes argued that the economy and control over economic resources and opportunities has also been at least in part responsible for the societal divisions and conflict. It is certainly the case that the economic structure in Northern Ireland long disfavored the Catholic population. In 1972, for example, the rate of Catholic unemployment was more than double that of Protestant unemployment. Catholics were also excluded from holding skilled manual labor and engineering jobs. Many found employment in unskilled jobs that were vulnerable to periodic unemployment.[85] This trend of high Catholic unemployment continued into the 1980s. However, by the 1990s, the gap between Catholic and Protestant unemployment levels started to close. This was mainly a result of successive British governments creating legislation that prevented discrimination based on religion.[86] Whatever the relative importance of economic factors in the Northern Ireland conflict, it is certainly the case that the peace process has included attempts to promote economic growth in Northern Ireland and emphasize equality of economic opportunity across the two communities.

In sum, the question of territorial control overlaps with and is permeated with sectarian, national, political, and economic divisions within the community. It is this complicated environment that the peacemakers faced as they sought to end the conflict.

The peace process: changes to the structure of the state

The Good Friday Agreement introduced a marked change to the governance of Northern Ireland. In place of direct rule from London, the agreement established a new devolved form of government that became operational in December 1999.[87] The British government, as noted above, introduced direct rule in 1972 in response to "the Troubles." The reintroduction of devolved government in 1999 was not, however, a return to the governing structures that had existed prior to 1972. In place of a devolved government dominated by unionists, which had been a target of republican protests and thus one of the causes of "the Troubles," the Good Friday Agreement established an elected assembly based on consociationalism.[88] It aimed at creating a political system that established balance between the unionist and republican communities and thus creating a shared stake in the political system.

The Agreement established a devolved 108-member Northern Ireland Assembly elected by a system of proportional representation to ensure fair representative for the different groups in Northern Ireland.[89] It is important to note that although this Assembly was created alongside the other two devolved institutions in the UK, it is the only one that has been suspended on numerous occasions.[90] The Assembly was suspended, for example, after the resignation of Deputy First Minister, Martin McGuinness on January 9, 2017. McGuinness resigned over the Democratic Unionist Party's handling of the Renewable Heat Incentive. After Sinn Féin refused to replace McGuinness, the Assembly collapsed. This led to a snap election, held in March 2017. Since the election, which saw the Democratic Unionist Party finish with just one more seat than Sinn Féin, no deal has been reached between the two parties to restore the power-sharing agreement, leaving Northern Ireland without a devolved government.[91]

One of the distinct features of the Assembly is that all elected members must identify as "unionist," "nationalist," or "other"; a feature that is central to consociationalism. For important legislation to pass in the Northern Ireland Assembly, a weighted majority is required, demonstrating support from both the unionist and nationalist blocs. This either takes the form of a majority of the entire Assembly plus a majority of both the unionist and nationalist bloc, or a 60 percent majority of the Assembly with a minimum of 40 percent support in both the unionist and nationalist blocs. In these sensitive legislative areas, therefore, "parallel consent" is required for a measure to be passed.

Consociationalism is also evident in the Executive comprising a First Minister and a Deputy First Minister and up to 10 ministers. The appointment process for the posts of First Minister and Deputy First Minister, as revised in 2007, has resulted in a situation where one of the posts goes to the unionist community and one to the nationalists.[92] The First Minister's position has always been held by either an Ulster Unionist or a Democratic Unionist. The Deputy First Minister's position has always been held by the leader of the SDLP or of Sinn Féin.[93] The 10 ministers on the executive are selected based on the relative weight of the political parties in Northern Ireland so that no one party, or no one bloc, dominates the executive. As with the positions of First Minister and Deputy First Minister, the competing communities in Northern Ireland share power.

The history of the devolved political structure in practice in Northern Ireland demonstrates that while some form of power-sharing arrangement may be essential to a peace agreement within divided communities, it does not guarantee that such arrangements will be easily achieved or will run smoothly. The political system emerging out of the Good Friday Agreement has witnessed frequent intense disagreement and conflict among the rival political parties across the unionist/nationalist divide.[94] These disagreements have included conflicts over symbolic issues, such as the number of days the British union flag is to be flown over city hall in Belfast,[95] to accusations over the existence of a Sinn Féin spy ring for the IRA and disagreements about the legitimacy and speed of IRA disarmament. On several occasions, unionist parties have refused to continue to work with their republican counterparts, especially Sinn Féin, which has resulted in the suspension of the Assembly and the reinstatement of direct rule from London. The longest of these suspensions lasted from 2002 until 2007, when both the British and Irish governments, along with unionist and republican parties, signed the St Andrews Agreement, which reestablished the Assembly.[96]

In spite of these problems, the devolved arrangements have continued to exist and evolve and have facilitated peace in Northern Ireland. Responsibility for policing in Northern Ireland is one example of this transformation. The British military is still present in Northern Ireland but no longer has a role in policing in Northern Ireland, as had been the case throughout the Troubles. Responsibility for policing now lies with the Police Service of Northern Ireland, which replaced the Royal Ulster Constabulary as one of the reforms emerging out of the St Andrews Agreement.[97]

External dimension to the conflict and the peace process

A key element in understanding the conflict in Northern Ireland and its peace process is the recognition of the role of external actors. The Irish Republic was involved in various aspects of the conflict and the peace process. It is also the case that different actors within the United States government and society played key roles at different times and in different ways in Northern Ireland.

The Irish-American community is one of the largest communities in the United States. According to the *Washington Post*, there were over 35 million Irish-Americans in 2013,[98] which represents a slight drop in the reported 40 million Irish-Americans in the 1980s. With such a large population living in the United States, it is no surprise that there was considerable interest in events in Northern Ireland as well as support for the different sides in the conflict. This interest and support took different forms, but included the channeling of money from the United States to the IRA. The Irish Northern Aid Committee

(NORAID) is perhaps the best known and most prominent example of this.[99] Michael Flannery (who was a member of the North Tipperary brigade of the IRA in the 1920s) founded NORAID in 1970. To raise funds for the IRA, NORAID sold tickets to annual dinners attended by US politicians. NORAID also collected money for the IRA in Irish-American owned bars, benefit dinners, and through solicitation by mail. From its formation to 1986, NORAID sent $3.5 million to the IRA. In the following five years, NORAID sent an additional $600,000. To get the money to the IRA, NORAID would donate to the An Cumann Cabhrach charity, which was in the orbit of the IRA. Although most funds were sent directly to Northern Ireland, a proportion of the money raised stayed in the United States for the purpose of purchasing weapons for the IRA.[100]

Citizen groups in the United States not only contributed to the conflict through their support of the IRA, they also contributed to the peace process. During the 1992 presidential election campaign, for example, Niall O'Dowd, a publisher at an Irish-American newspaper, created a new Irish-American pro-Clinton group. The group, called Irish-Americans for Clinton, lobbied the presidential candidate to make the Northern Ireland issue a top priority. The group was successful in getting Bill Clinton to promise to send a special envoy to Northern Ireland if elected, and later in drawing Sinn Féin into the peace process through the 1994 granting of a visa to Gerry Adams (the party's leader). This in turn helped to secure the IRA's ceasefire and commitment to peace.[101]

President Clinton himself was a central participant in the Good Friday peace negotiations and visited Northern Ireland on multiple occasions,[102] reflecting the important role played by US politicians in the Northern Ireland peace process both before and after the Good Friday Agreement. The United States provided one of the external mediators—former senator George Mitchell—in the talks that resulted in the Good Friday Agreement.[103] To ensure the support of republicans in the peace process, the United States played a secondary role in the Humes-Adams Agreement of 1993. The prospect of United States financial support and the ties between the Clinton administration and the government in Dublin were instrumental in getting these two rival political leaders to come together to agree on a "new" peace process. It has also been stated that Washington may have placed pressure on London to release republican prisoners.

In addition, the United States also wanted to ensure the support of loyalists in the peace process. To accomplish this, James Molyneaux, leader of the Ulster Unionist Party, was invited to Washington to meet Vice-President Al Gore. During these discussions, Molyneaux was promised that the United States would not seek to impose an unwanted settlement on the Protestant majority in Northern Ireland. To further the peace process, the Clinton administration hosted a White House investment conference, which provided an opportunity for the Secretary of State for Northern Ireland, Sir Patrick Mayhew, and Gerry Adams to meet. The work of the Clinton administration was one of the reasons for the successful negotiation of the Good Friday Agreement.[104]

United States presidents and Congressional leaders continued to play a role after the formal acceptance of the Good Friday Agreement. This role was, for example, evident in the 2010 "Hillsborough Agreement" that led to the devolution of responsibility for justice and policing. Securing Catholic acceptance of the newly established Police Service of Northern Ireland depended in part on US intervention. A second example is the 2013 appointment of the former U.S. diplomat, Richard Haas, by the Northern Ireland Executive to chair talks aimed at reaching agreements over issues, such as the Orange Order marches, that continued to cause inter-group division in Northern Ireland.[105]

The European Union (EU) has also been active in Northern Ireland through a financial contribution to the peace process and through facilitating the opening of the border between the north and south as part of the single market.[106] Following the IRA's 1994 ceasefire, the European Commission established a special task force that produced a program called the Special Support Programme for Peace and Reconciliation in Northern Ireland.[107] The special task force stated that to take advantage of the economic and social opportunities created by the ceasefire and to push the region into permanent peace, a financial assistance package was required from the EU. This financial package would assist in employment creation, cross-border development, social inclusion and investment, urban and regional regeneration, and industrial development. This program was presented to the European Council in December 1994 and established by EU member states in 1995.[108] The goal of this program is to fund projects aimed at promoting reconciliation and long-lasting peace in Northern Ireland. The PEACE program has been renewed three times since its introduction in 1995.

In 1995, the PEACE program received €667 million over three years. The first renewal phase occurred in 2000 and received €995 million over a four-year period. In 2005, this phase was granted a one-year extension and received €160 million. The second renewal phase occurred in 2007. The program received €225 million over a period of six years. The third renewal phase occurred in 2014 and will last up until 2020. The program will receive a total of €269 million during this phase.[109]

The European Union was also involved in the peace process indirectly through the contribution of the EU single market to facilitating the opening of the border between Northern Ireland and the Republic. As noted earlier, the removal of border controls was a main feature of the Good Friday Agreement and this, combined with the single market project, helped to facilitate extensive legitimate economic links across the border. As a result of the 2016 UK referendum and the ongoing Brexit negotiations that will ultimately see the UK leave the European Union while the Republic remains a member state, there is a concern that a hard border may return to the island, and that this will hurt the peace process.[110] According to Máirtín Ó Muilleoir, former Sinn Féin MP and former mayor of Belfast

> any attempt at replacing borders on the island of Ireland is a mistake, not just because it's a threat to the peace process, but because it damages the process of reconciliation, of the healing of wounds, of building a new type of society.

Former Prime Minister of Ireland, Enda Kenny, and former Chief Constable of the Police Service of Northern Ireland, George Hamilton, also echoed these concerns. Both claim that a border between Northern Ireland and the Republic could become a target for dissident republicans. These fears eventually led to a meeting between Theresa May and Kenny in January 2017, where May pledged that the border will be "friction-free and fluid." May repeated that pledge when she met with the President of the European Commission, Jean-Claude Juncker in December 2017. May stated that the UK is committed to avoiding a hard border, including any "physical infrastructure or related checks and controls."[111] These promises, however, are difficult if not impossible to reconcile with May's other promises that the UK will leave the customs union and not be subject to rulings from the European Court of Justice. Unionists, in particular, are opposed to any form of special status for Northern Ireland that would see it remain part of the single market unlike the rest of the United Kingdom. There therefore remain key questions as to what kind of border will exist between Northern Ireland and the Republic and whether or not that border will hurt the peace process.

Conclusion

An uneasy peace was reached in Northern Ireland with the Good Friday Agreement and, in spite of continued low-level violence as well as occasional political disagreements that have led to the periodic suspension of the devolved institutions, the peace agreement has held. Central questions for those directly or indirectly interested in Northern Ireland are whether this peace will continue to hold and what will be the ultimate outcome in terms of the constitutional status of Northern Ireland.

Making predictions is always a risky proposition in any political situation. That said, there are several reasons for optimism that the peace agreement will hold and that there will not be a return to the violence of the Troubles. The Good Friday Agreement is not without its critics, particularly with respect to its impact, or lack of impact, on societal divisions. One prominent criticism relates to the consociational power-sharing institutions. In this critical perspective, these institutions cement in place the divisions between the two communities and do nothing to overcome these divisions at the societal level.[112] Thus, the republican and loyalist groups continue to live in segregated communities and indeed in some cases, through the continued construction of peace walls after the signing of the Good Friday Agreement, these communities are even more clearly separated than during the Troubles.[113]

There is, nevertheless, reason to be hopeful. There has been a slight increase in the political support given to non-denominational political parties—parties that declare themselves to be "other"—within the Northern Ireland legislature. Moreover, although the system has resulted in the militant political parties on either side of the divide (the Democratic Unionist Party and Sinn Féin) becoming the two largest parties, they have, to some extent, moderated their views. The power-sharing arrangements have forced the two sides to work together.[114] The

DUP, for example, once refused to negotiate directly or work with Sinn Féin and its representatives, but they have since worked together as First Minister and Deputy First Minister. A second reason to be hopeful is the decline in violence in Northern Ireland, and especially the paramilitary violence that was so prominent during the Troubles. Violence continues to occur but it is limited and confined to small dissident groups of the earlier paramilitary groups including the IRA. One sign of this more positive situation is that the Independent Monitoring Commission, established by the British and Irish governments to study and report on the possibility of violence in Northern Ireland, issued its final report in 2011.[115]

A second question relates to the ultimate constitutional status of Northern Ireland. In short, will the secession sought by the IRA using violence be achieved by peaceful means? This possibility is clearly provided for in the Good Friday Agreement, where it is established that if a majority of the population in Northern Ireland freely express the desire to secede from the United Kingdom and this is accepted by a majority in the Republic of Ireland, then the parties to the agreement will allow this to happen. The Catholic population is increasing in size relative to the Protestant population. The 2012 census indicated that the Protestant population comprised 48 percent of the population compared with the 45 percent of the population who identified as Catholic. It is possible therefore that at some point in the future the Catholic population will outnumber the Protestant community. What is less clear, however, is whether such a majority will result in a constitutional change. As Coakley identified, it is important to be cautious about assuming that a Catholic majority will inevitably mean secession and unification with the Republic.[116]

It is of course impossible to predict with absolute certainty what the future holds for Northern Ireland. What the Northern Ireland case does suggest, however, is the optimistic message that violent secessionist movements are not inevitably condemned to remain violent. Peaceful political change is possible even in a setting where disagreement, conflict, and violence appear intractable.

Notes

1 Mark Devenport, "Census figures: NI Protestant population continuing to decline," *British Broadcasting Company*, December 11, 2012, www.bbc.com/news/uk-northern-ireland-20673534; Gerard Murray and Jonathan Tonge, *Sinn Féin and the SDLP: From Alienation to Participation* (New York City, New York: Palgrave Macmillan, 2005), 1–3, 5; Martin Wallace, *Northern Ireland: 50 Years of Self-Government* (New York: Barnes & Noble Inc, 1971), 24.

2 Brendan O'Leary and John McGarry, *The Politics of Antagonism: Understanding Northern Ireland* (London: Bloomsbury Academic, 2016).

3 Landon E. Hancock, Joshua N. Weiss, and Glen M.E. Duerr, "Prospect Theory and the Framing of the Good Friday Agreement," *Conflict Resolution Quarterly* 28, no. 2 (2010): 183–203, doi: 10.1002/crq.20019.

4 Landon E. Hancock, "The Northern Irish Peace Process: From Top to Bottom," *International Studies Review* 10, no. 2 (2008): 203–238, doi: 10.1111/j.1468-2486.2008.00771.x.

5 This is evident, for example, in recent conflicts over parades and their routes and flags in Northern Ireland. For detailed histories on Northern Ireland, see: John McGarry and Brendan O'Leary, *Explaining Northern Ireland: Broken Images* (Oxford: Wiley-Blackwell, 1995); John Coakley, "Ethnic Conflict and its Resolution: The Northern Ireland Model," *Nationalism and Ethnic Politics* 93, no. 3 (2003): 25–53, doi: 10.1080/13537110412331301465; Jonathan Tonge, *Northern Ireland* (Cambridge: Polity Press, 2006); Arthur Aughey, *The Politics of Northern Ireland: Beyond the Belfast Agreement* (London: Routledge, 2005).
6 J.B.E Hittle, *Michael Collins and the Anglo-Irish War* (Dulles, Virginia: Potomac Books, 2011), 1.
7 Ibid., 4.
8 Ibid., 8.
9 Brian Hanley, *The IRA: A Documentary History 1916–2005* (Dublin: Gill & Macmillan Publishing, 2010), 3.
10 Ibid., 3.
11 Ibid., 4.
12 Hittle, *Michael Collins and the Anglo-Irish War*, 8.
13 Ibid., 8–9. The first Home Rule Bill for Ireland had been introduced in 1885 and passed in 1886 by the government of William Gladstone. See Duncan Morrow, "Reconciliation and After in Northern Ireland: The Search for a Political Order in an Ethnically Divided Society," *Nationalism and Ethnic Politics* 23, no. 1 (2017): 98–117, doi: 10.1080/13537113.2017.1273688.
14 Ibid., 9.
15 Hanley, *The IRA: A Documentary History 1916–2005*, 4.
16 Ibid.
17 Brian Feeney, *Sinn Féin: A Hundred Turbulent Years* (Madison, Wisconsin: The University of Wisconsin Press, 2003), 18–19, 44.
18 Hanley, *The IRA: A Documentary History 1916–2005*, 6.
19 Colin Gray, "The Anglo-Irish War, 1919–21: Lessons from an Irregular Conflict," *Comparative Strategy* 26, no. 5 (2007): 374, doi: 10.1080/01495930701750208.
20 Andrew McGrath, "The Anglo-Irish War (1919–1921): Just War or Unjust Rebellion?," *Irish Theological Quarterly* 77, no. 1 (2012): 67–68, doi:10.1177/002.
21 Hittle, *Michael Collins and the Anglo-Irish War*, 210.
22 Mary E. Daly, "The Irish Free State/Éire/Republic of Ireland/Ireland: 'A Country by Any Other Name'?" *Journal of British Studies* 46, no. 1 (2007): 81–84, www.jstor.org/stable/10.1086/508399.
23 Hittle, *Michael Collins and the Anglo-Irish War*, 210.
24 Gray, "The Anglo-Irish War, 1919–21: Lessons from an Irregular Conflict," 372.
25 Tonge, *Northern Ireland*, 41; Henry Patterson, "Sectarianism Revisited: The Provisional IRA Campaign in a Border Region of Northern Ireland, "*Terrorism and Political Violence* 22, no. 3 (2010): 343, doi: 10.1080/09546551003659335.
26 Although the title Provisional IRA was used by both participants and commentators, the more usual situation was to refer to this group simply as the IRA. This is the form used here.
27 This discrimination was particularly evident in terms of employment opportunities and access to housing.
28 Tonge, *Northern Ireland*, 41.
29 Graham Dawson, "Trauma, Place and the Politics of Memory: Bloody Sunday, Derry, 1972–2004," *History Workshop Journal* 59, no. 1 (2005): 151, http://journals2.scholarsportal.info.ezproxy.uwindsor.ca/pdf/13633554/v59i0001/151_tpatpombsd1.xml; Rod Thornton, "Getting it Wrong: The Critical Mistakes Made in the Early Stages of the British Army's Deployment to Northern Ireland (August 1969 to March 1972)," *Journal of Strategic Studies* 30, no. 1 (2007): 100, doi: 10.1080/01402390701210848.

30 Gary MacEoin, *Northern Ireland: Captive of History* (New York: Holt, Rinehart and Winston Limited, 1974), 259–260.
31 Henry Patterson, "The Provisional IRA, the Irish Border, and Anglo-Irish Relations During the Troubles," *Small Wars & Insurgencies* 24, no. 3 (2013): 493, doi: 10.1080/09592318.2013.802607.
32 Ignacio Sanchez-Cuenca, "The Dynamics of Nationalist Terrorism: ETA and the IRA," *Terrorism and Political Violence* 19, no. 3 (2007): 291, doi: 10.1080/09546550701246981.
33 Anthony Oberschall, "Explaining Terrorism: The Contribution of Collective Action Theory," *Sociological Theory* 22, no. 1 (2004): 28, http://journals1.scholarsportal.info.ezproxy.uwindsor.ca/pdf/07352751/v22i0001/26_ettcocat.xml.
34 See John Coakley, "Has the Northern Ireland Problem Been Solved?" *Journal of Democracy* 19, no. 3 (2008): 98–112, https://muse-jhu-edu.ledproxy2.uwindsor.ca/article/241802/pdf.
35 Gary McGladdery, *The Provisional IRA in England: The Bombing Campaign 1973–1997* (Dublin: Irish Academic Press, 2006), 3.
36 Ibid., 68; Richard English, "Terrorist Innovation and International Politics: Lessons from an IRA Case Study?" *International Politics* 50, no. 4 (2013): 499, http://search.proquest.com.ezproxy.uwindsor.ca/docview/1364541793/fulltextPDF/BDC77F1897B94CC0PQ/1?accountid=14789.
37 McGladdery, *The Provisional IRA in England: The Bombing Campaign 1973–1997*, 70.
38 Ibid., 79.
39 Ibid., 86.
40 Ibid., 87.
41 Ibid., 90.
42 Ibid., 99.
43 Ibid., 228.
44 Kevin O'Brien, "Assessing Hostile Reconnaissance and Terrorist Intelligence Activities," *The RUSI Journal* 153, no. 5 (2008): 36, doi: 10.1080/03071840802521903; McGladdery, *The Provisional IRA in England: The Bombing Campaign 1973–1997*, 117.
45 David Altheide, "Format and Symbols in TV Coverage of Terrorism in the United States and Great Britain," *International Studies Quarterly* 31, no. 2 (1987): 168, www.jstor.org.ezproxy.uwindsor.ca/stable/pdf/2600451.pdf; McGladdery, *The Provisional IRA in England: The Bombing Campaign 1973–1997*, 119.
46 Ibid., 122.
47 McGladdery, *The Provisional IRA in England: The Bombing Campaign 1973–1997*, 126.
48 Ibid., 127.
49 Catherine Switzer and Sara McDowell, "Redrawing Cognitive Maps of Conflict: Lost Spaces and Forgetting in the Centre of Belfast," *Memory Studies* 2, no. 3 (2009): 344, doi: 10.1177/1750698008337562.
50 Brendan O'Duffy, "Violence in Northern Ireland 1969–1994: Sectarian or Ethno-National," *Ethnic and Racial Studies* 18, no. 4 (1995): 751, doi: 10.1080/01419870.1995.9993889; see also Alferd McClung Lee, *Terrorism in Northern Ireland* (Bayside, New York: General Hall, Inc. Publishers, 1983), 183.
51 McGladdery, *The Provisional IRA in England: The Bombing Campaign 1973–1997*, 114.
52 O'Duffy, "Violence in Northern Ireland 1969–1994: Sectarian or Ethno-National," 760; Andrew Silke, "Beyond Horror: Terrorist Atrocity and the Search for Understanding – The Case of the Shankill Bombing," *Studies in Conflict & Terrorism* 26, no. 1 (2003): 41, doi: 10.1080/10576100390145152.
53 Silke, "Beyond Horror: Terrorist Atrocity and the Search for Understanding – The Case of the Shankill Bombing," 42.

54 See Paul Dixon, "British Policy Towards Northern Ireland 1969–2000: Continuity, Tactical Adjustment and Consistent 'Inconsistencies.'" *British Journal of Politics and International Relations* 3, no. 3 (2001): 340–368, doi: 10.1111/1467-856X.00063.

55 McGrath, "The Anglo-Irish War (1919–1921): Just War or Unjust Rebellion?" 67–68; Gray, "The Anglo-Irish War, 1919–21: Lesson from an Irregular Conflict," 372.

56 See Morrow, "Reconciliation and After in Northern Ireland: The Search for a Political Order in an Ethnically Divided Society," 98–117.

57 Tonge, *Northern Ireland*, 41.

58 McGladdery, *The Provisional IRA in England: The Bombing Campaign 1973–1997*, 96.

59 Ibid., 94; see also Jessie Blackbourn, "The Evolving Definition of Terrorism in UK Law," *Behavioral Sciences of Terrorism and Political Aggression* 3, no. 2 (2011): 132, doi: 10.1080/19434472.2010.512149.

60 Ibid., 96.

61 Ibid., 97.

62 Ibid., 97.

63 See Niall Ó Dochartaigh, "The Longest Negotiation: British Policy, IRA Strategy and the Making of the Northern Ireland Peace Settlement," *Political Studies* 63, no. 1 (2015): 202–220, http://journals.sagepub.com/doi/full/10.1111/1467–9248.12091.

64 Gerard Murray and Jonathan Tonge, *Sinn Féin and the SDLP: From Alienation to Participation* (New York: Palgrave Macmillan, 2005), 69–70; Robert Perry, "The Devolution of Policing in Northern Ireland: Politics and Reform," *Politics* 31, no. 3 (2011): 174, doi: 10.1111/j.1467-9256.2011.01416.x.

65 John Coakley, "Ethnic Conflict and its Resolution: The Northern Irish Model," *Nationalism and Ethnic Politics* 9, no. 3 (2003): 25–53, doi: 10.1080/13537110 412331301465.

66 The three Unionist parties were the Alliance Party, the Ulster Unionist Party (UUP), and the Democratic Unionist party (DUP). The Catholic party was the SDLP and later Sinn Féin.

67 Murray and Tonge, *Sinn Féin and the SDLP: From Alienation to Participation*, 175.

68 Coakley, "Ethnic Conflict and its Resolution: The Northern Irish Model," 40–41; Ciaran Mullan, "Joint Declaration on Peace: The Downing Street Declaration, Wednesday 15 December 1993," *CAIN*, January 9, 2016, http://cain.ulst.ac.uk/events/peace/docs/dsd151293.htm.

69 There is a lot written on the Good Friday Agreement. See Morrow, "Reconciliation and After in Northern Ireland: The Search for a Political Order in an Ethnically Divided Society," 98–117; Coakley, "Ethnic Conflict and its Resolution: The Northern Ireland Model," 25–53. Murray and Tonge, *Sinn Féin and the SDLP: From Alienation to Participation*, 189, 196–197; Etain Tannam, "Explaining the Good Friday Agreement: A Learning Process," *Government and Opposition* 36, no. 4 (2001): 505, doi: 10.1111/1477-7053.00078; Stefan Wolff, "The Road to Peace? The Good Friday Agreement and the Conflict in Northern Ireland," *World Affairs* 163, no. 4 (2001): 168–169, www.jstor.org/stable/20672614; Andrew Reynolds, "A Constitutional Pied Piper: The Northern Irish Good Friday Agreement," *Political Science Quarterly* 114, no. 4 (1999–2000): 619, www.jstor.org/stable/2657786; William Hazleton, "Encouragement from the Sidelines: Clinton's Role in the Good Friday Agreement," *Irish Studies in International Affairs* 11, (2000): 112, www.jstor.org/stable/30001915; Ian Somerville and Andy Purcell, "A History of Republican Public Relations in Northern Ireland from 'Bloody Sunday' to the 'Good Friday Agreement,'" *Journal of Communication Management* 15, no. 3 (2011): 205–206, doi: 10.1108/13632541111150970; An Taoiseach and Bertie Ahern, "The Good Friday Agreement: An Overview," *Fordham International Law Journal* 22,

no. 4 (1999): 1197–1198, http://heinonline.org.lawlibrary.laws.uwindsor.ca/HOL/Page?public=false&handle=hein.journals/frdint22&page=1196&collection=journals; Axel Schmit, "The Impact of Terrorism on Democracy in Northern Ireland," *Perspectives on Terrorism* 4, no. 2 (2010): 12, www.terrorismanalysts.com/pt/index.php/pot.

70 Jonathan Tonge, "From Sunningdale to the Good Friday Agreement: Creating Devolved Government in Northern Ireland," *Contemporary British History* 14, no. 3 (2000): 51, doi: 10.1080/13619460008581593.

71 The British–Irish Council included representatives from the United Kingdom and the Republic of Ireland as well as from the three devolved governments in the UK (Scotland, Wales, and Northern Ireland) and the three autonomous crown territories (the Isle of Man, and Jersey and Guernsey).

72 Murray and Tonge, *Sinn Féin and the SDLP: From Alienation to Participation*, 197.

73 Tonge, "From Sunningdale to the Good Friday Agreement: Creating Devolved Government in Northern Ireland," 51–52.

74 Over 94 percent of those voting in the Republic of Ireland supported the peace agreement.

75 This is not to say that violence has not continued to be a feature of life in Northern Ireland. It has, however, tended to be of a different order than the violence of "the Troubles." See Laia Balcells, Lesley-Ann Daniels and Abel Escribà-Folch, "The Determinants of Low-Intensity Intergroup Violence: The Case of Northern Ireland," *Journal of Peace Research* 53 no. 1 (2016): 33–48, doi: 10.1177/0022343315610399.

76 Tonge, *Northern Ireland*, 13–15.

77 Ibid., 15.

78 Ibid., 13–14.

79 Coakley, "Has the Northern Ireland Problem Been Solved," 98–112.

80 See, for example, Jennifer Todd, "Partitioned Identities? Everyday National Distinctions in Northern Ireland and the Irish State," *Nations and Nationalism* 21, no. 1 (2015): 21–42, doi: 10.1111/nana.12083.

81 John Coakley, "National Identity in Northern Ireland: Stability or Change?" *Nations and Nationalism* 13, no. 4 (2007): 573–597, doi: 10.1111/j.1469-8129.2007.00316.x.

82 See John D. Brewer and Bernadette C. Hayes, "The Influence of Religion and Ethnonationalism on Public Attitudes towards Amnesty: Northern Ireland as a Case Study," *Nationalism and Ethnic Politics* 22, no. 4 (2016): 393–411, doi: http://dx.doi.org/10.1080/13537113.2016.1239444.

83 McGarry and O'Leary, *Explaining Northern Ireland: Broken Images*. See also Brendan O'Leary and John McGarry, *The Politics of Antagonism: Understanding Northern Ireland*, 2nd ed. (London: Athlone, 1996).

84 Cera Murtagh, "Reaching Across: Institutional Barriers to Cross-Ethnic Parties in Post-Conflict Societies and the Case of Northern Ireland," *Nations and Nationalism* 21, no. 3 (2015): 544–565, doi: 10.1111/nana.12129.

85 Tonge, *Northern Ireland*, 20–21.

86 R.D. Osborne and R.J. Cormack, "Unemployment and Religion in Northern Ireland," *The Economic and Social Review* 17, no. 3 (1986): 220, http://search.proquest.com.ezproxy.uwindsor.ca/docview/1298043842/fulltextPDF/76C19AF28BBC4C8APQ/1?accountid=14789; Tonge, *Northern Ireland*, 22–23; D. O'Reilly and M. Stevenson, "The Two Communities in Northern Ireland: Deprivation and ill Health," *Journal of Public Health Medicine* 20, no. 2 (1998): 167, doi: https://doi-org.ledproxy2.uwindsor.ca/10.1093/oxfordjournals.pubmed.a024737; Richard Breen, "Class Inequality and Social Mobility in Northern Ireland, 1973 to 1996," *American Sociological Review* 65, no. 3 (2000): 397, www.jstor.org/stable/2657463; A.M. Gallagher, "Employment, Unemployment and Religion in Northern Ireland," *CAIN*, January 9, 2016, http://cain.ulst.ac.uk/csc/reports/mm28.htm#data13.

87 The Tony Blair-led Labour Government introduced experiments with devolved government in different parts of the United Kingdom during this time period. The establishment of devolved institutions in Northern Ireland was paralleled by the establishment of the Scottish Parliament and Welsh Assembly.

88 John McGarry and Brendan O'Leary, "Consociational Theory, Northern Ireland's Conflict, and its Agreement. Part 1: What Consociationalists Can Learn from Northern Ireland," *Government and Opposition* 41, no. 1 (2006): 43–63, doi: 10.1111/j.1477-7053.2006.00170.x; John McGarry and Brendan O'Leary, *The Northern Ireland Conflict: Consociational Engagements* (Oxford: Oxford University Press, 2004).

89 "Cross-Community Voting," *Northern Ireland Assembly*, http://education.niassembly.gov.uk/post_16/the_work_of_the_assembly/scrutinise/committees/voting/cross.

90 Chris Paris, "The Changing Housing System in Northern Ireland 1998–2007," *Ethnopolitics* 7, no. 1 (2008): 126, doi: 10.1080/17449050701847269.

91 At the time of writing, the assembly has been suspended for just over one year. Mark Devenport, "What caused the Stormont stalemate?" *The British Broadcasting Corporation*, July 5, 2017, www.bbc.com/news/uk-northern-ireland-politics-40506189; Cormac Fitzgerald, "One year on from Stormont collapse, there's still no sign of a deal," *The Journal*, January 9, 2018, www.thejournal.ie/northern-ireland-government-3789320-Jan2018/; Siobhan Fenton, "Power-sharing collapses in Northern Ireland, after Sinn Fein refuse to return to Stormont executive," *Independent*, January 16, 2017, www.independent.co.uk/news/uk/politics/northern-ireland-power-sharing-latest-collapse-end-sinn-fein-refuse-stormont-dup-martin-mcguinness-a7529111.html; "Stormont crisis: Northern Ireland heads for fresh Assembly election just 10 months after last poll," *Belfast Telegraph*, January 16, 2017, www.belfasttelegraph.co.uk/news/northern-ireland/stormont-crisis-northern-ireland-heads-for-fresh-assembly-election-just-10-months-after-last-poll-35370985.html; Henry McDonald and Jamie Grierson, "Sinn Féin makes major gains in Northern Ireland elections," *Guardian*, March 4, 2017, www.theguardian.com/politics/2017/mar/03/dup-and-sinn-fein-on-course-to-dominate-northern-ireland-assembly; "Significant gaps in Stormont talks, says Theresa May," *The British Broadcasting Corporation*, October 30, 2017, www.bbc.com/news/uk-northern-ireland-41797388; "Martin McGuinness resigns as NI deputy first minister," *The British Broadcasting Corporation*, January 10, 2017, www.bbc.com/news/uk-northern-ireland-38561507; "Stormont deadlock: Sinn Féin rejects DUP proposal," *The British Broadcasting Corporation*, September 1, 2017, www.bbc.com/news/uk-northern-ireland-41122078; Harry McGee, Amanda Ferguson, Vivienne Clarke, Rodney Edwards, and Éanna Ó Caollaí, "NI Assembly election: DUP finish just one seat ahead of Sinn Féin," *The Irish Times*, March 3, 2017, www.irishtimes.com/news/politics/ni-assembly-election-dup-finish-just-one-seat-ahead-of-sinn-f%C3%A9in-1.2996479; "DUP and Sinn Féin largest parties in poll," *The British Broadcasting Corporation*, March 4, 2017, www.bbc.com/news/election/2016/northern_ireland; Vince Chadwick, "Martin McGuinness resigns as Northern Ireland deputy first minister," *Politico*, January 9, 2017, www.politico.eu/article/martin-mcguinness-resigns-as-northern-ireland-deputy-first-minister/; Benjamin Kentish, "Northern Ireland power-sharing: DUP leader Arlene Foster says no agreement reached and Stormont talks will continue over summer," *Independent*, July 4, 2017, www.independent.co.uk/news/uk/politics/northern-ireland-power-sharing-dup-leader-arlene-foster-no-agreement-stormont-sinn-fein-summer-a7823246.html.

92 "Cross-Community Voting," *Northern Ireland Assembly*.

93 Murtagh, "Reaching Across: Institutional Barriers to Cross-Ethnic Parties in Post-Conflict Societies and the Case of Northern Ireland," 544–565. Despite the titles, the two positions hold identical powers.

94 Coakley, "Has the Northern Ireland Problem Been Solved," 98–112.

95 Donna Halliday and Neil Ferguson, "When Peace is Not Enough: The Flag Protests, the Politics of Identity & Belonging in East Belfast," *Irish Political Studies* 31 no. 4 (2015): 525–540, doi: 10.1080/07907184.2015.1084291.

96 Jonathan Bradbury and Neil McGarvey, "Devolution: Problems, Politics and Prospects," *Parliamentary Affairs* 56, no. 2 (2003): 227–232, doi: 10.1093/parlij/gsg015; Rick Wilford, "Northern Ireland: The Politics of Constraint," *Parliamentary Affairs* 63, no. 1 (2010): 144–146, doi: 10.1093/pa/gsp046; Gordon Anthony, "The St. Andrews Agreement and the Northern Ireland Assembly," *European Public Law* 14, no. 2 (2008): 157, www.kluwerlawonline.com.ezproxy.uwindsor.ca/document.php?id=EURO2008013.

97 The acceptance of the Police Service for Northern Ireland by the republican parties was a central part of the 2006 St Andrew's Agreement, which helped to restore devolved government to Northern Ireland after the 2002 suspension.

98 Sarah Kliff, "The Irish-American Population is Seven Times Larger than Ireland," *Washington Post*, March 17, 2013, www.washingtonpost.com/news/wonk/wp/2013/03/17/the-irish-American-population-is-seven-times-larger-than-ireland/.

99 Adrian Guelke, "The United States, Irish Americans and the Northern Ireland Peace Process," *International Affairs* 72, no. 3 (1996): 523, www.jstor.org.ezproxy.uwindsor.ca/stable/pdf/2625555.pdf.

100 Feargal Cochrane, Bahar Baser and Ashok Swain, "Home Thoughts From Abroad: Diasporas and Peace-Building in Northern Ireland and Ski Lanka," *Studies in Conflict & Terrorism* 32, no. 8 (2009): 688–689, doi: 10.1080/10576100903040716; Guelke, "The United States, Irish Americans and the Northern Ireland Peace Process," *International Affairs* 72, no. 3 (1996): 524–526, www.jstor.org.ezproxy.uwindsor.ca/stable/pdf/2625555.pdf.

101 Murray and Tonge, *Sinn Féin and the SDLP: From Alienation to Participation*, 190; William Hazleton, "Clinton's Role in the Good Friday Agreement," *Irish Studies in International Affairs* 11, (2000): 103–119, www.jstor.org/stable/30001915.

102 Roger MacGuinty, "American Influence on the Northern Ireland Peace Process," *Journal of Conflict Studies* 17, no. 2 (1997), https://journals.lib.unb.ca/index.php/JCS/article/view/11750/12521; Andrew Wilson, "The Billy Boys Meet Slick Willy: The Ulster Unionist Party and the American Dimension of to the Northern Ireland Peace Process, 1993–1998," *Policy Studies Journal*, 11 (2000): 121–136, www.jstor.org/stable/30001916.

103 The other mediators were Canadian General John de Chastelain and former Finnish Prime Minister Harry Holkerri. De Chastelain played a central role in the process that led to the decommissioning of the IRA's weapons.

104 MacGuinty, "American Influence on the Northern Ireland Peace Process,"; Tannam, "Explaining the Good Friday Agreement: A Learning Process," 514; John Dumbrell, "The United States and the Northern Irish Conflict 1969–94: From Indifference to Intervention," *Irish Studies in International Affairs* 6 (1995): 123, www.jstor.org/stable/30001841; James F. Clarity, "Initiative on Northern Ireland Stirs Optimism," *New York Times*, October 6, 1993, www.nytimes.com/1993/10/06/world/initiative-on-northern-ireland-stirs-optimism.html.

105 Schmit, "The Impact of Terrorism on Democracy in Northern Ireland," 11–12; Perry, "The Devolution of Policing in Northern Ireland: Politics and Reform," 167–178; Dominic Bryan, "Parades, Flags, Carnivals, and Riots: Public Space, Contestation, and Transformation in Northern Ireland," *Peace and Conflict* 21, no. 4 (2015): 565–566, doi: http://dx.doi.org/10.1037/pac0000136; John Coakley, "The Challenge of Consociation in Northern Ireland," *Parliamentary Affairs* 64, no. 3 (2011): 485, http://journals2.scholarsportal.info.ezproxy.uwindsor.ca/pdf/00312290/v64i0003/473_tcocini1.xml.

106 See Sean Byrne, *Economic Assistance and the Northern Ireland Conflict: Building the Peace Dividend* (Lanham, Maryland: Rowman & Littlefield, 2008).

107 Paul Teague, "The European Union and the Irish Peace Process," *The Journal of Common Market Studies* 34, no. 4 (1996): 550–551.

108 Ibid., 551.

109 See Michael Potter and Leigh Egerton, "The EU PEACE and INTERREG Programmes in Northern Ireland," *The Northern Ireland Assembly*, October 14, 2011, www.niassembly.gov.uk/globalassets/Documents/RaISe/Publications/2011/OFMdFM/12611.pdf; "Programme Factsheet," *Special EU Programmes Body*, www.seupb.eu/Libraries/PEACE_IV_Programme_Guidance/PIV_ProgrammeFactsheet.sflb.ashx; "PEACE IV Programme: Overview," *Special EU Programmes Body*, www.seupb.eu/2014–2020Programmes/PEACEIV_Programme/PEACEIV_Overview.aspx; "PEACE IV: a new EU funding programme for Northern Ireland and the border region of Ireland," *European Commission*, February 1, 2016, www.creativeeuropeuk.eu/news/peace-iv-new-eu-funding-programme-northern-ireland-and-border-region-ireland; Filipa Azevedo and Diana Haase, "Northern Ireland PEACE Programme," *European Parliament*, December 2016, www.europarl.europa.eu/atyourservice/en/displayFtu.html?ftuId=FTU_5.1.9.html.

110 Cathy Gormley-Heenan and Arthur Aughey, "Northern Ireland and Brexit: Three Effects on 'The Border in the Mind *The British Journal of Politics and International Relations* 19, no. 3 (2017): 499, doi: 10.1177/1369148117711060; Jonathan Tonge, "The Impact of Withdrawal from the European Union upon Northern Ireland," *Political Quarterly* 87, no. 3 (2016): 340, doi: 10.1111/1467-923X.12288; Artur Tielmann and Dirk Schiereck, "Arising Borders and the Value of Logistic Companies: Evidence from the Brexit Referendum in Great Britain," *Finance Research Letters* 20, (2017): 22, doi: 10.1016/j.frl.2016.08.006; Gavin Cordon, "Return of border checks in Ireland 'inevitable' after Brexit, warn MPs," *The Irish News*, December 1, 2017, www.irishnews.com/news/northernirelandnews/2017/12/01/news/return-of-border-checks-in-ireland-appears-inevitable-following-brexit-warn-mps-1200839/; James Rodger, "Brexit: Return of border checks between Northern Ireland and the Republic 'inevitable' when Britain leaves EU," *Coventry Telegraph*, December 1, 2017, www.coventrytelegraph.net/news/uk-world-news/brexit-border-news-13980058; Katy Hayward, "Brexit deal allows for three different types of Irish Border," *Irish Times*, December 8, 2017, www.irishtimes.com/news/ireland/irish-news/brexit-deal-allows-for-three-different-types-of-irish-border-1.3320497; Chris Morris, "Brexit Countdown: Why is the Northern Ireland border question so hard?" *The British Broadcasting Corporation*, November 30, 2017, www.bbc.com/news/uk-politics-42180074; Kathleen Moore, "In Northern Ireland, Border Looms Large in Brexit Vote," *RadioFreeEurope, RadioLiberty*, June 21, 2016, www.rferl.org/a/uk-brexit-northern-ireland-border-worries/27811595.html.

111 Negotiators of the European Union and the United Kingdom Government, *Joint report from the negotiators of the European Union and the United Kingdom Government on progress during phase 1 of negotiations under Article 50 TEU on the United Kingdom's orderly withdrawal from the European Union*, [Brussels], 2017, 7–8, https://ec.europa.eu/commission/sites/beta-political/files/joint_report.pdf; "This is what the Brexit deal means for Ireland and Northern Ireland," *The Journal*, December 8, 2017, www.thejournal.ie/brexit-deal-ireland-northern-ireland-3738759-Dec2017/; Rob Merrick, "Brexit: Theresa May agrees on breakthrough Irish border deal with EU leaders," *Independent*, December 8, 2017, www.independent.co.uk/news/uk/politics/brexit-latest-theresa-may-northern-ireland-border-talks-brussels-eu-jean-claude-michel-barnier-a8098396.html; Henry McDonald, "Police chief says 'hard Brexit' Irish border would be paramilitary target," *Guardian*, February 7, 2018, www.theguardian.com/uk-news/2018/feb/07/n-ireland-police-chief-says-hard-brexit-border-posts-would-be-paramilitary-target; Natasha Turak, "The Irish border and Brexit: Here's what you need to know," *CNBC News*, December 6, 2017, www.cnbc.com/2017/12/06/irish-border-and-brexit-heres-what-you-need-to-know.

html; Henry McDonald, "Brexit: Irish taoiseach spells out fears over 'hard border' with north," *Guardian*, January 30, 2017, www.theguardian.com/world/2017/jan/30/brexit-irish-taoiseach-spells-out-fears-over-hard-border-with-north.

112 Wilford, "Northern Ireland: The Politics of Constraint," 134–155; Peter Shirlow and Brendan Murtagh, *Belfast: Segregation, Violence and the City* (London: Pluto Press, 2006).

113 Jonny Byrne and Cathy Gormley-Heenan, "Beyond the Walls: Dismantling Belfast's Conflict Architecture," *City* 18, no. 4–5 (2014): 447–448, doi: 10.1080/13604813.2014.939465; Cathy Gormely-Heenan, Jonny Byrne, and Gillian Robinson, "The Berlin Walls of Belfast," *British Politics* 8, no. 3 (2013): 361–366, doi: 10.1057/bp. 2013.11; F.W. Boal, "Belfast: Walls Within," *Political Geography* 21, no. 5 (2002): 687–694, doi: 10.1016/S0962-6298(02)00013-6; John Nagle, "Sites of Social Centrality and Segregation: Lefebvre in Belfast, a 'Divided City,'" *Antipode* 41, no. 2 (2009): 326–327, doi: 10.1111/j.1467-8330.2009.00675.x.

114 John Nagle and Mary-Alice C. Clancy, "Constructing a Shared Public Identity in Ethno Nationally Divided Societies: Comparing Consociational and Transformative Perspectives," *Nations and Nationalism* 18 no. 1 (2012): 78–97, doi: 10.1111/j.1469-8129.2010.00474.x.

115 See Independent Monitoring Commission (2011). *Twenty-Sixth and Final Report of the Independent Monitoring Commission: 2004–2011 – Changes, Impact and Lessons*. London: The Stationary Office.

116 Coakley, "Has the Northern Ireland Problem Been Solved," 98–112.

3 Contingent violence

Arana, Franco, and ETA's terrorist actions in the Basque Country

Britt Cartrite

General overview

Basque nationalism can easily be understood as a near-perfect archetype of a European ethno-nationalist movement. The Basque language is a language isolate pre-dating the arrival of Indo-European languages. The Basque people, residing in the isolated western littoral of the Pyrenees Mountains, are attested to by the earliest written sources. They appear to have successfully resisted integration into the various political powers that conquered neighboring areas, from the Romans to modern Spain and France, while also never quite having the power to establish a lasting independent state. Given these millennia of recorded political resistance punctuated by occasional periods of independence, the emergence of a violent organization, *Euzkadi ta Askatasuna* (Basque Homeland and Freedom, ETA) from within the broader Basque nationalist movement during the harsh dictatorship of Francisco Franco is, for some, almost a foregone conclusion.

However, while such a perspective does draw from historical, cultural, and geographical realities, the suggestion of the inevitability of Basque nationalism, yet alone a violent faction within it, drastically overstates the case. Politicized Basque nationalism emerged at the end of the nineteenth century, relatively late in comparison with many other movements in Western Europe. It appeared amid a severe crisis within the Spanish state itself. The nineteenth century had seen a series of "Carlist" wars in which the dual cleavages of monarchism-liberalism and centralization-decentralization spawned a variety of differing political factions competing for power, in which the Basque region played a central role; the twentieth century would see alternations between centralizing authoritarianism and federalizing democracy reproduce some of these earlier cleavages. The Spanish Empire, which had once been among the largest in human history, came to an ignominious end in the Spanish-American war. Industrialization had begun, but rather as in many other European states being concentrated in the core, in Spain the most rapid gains were in the Basque and Catalan peripheries, leading to significant levels of immigration from the Castilian core to these regions. And, across Europe, older ethnic movements had politicized, articulating demands for protections, autonomy, or even outright independence, a trend which would accelerate following the end of the World War I. Thus Basque nationalism emerged precisely during one of the deepest crises of Spanish state-nation building, following the examples of numerous other movements. The timing of Basque nationalism must, therefore, be understood as part of a complex co-evolution with Spanish state-nation building and, indeed, of European norms and institutions regarding ethnic minorities.

So too, the inevitability of nationalist violence would be to overstate the case. As will be seen below, the timing of the emergence of modern Basque nationalism, coming during periods of violent resistance in Cuba, Puerto Rico, the Philippines, and Ireland, and the celebration of violent resistance by its founder, Sabino Policarpo de Arana y Goiri (hereafter Arana), arguably increased the probability that violence would become a prominent theme in Basque nationalism. Yet violence among ethnopolitical movements in Europe is reasonably rare; most such movements for most of their history have been overwhelmingly, if not entirely, peaceful, including other movements in Spain (such as the Catalans and Galicians) and indeed Basques just over the border in France. This chapter will address the rise of Basque nationalism within the broader European and Spanish contexts, then turn to the violence of ETA and Spanish responses to the movement, concluding with an assessment of the current peaceful status of the "Basque problem."

The European context

While nationalism and state-nation building have clear antecedents preceding the modern, Westphalian period, John Locke argued in the *Second Treatise of Government* for legitimacy arising from the "consent of the governed," rather than legitimacy through genealogy or claims to divine right (Locke 1988, 50–51). Rousseau subsequently argued in *The Social Contract* that the State draws its legitimacy through an (implicit) voluntary contract by individuals to be governed (Rousseau 1968, 61), related to a longer tradition of citizenship tracing back to Roman thought and law (Geary 2002, 49–50). However, Johann Gottfried Herder, a contemporary of Rousseau's, developed the argument that humans subdivide into groups on the basis of language; in this sense a "people" is a linguistic community, not a voluntary political association.

As a result, for many nineteenth-century Liberals, the legitimacy of the state rested on its connection to its "people," often defined in ethnic or linguistic terms. Will Kymlicka argues:

> [I]n the nineteenth-century, the call for a common national identity was often tied to an ethnocentric degeneration of smaller national groups. It was commonplace in nineteenth-century thought to distinguish the "great nations," such as France, Italy, Poland, Germany, Hungary, Spain, England, and Russia, from smaller "nationalities," such as the Czechs, Slovaks, Croats, Basques, Welsh, Scots, Serbians, Bulgarians, Romanians, and Slovenes. The great nations were seen as civilized, and as the carriers of historical development. So some nineteenth-century liberals endorsed

> national independence for great nations, but coercive assimilation for smaller nationalities.
>
> (Kymlicka 1995, 52)

Over the course of the nineteenth century many small polities were absorbed into existing or, in the case of Germany and Italy, altogether novel larger political institutions. Languages were increasingly standardized and efforts undertaken to homogenize populations. For example, as Eugen Weber documents, despite linguistic homogenization having been official government policy in France back to the First Republic, it was the establishment of compulsory public schools in the 1870s under the Third Republic that caused the marked decline in regional dialects and languages (Weber 1976, 303; Ager 1999, 26). Thus nineteenth-century Liberalism was associated with democratization, centralization, and homogenization; indeed, the argument was that there could be no democratic freedom without homogeneity (Kymlicka 1995, 52). Conversely, nineteenth-century conservativism, while typically continuing to support monarchism against democratization, at least in some contexts was increasingly linked to the preservation of regional political institutions and traditions against the centralizing liberal state.

However, countervailing trends became increasingly evident in cases where existing states, particularly the "sick man of Europe," the Ottoman Empire, began to lose control over their populations. Greece became independent in 1830 with the support of the European great powers, followed by Belgium in 1832; in both cases religion played a central role in defining the territory of the new state, but linguistic distinctiveness, tied to some degree to religion, was a crucial element. The Berlin Treaty of 1878 led to the creation of a number of new states in the Balkans, each of which contained a titular ethnolinguistic "nation" alongside considerable linguistic and religious diversity; while protections for minorities were expressly included in the provisions, in practice assimilation was tolerated and, indeed, expected (Jackson Preece 1998; Alcock 2000).

The tension between "minority rights" and centralizing, democratizing liberal states was made manifest following World War I. U.S. President Woodrow Wilson, in a speech following his famous "Fourteen Points" speech, argued:

> Peoples are not to be handed about from one sovereignty to another by an international conference or an understanding between rivals and belligerents. National aspirations must be respected; peoples may now be dominated and governed only by their own consent. "Self-determination" is not a mere phrase. It is an imperative principle of action.... This war had its roots in the disregard of the rights of small nations and of nationalities which lacked the union and the force to make good their claim to determine their own allegiances and their own forms of political life. Covenants must now be entered into which will render such things impossible for the future....
>
> (Alcock 2000, 40)

Liberal Western states, many of which had significant minorities increasingly mobilized around their cultural distinctiveness and challenging existing political arrangements (notably but not solely the Irish in the United Kingdom), attempted to argue that the self-determination of "peoples" should apply only to the formation of new states; further, these new states, which would inevitably be heterogenous given the cultural geography of Eastern Europe, should be expected to undertake policies of assimilation within them (Jackson Preece 1998, 88–89). Thus, the League of Nations Minority Treaties system attempted to recognize the rights of "small nations," in part by allowing outside "kin" states to intervene on the behalf of minorities in new states, and the right of states to engage in cultural homogenization processes. As a result, group minority rights became enshrined in both international law and institutions, despite the intent that they only be applied in the defeated powers of Eastern Europe (Claude 1955, 16–17).

As conservative monarchism declined in the wake of World War I, twentieth-century fascist and other varieties of authoritarian regimes articulated policies of centralization and homogenization as an extension of strengthening the nation through its associated state. Conversely, and particularly following World War II, liberal democracy came to increasingly accept, but not resolve, the tension between group rights and democratic rule. The horrors of genocide, massive post-war population transfers, and the break-up of European empires (often in the name of democratic self-determination) forced the issue, and both European institutions and the United Nations established and refined institutions designed to protect ethnic and linguistic minorities wherever such groups exist *as an extension of* individual human rights and democratic institutions. Thus on the dimension of ethnic and linguistic group rights, liberalism moved from supporting centralization and homogenization as necessary conditions for stable democracy to (somewhat uneasily) associating group rights with individual human rights, while nineteenth-century conservatism and its support for regional cultural variation and institutional distinctiveness gave way to twentieth-century authoritarian efforts to centralize and homogenize. Not surprisingly, therefore, Basque nationalism would be associated with monarchism and conservatism in the nineteenth century, but with democratization and federalism in the twentieth.

Spanish state-nation building

The emergence of Basque nationalism is closely associated with the writings and political efforts of Arana near the end of the nineteenth century. But this somewhat belated beginning, at least in comparison with other movements in Western Europe, including nearby Catalonia, began amid a longer trajectory of Spanish state-nation building and at a time of crisis within the Spanish state. The prominence of ethnopolitical mobilization in contemporary Spain leads many observers to conclude that nation-building in Spain is incomplete and this failure has now been institutionalized (Moreno 2001, 38–39). In particular, the weak nineteenth-century Spanish state, when nation-building began in a number of liberal states, represents for many the primary culprit. However, a much longer historical analysis illustrates that Spanish national identity has included, for centuries, a strong regionalist dimension compatible with the larger identity. Furthermore, to argue that nation-building was not completed is to assume that Spanish identity could have become unitary along the lines, for example, of France, an assumption that may not hold up under historical scrutiny.

Although the Spanish state emerged relatively early compared with many other European states, its various political antecedents formed as separate Catholic entities during the process of the *Reconquista*, in which Muslim control of the peninsula was slowly pushed southward over a period of many centuries. With the end of the *Reconquista*, and at the start of Spanish imperial expansion, the various political entities of the peninsula were joined through the marriage of Ferdinand of Aragón to Isabella of Castile-León (with Portugal remaining an independent entity). Unlike in neighboring France, in which the French state would expand from core territories around Paris to absorb other entities, or in the United Kingdom, in which the overwhelmingly dominant English state absorbed most of its rivals and entered into a union with the much smaller Scottish crown, the Spanish crown was from the beginning a joining of two distinct polities with varying interests and concerns: for example, while Castile invested heavily in the development of the nascent overseas empire, Aragón continued pursuing its centuries-long dynastic concerns in Sicily, Flanders, and Corsica. The ascension of Charles I, grandson of Ferdinand and Isabella, to head the Holy Roman Empire as the head of the Hapsburg family merely continued the differentiation of external concerns for the Spanish monarchy; as a result, while other states were beginning to consolidate themselves as coherent nation states, the varying components of the Spanish crown, with their differing interests, undermined any similar dynamic on the peninsula.

Centralization and unification began in the eighteenth century under Philip V: during the War of the Spanish Succession (1702–1714), which ultimately saw Philip confirmed as the monarch of Spain while renouncing claims to the French crown and Hapsburg possessions in the Italian peninsula, Philip conquered the rebellious peninsular kingdoms, stripping Aragón, Valencia, and Catalonia of their ancient privileges and centralizing the monarchy along the lines of France. These historic kingdoms were transformed into administrative regions, while further subdivisions resulted in the creation of 30 administrative provinces. Yet this process of centralization and standardization was to be interrupted by the French Revolution, the occupation of Spain by Napoleon's forces, and the brief rule of Joseph Bonaparte. During the French occupation, the liberal Constitution of 1812 was published in Cádiz; however, conservatives opposed the institutions, desiring instead for a restoration of Fernando and the resumption of the Inquisition; Fernando regained the throne in 1814 and immediately voided the Constitution.

Political ineptitude and corruption characterized the rule of Fernando VII (1808–1833) and his daughter Isabel II (1833–1868). Spain lost most of its overseas empire to independence movements; by 1825 all that remained were Cuba, Puerto Rico, Guam, and the Philippines. Liberal resistance to the conservative monarchy dominated nineteenth-century Spanish politics. In 1820 disgruntled military officers marched on Madrid and demanded the Constitution of 1812 be reinstated, to which the King acceded. Moderate liberals lost to more extremists in the election of 1822, and the government turned against the Jesuits. Civil war threatened when France, sanctioned by the Quadruple Alliance, intervened to put down the government and restore the absolute monarch. Liberal revolts persisted in the 1830s, albeit with no success.

When Fernando died without a male heir, his daughter Isabel took the throne; a new constitution represented a limited move towards liberalization of the Cortes (the national legislature). However, her uncle Don Carlos declared himself king; his conservative supporters, mainly in the Basque Country, Navarre, Aragón, and rural Catalonia, argued for the restoration of regional privileges (*fueros*) in the latter three areas alongside the continuing preservation of Basque fueros. The First Carlist War (1833–1839) therefore pitted conservatives in favor of the fueros, with the Church as an ally, against Moderates and Progressives supporting the centralized and liberalizing monarchy; the war ended with Don Carlos fleeing to France. Isabel's marriage in 1846 led to the Second Carlist War (1846–1849) with a peasant uprising in Catalonia, although it again ended in failure.

Political instability returned with a vengeance in the Glorious Revolution of 1868, when the military and main opposition parties overthrew the government and Isabel II fled to France. Monarchists brought in Prince Amadeo, son of King Victor Emmanuel II of Italy, to establish a constitutional monarchy, while Carlists promoted Don Carlos María. Continued instability and political division led to the creation of a Republic in 1873. The Third Carlist war erupted in 1872; after a protracted conflict mainly in the Basque Country, the Carlists were defeated in 1875 and the Basque fueros subsequently revoked. Restoration of the monarchy under Alfonso XII, son of Isabel, was achieved in 1876.

Fears of radicalism and centrifugal policies brought conservatives and liberals together in the restoration of the Bourbon monarchy under Alfonso XII and his son Alfonso XIII, which lasted until the dictatorship of Primo de Rivera in 1923. Revolts in Cuba and the humiliating defeat to the United States in 1898 provided exogenous shocks to the Spanish political environment, while nascent industrialization generated internal pressures. After protests and bloody reprisals in Barcelona during the *Setmana Trágica* (Tragic Week) of 1909, Liberals swept to power in the national Cortes in 1910 and expanded the limited local autonomy of Catalonia in the *Mancomunitat*. However, the Communist Revolution in Russia, in conjunction with increasing labor union activity in Spain during World War I, generated first a highly divided Cortes in 1918 and then a Conservative victory in 1920. After a military debacle in Morocco in protection of the two remaining Spanish enclaves there, anti-war sentiment flared in Catalonia, which was put under martial law. After a series of governments, Liberals again came to power; after easing restrictions on Catalonia, however, violence escalated. Elections were held in April 1923, but only 40 percent of the electorate turned out; the Liberals were returned with a slim majority. On September 13, the captain-general of Catalonia, Miguel Primo de Rivera was appointed Prime Minister by King Alfonso and given dictatorial powers similar to those granted to Mussolini by Victor Emanuel III a year earlier.

By the time of the Primo de Rivera dictatorship, ethnopolitical mobilization in Spain anticipated that of other movements in Western Europe: a decisive shift from conservatism to democracy. While Basque nationalism retained its conservative allegiance through the Restoration, Galician and Catalan nationalism emerged clearly associated with advocates of democracy; periods of democratic reforms represented, therefore, the realization of institutional accommodations for the three linguistically distinct areas of Spain: Catalonia, the Basque Country, and Galicia. Conversely, the dictatorships of Primo de Rivera and Franco were predicated, in part, on centralization and the advancement of Spanish identity.

Primo de Rivera's dictatorship (1923–1929) entailed the complete reversal of Catalan institutional accommodation and the quashing of ethnopolitical organizations and suppression of ethnic expression. After the forced resignation of Rivera in 1929, an interregnum period under Berenguer, and the abdication of Alfonso XIII and the establishment of the Second Republic in 1931, in which ethnopolitical parties established coalitions with various republican parties, ethnopolitical mobilization surged. Indeed, on the same day that the Republic was declared, Francesc Macià, leader of *Estat Catalá*, declared a Catalan Republic and Iberian confederation. After negotiations with the Spanish government the regional *Generalitat* was reestablished in 1932 in place of the Catalan Republic and a Statute of Autonomy for the region was put to a referendum and approved later that year. Basque activists also declared their right to autonomy in 1931, but divisions arose between leaders in Bilbao and San Sebastian and those of Navarre; eventually the Statute of Autonomy approved by referendum and the Spanish parliament excluded Navarre from the Basque Region.

Catalonia provided the example for Basques and Galicians, who would also realize Statutes of Autonomy during the Second Republic (1931–1939). Interestingly, these successes generated movements in other, less distinctive regions, as well, notably in Andalusia. This model, labeled the "integral state," represented a compromise between centralism and federalism and anticipated the "State of Autonomous Communities" of the 1978 Constitution (Beramendi 2000, 93).

The years of the Second Republic were tumultuous. Martial law was imposed in 1934 after violence again erupted. Monarchists, Falangists (fascists led by Primo de Rivera's son), and even Carlists reappeared. Anarchist and communist activism generated a reactive formation of a National Front by conservatives to oppose the coalition of leftist parties in the Popular Front; in the 1936 elections the Popular Front narrowly won the first round of elections and then expanded their dominance after runoffs. While the state of emergency was continued, land reforms and amnesty for prisoners from the October 1934 violence were implemented amid escalating political violence and strikes.

Premised on what they saw as internal fragmentation and the expansion of "communist" power, conservatives in the military acted in July 1936 to overthrow the Republic. General Franco declared from Spanish Morocco the necessity of military intervention, initiating the Civil War. In the early days, as Madrid's power collapsed, local authorities and workers' juntas in Catalonia, the Basque Country, Valencia, La Mancha, and Extremadura took the lead in resisting the rebels. The rebels under Franco received aid from both Hitler and Mussolini, but France, Great Britain, and the United States promoted non-intervention, with only the Soviet Union sending aid to the Republicans. Despite early gains, however, the self-styled Nationalists were unable to quickly defeat the Republicans, subjecting Madrid to a two-year siege. By 1939, however, Republican forces were decimated and retreating into France; Franco proclaimed total victory on April 1.

In the wake of the Nationalist victory, reprisals against the Republicans included actions against ethnopolitical leaders. The Statutes of Autonomy for Catalonia, the Basque Country, and Galicia were revoked, regional languages were forbidden in public, and even the distinctively Catalan dance, the sardana, was forbidden. Local government was based on appointments rather than elections, with military officers often serving in civil administration posts. And the Franco regime relied heavily on Falangists, military officers, old conservatives, church leaders, technocrats, and, after 1957, Opus Dei to govern, with periodic reshuffling of the cabinet to prevent rivals from establishing a support base.

The long years of Franco's rule saw persistent attempts to homogenize Spanish culture and identity at the expense of the national minorities and regional differentiation. Using education and mass media, Francoism pushed assimilationist policies in an attempt to eradicate local identities; ironically, after decades of such policies ethnopolitical mobilization reemerged under the dictator and became increasingly political in the 1960s. Interestingly, in 1966, after some 27 years of homogenizing policies, the "Freedom of Expression Law" permitted the private and limited use of non-Castilian languages and dialects; Mar-Molinero argues that this small opening reflected the self-confidence of the Franco regime and, in part, served to trivialize local cultures in the mass media (Mar-Molinero 1996, 81–82). Also at this time, manifestations of regionalism were reemerging throughout Spain, with the most visible being, of course, the terrorism of newly founded Basque separatist ETA.

As with the collapse of the Primo de Rivera dictatorship, the demise of Francoism after his death in 1975 unleashed a remarkable resurgence in ethnopolitical mobilization. Indeed, Basque, Catalan, and Galician groups were at the forefront in calling for the restoration of democracy even prior to Franco's death and were particularly active in the 1975–1978 transition period. These three groups are referred to as "historical nationalities" in the 1978 Constitution; the designation singles out these areas for institutional accommodations beyond those granted to other regions. Few in the transition period espoused the preservation of the centralist state (Gibbons 1999, 13); as a result, ethno-nationalism in particular and regionalism more generally were to have a significant influence on the Third Republic (Muñoz 2009, 621). The old cleavage between centralists and decentralists that had cut across conservative, liberal, and socialist lines appeared decisively resolved in favor of decentralization.

Interestingly, while centralization was off the political table, there was a division between those desiring to emphasize Spanish unity versus those conceptualizing Spain as an "ensemble of diverse peoples, historic nations and regions" (Moreno 2001, 60). Rather than a federal constitution, in which authorities are clearly delineated to the varying levels of administration and guaranteed by the constitution, the tension between these two visions of post-Franco Spain resulted in the *Estado de las Autonomías*, which outlines various paths by which regional competencies can be decided, including the possibility of asymmetrical devolution. Indeed, the expectation in the Constitution is that the "historical nationalities" will have regional competencies more extensive than those of the other regions.

However, the nascent regionalism evident in the Second Republic remerged in the Third as well, most notably in Andalusia; that region successfully met the conditions of the "fast track" devolutionary process intended solely for the "historical nationalities." As a result, a call for "*café para todos*" ("coffee for everyone"), increased decentralization for the remaining areas of Spain, emerged. After the failed coup attempt of February 23, 1981 (F23), the two main Spanish parties agreed on the need to harmonize the devolution process, passing the Organic Law on the Harmonization of the Autonomy Process (Ley Orgánicia del Armonización del Proceso Autonómico, LOAPA) in 1982. However, Basque and Catalan ethnopolitical leaders continue to assert the need for additional accommodations for the "historical nationalities" beyond those of the other Autonomous Communities to reflect their ethnic distinctiveness. Thus, the evolution of Spanish nation-building remains stressed between an emphasis on a superordinate Spanish identity, closely associated with the Castilian language, and the contemporary diversity of linguistic and ethnic identities that, for some at least, remained under threat from the larger, hegemonic identity. These pressures are manifest in fears of too much centralization on the one hand and the possible break-up of the Spanish state on the other.

The emergence of Basque nationalism

Basque nationalism emerged at a critical moment in Spanish nation-building. The turmoil of military occupation and the Carlist wars had, by the late nineteenth century, exhausted the Spanish state and contributed to the independence of much of the empire. Spain remained divided between liberals and monarchists, each of which was also divided between centralizers and those seeking to preserve regional distinctiveness. In addition, Catalan nationalism had emerged, as did many other ethno-nationalist movements, with the literary *Renaixença* in 1833, followed by the (re)establishment of the *Jocs Forals* games in 1859, the First Catalanist Congress in 1880, the subsequent formation of an explicit political movement during the 1880s, and the publication of Valentí Almirall's *Lo Catalanisme* in 1886. These trends thus represent the context in which Arana initiated a formalized Basque nationalism which, some scholars contend, had from the beginning an acceptance of violence in the cause of national liberation.

For primordialists, the Basques likely represent the archetype of an ethnonationalist group. The Basque language, a linguistic isolate, predates all Indo-European languages (MacClancy 1996, 208). As with other linguistic minorities in Western Europe, Basque ethnopolitical mobilization began with a literary movement. Although not as widespread or influential as other literary movements, the *renacimiento euskerista*, centered in the province of Navarre and Biskaia in the late 1870s, was an attempt by early activists to study and propagate Basque, which was becoming marginalized, in part, because of industrialization and an influx of workers from other areas of Spain. Basque Foral games were organized in 1879; *itz-jostaldiak* (literary contests) were added soon thereafter. The movement remained largely intellectual, however, and its political concerns were foralist rather than ethnopolitical. Thus one finds evidence that Basque nationalism emerged from Basque cultural and linguistic consciousness, with roots extending back to pre-history.

Similarly, constructivists and ethno-symbolists find within the Basque nationalist trajectory evidence supporting their arguments (Muñoz 2009, 636). Interestingly, Arana downplayed the centrality of the language as differentiating the Basques from the Spanish; rather, Arana conceived the Basques in racial and religious terms. Arguments of genetic purity are, of course, difficult to maintain even in the relatively isolated Basque Country and were largely discredited by the end of World War II, while Catholicism represents a dimension of unity with Spain. However, Arana also constructed elements of Basque identity that persist as differentiating symbols, including designing the Basque flag and composing the anthem (1895, adopted in 1980) and, indeed, the very name of the group. The day of his "nationalist conversion" on Easter Sunday, in 1882, is celebrated as the national holiday, *Aberri Eguna*. There are even some indications that language was becoming increasingly central to Arana's conceptualization of Basque identity, but his suffering from Addison's disease and early death leave such interpretations to speculation.

Modernists also find support for their hypothesis that nationalist movements are a result of modern political ideas and institutions rather than continuations of ancient cultures and polities. Clearly Basque nationalism emerges in the context of, and partially in reaction against, modern Spanish state-nation building. The shift from an emphasis on preserving older *foral* institutions to demands for institutions based on Basque distinctiveness occurs late in the nineteenth century: indeed, Arana himself was initially a Carlist before adopting Basque nationalism as a political cause (Watson 2007, 49). Spanish state formation left intact local provisions for the Basques, the fueros, until comparatively recently: Basque autonomy officially ended with the end of the Third Carlist War in 1876. Yet it was the ending of Basque autonomy which provided the genesis for Basque ethnic mobilization (Conversi 1997, 48): "foralism" (Sp. *fuerismo*), which sought to protect the Basque fueros, was an ideology in favor of preserving particular institutional rights rather than a movement for the protection and advancement of Basque identity through political institutions. Indeed, while later foralists were leaders in the emerging Basque movement, their priority and allegiance was with any political movements opposed to centralization rather than to an articulation of Basque identity and the need for its preservation.

The centrality of Arana to the emergence of Basque nationalism is difficult to overstate: while political *fuerismo* leaders obviously predate him, the shift from support for decentralized institutions to arrangements specifically to protect and preserve Basque distinctiveness clearly occurs with Arana. His early political writings focused on asserting *Biscayan*, rather than Basque, independence. However, his thinking soon expanded to encompass all Basques in the *Euzkadi*, the name he gave for the four Spanish Basque provinces and, vaguely by extension, the three French Basque areas. Arana formed the first Basque political party, the Partido Nacionalista Vasco (Basque Nationalist Party, PNV), in 1895. Interestingly, Arana's early views on Basque identity were religious and vaguely racist rather than ethnic (Zabalo Bilbao and Odriozola Irizar 2017, 138).[1] Indeed, all members of the PNV had to be Catholic and have at least four Basque surnames or one grandparent who was native Basque (Conversi 1997, 61); this position appears in some of his writings to have resulted from what seemed to Arana as the imminent demise of the Basque language, which was always a secondary consideration.

Basque political mobilization increased after Arana and, seeing the relative success of the moderate Catalans in 1901, moved away from a clearly separatist position. The PNV enjoyed limited electoral success in the provinces, primarily in Bizkaia and its capital, Bilbao. In 1918, after years of industrial expansion as neutral Spain sat out World War I, the first *Eusko Ikaskuntza* (Basque Studies Society) and *Euskaltzaindia* (Basque Language Academy) were established; jointly, their efforts focused on the expansion of Basque literature, language standardization, and improving the status of the language in the region. Despite these joint efforts on the cultural front, however, politically the Basque movement split in 1921 into moderates, under the *Comunión Nacionalista Vasca* (CNV, the renamed PNV) and radicals, inspired by Sinn Féin in Ireland, advocating anti-capitalism and independence and adopting the old PNV name.[2] The latter group more closely adhered to Arana's thought until it finally turned towards Marxism in the 1960s. While the Basque ethnic parties were relatively minor political players at this time, their political successes were increasing.

The Primo de Rivera dictatorship (1923–1930) forced ethnopolitical activism underground: political publications were banned and leaders fled the country. However, this repression also forced the CNV and PNV to cooperate, both with each other and with other pro-democracy parties. By 1930 the two groups had officially reunited under the "*Reunificación de Vergara*," which represents a revival of much of Arana's thought (Medrano 1995, 83–84). While internal divisions within the reunited PNV persisted, especially with regards to strategy and social programs, the Basque nationalists became the largest party in the Basque Country in the elections of 1931, 1933, and 1936; interestingly, this surge in support came largely from conservative voters, especially farmers. In this respect the Basque movement was returning to its *foralist* roots; indeed, in 1931 the Basques ran with the Carlists, although the latter turned to the far right by 1933 and the PNV ran alone in subsequent elections. The leftward shift of the PNV towards pro-republicanism resulted, however, in a decline in voter support between 1933 and 1936, suggesting the political conservatism of the Basque electorate.

The Basque nationalists also held a plebiscite for creation of a Basque Autonomous Community. Support in three of the provinces was overwhelming, but voters in Navarre rejected the statute; while voters in Alava supported the proposal, their support was much lower than in the two provinces of Bizkaia and Guipúzcoa. Rather than rework the proposal, Basque leaders chose to exclude Navarre from the project. In any event, Basque autonomy was short-lived: Implemented in October 1936, nationalist forces in the Civil War occupied Bilbao in June 1937, ending Basque autonomy and ushering in Franco's dictatorship. Basque leaders subsequently formed a government-in-exile across the border in France.

As with the Rivera dictatorship, General Franco sought to quash all regionalist identity and sentiment as part of a program of centralization and national unification. From 1939 to 1945 the Basques were subject to extreme state terror as part of Franco's anti-ethnic agenda; emigration surged as a result of this repression. After World War II ended, the government-in-exile tried to bring pressure on the Allies to address Franco's oppression, including appealing to newly created international institutions; however, the onset of the Cold War rehabilitated Franco, a staunch anti-communist, in Western eyes; this window of opportunity quickly closed.

The suppression of Basque ethnopolitical mobilization continued under Franco. By the mid-1950s, however, small student groups began to emerge, some associated with the underground PNV, initially advocating the study of Basque language and culture. One such group, *Ekin* (to do), formed outside the PNV in 1952 and quickly adopted political objectives. This group merged in early 1959 with the culturalist PNV youth cell, the *Euzko Gastedi del Interior* (EGI). However, PNV attempts to control these groups failed: *Ekin* formally split with the PNV and took most of the EGI members with it and on July 31, 1959 this group renamed itself ETA.

ETA's political position was a reaction to two important factors: the conservatism and perceived inertia of the PNV and the failure of the West to aid the Basques against Franco. While the group incorporated some of Arana's myths, especially his intransigence to Spanish identity and rule, it rejected the centrality of race and religion as the defining characteristics of Basque identity; language became the central concern (Zabalo Bilbao and Odriozola Irizar 2017, 140). The movement soon adopted violent tactics, attempting in 1961 to derail trains carrying Francoist Civil War veterans. While the plot failed and 110 ETA members were quickly arrested and tortured with another 100 forced into exile, it also highlighted the remarkable growth of the group: from approximately 10 *Ekin* members in 1953 the group had expanded to over 300 militants in 1960.

In 1960, in a separate action, 339 priests from the region signed a joint petition denouncing official Church support for the Franco regime and the atrocities committed against the Basques. While this action was not associated with ETA, Basque resentment towards Church complicity was manifest in ETA's increasingly secularist position. Additionally, ETA moved clearly in a Marxist direction, drawing upon the works of Franz Fanon and other "Third-Worldists" for ideological and tactical inspiration, including the adoption of guerrilla war as a strategy for liberation.

ETA dominated Basque ethnopolitical mobilization under the remaining years of Franco's rule; the group split numerous times but generally retained a leftist guerrilla approach. The Spanish government responded to escalating violence with arrests, torture, and forced expulsions. However, the PNV did not remain completely inert during this period: cultural activities were revived in the early 1970s and a new literary movement emerged. Basque language schools (*ikastolak*), initially operating underground, increased dramatically during the period. The Franco regime was clearly coming to an end and the two main segments of the Basque movement were mobilizing and positioning themselves to take advantage of the impending regime change.

During the "Transition" period (1975–1978) following Franco's death, the PNV regained much of the initiative and vitality it had lost to ETA; it also shed its racist and clerical roots and articulated a moderate, bourgeois line. Given its historical role as the leading Basque political structure, the PNV was the chief negotiator for the Basque Country on the region's status in the new constitution, although escalating ETA violence and repression by security forces constrained the negotiation positions of both sides. In the end, the resulting Statute of Autonomy did not include Navarre or the right to self-determination; thus although the Statute was approved in a referendum in 1979, many Basque nationalists were unsatisfied.

Basque ethnopolitical mobilization continues at a high level, with the PNV continuing to be the largest party in the region. The *Eusko Alkartasuna* (EA), which split from the PNV and advocates eventual independence, enjoyed significant support at its founding in 1985, but that support has slowly waned in the intervening years. ETA, through its political wing *Herri Batasuna* (HB), enjoys a relatively consistent degree of support, with violence continuing to be used. Thus the relatively early politicization of Basque ethnicity, punctuated by periods of dictatorship and repression, resulted in a high and continuing activism in contemporary Spain (Leonisio and Strijbis 2014, 61).

What is clear is that the movement generally shifted away from race and religion towards language as central to Basque identity (Ansolabehere and Socorro Puy 2016, 79). This represents the opening of group membership to immigrants: one need merely learn the language to become a Basque. Interestingly, Basque linguistic distinctiveness may work against itself in this regard: the language appears particularly difficult to learn, thereby limiting the potential for demographic extension. Furthermore, even Basque-speakers find Castilian more appropriate or useful than *Euskera* in many social contexts (MacClancy 1996, 216–217). Conversi argues that speaking Basque may be giving way to active participation in Basque ethnopolitical mobilization as indicative of membership in the community (Conversi 1997, 203–205), which can be linked to Arana's stress on patriotism as a moral obligation; this tendency may be more pronounced among supporters of HB than of more moderate Basques (MacClancy 1996, 213–214). Such a shift, should it come to represent the dominant Basque self-conception, would clearly expand the potential membership of the community, bolstering its potential ethnopolitical power. evidence of this shift is, however, considerably ambiguous (Conversi 1997, 205–208).

Finally there is the issue of territory. While many activists refer to the Basque Country, that region has been divided between France and Spain for centuries. Furthermore, Navarre's heterogeneous demography and resistance to inclusion in the Basque region, despite the considerable historical and linguistic connection to the rest of the Basque Country, serves to undermine the clarity of a Basque territory. Despite the relatively recent loss of political autonomy and shared experiences of repression, territoriality represents an important ambiguity. The Basque Autonomous Community, therefore, does not contain and cannot speak for all contiguous Basques. While language continues to represent the clearest marker of group differentiation, other cultural symbols, a historical and territorial identity, and contemporary political institutions facilitate the broadening of Basque membership. Ambiguities regarding the Basque community, however, work against the furtherance of ethnopolitical mobilization.

ETA's violence

ETA's first known violent attack was the unsuccessful attempt to derail trains in July 1961. The first death attributed to the group was in a gunfight with the *Guardia Civil* in June 1968, while the first successful assassination occurred the following August. Arguably the most impactful assassination was that of Prime Minister, and designated Franco successor, Admiral Luis Carrero Blanco on December 20, 1973. Since that time there have been over 3,300 reported ETA attacks, with over 2,000 people injured and, according to government sources, a total of 829 people killed (other organizations put the death toll as high as 952). While there have been multiple ceasefires over the decades, the current ceasefire was announced in October 2011; in early 2017, caches of arms were turned over to French police.

ETA's violence has taken a wide array of forms: bank robbery; kidnapping; extortion; letter, car, and other bombings; and targeted assassinations. Most assassinations have been of members of the security forces and politicians at various levels of government, including the Basque regional and local governments. Although ETA formed during the Franco dictatorship, violence during the period of dictatorship was very limited, both in terms of the number of attacks and fatalities. The early years of the Third Republic (1977-present) were the deadliest, while the volume of attacks has been highest since 2000, with ETA frequently warning police of bombings to give time for the areas to be cleared. ETA declared ceasefires in 1989, 1996, 1998, 2006, and 2011, with the latter still in force; in 2012 ETA announced it was ready to negotiate a definitive end to its activities, and in April 2017 surrendered what it claims to be the last of its

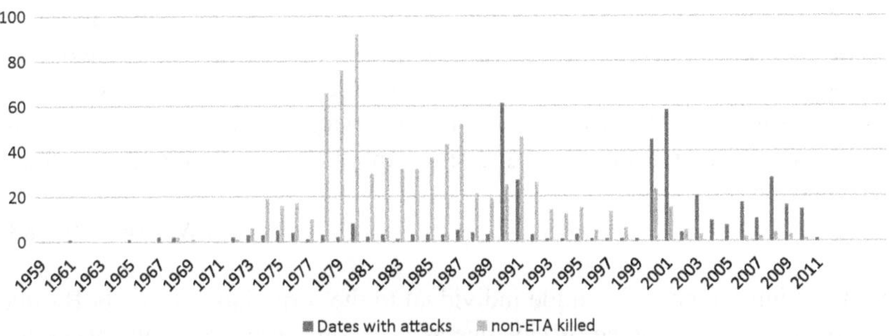

Figure 3.1 Number of dates and fatalities in ETA attacks by year.

arms and disbanded. Figure 3.1 provides a count of the number of days with attacks (taken from List of ETA Attacks 2017, which provides links to media sources for each attack) and fatalities (Government of Spain Ministry of the Interior 2010) annually, 1969–2011.

Thus ETA waged one of the longest and bloodiest campaigns for independence in modern Europe. However, ETA represents one of only a small number of violent secessionist movements in Europe, and is the only example in Spain. The adoption of violence as a strategy, and the persistent if very limited support for ETA among Basques, is perhaps partially explained by the timing of the emergence of the organization. ETA can be understood in the context of Marxist liberation movements around the globe, notably in Algeria and Cuba, based on an ideology informed by, among others, Frantz Fanon, Ernesto Guevara, and Mao Zedong; ETA statements make clear the aspiration for a socialist independent state (Zabalo and Saratxo 2015, 367). ETA can also be understood as a reaction against the inaction of the PNV under Franco, perhaps as the manifestation of a much longer divide within Basque nationalism between moderates and extremists dating (arguably) back 150 years or more (Molina 2010, 254). Other revolutionary organizations in Europe formed in this same period with a commitment to violence, including the Breton Liberation Front and the National Liberation Front of Corsica in France, the Provisional Irish Republican Army in the UK, the Red Brigades in Italy, and the Baader-Meinhof Gang in Germany. Notably, however, other secessionist movements formed or strengthened during this period without resorting to violence, including Scottish and Welsh nationalists in the UK; Alsatians, Basques, Catalans, and Occitans in France; and Catalans and Galicians in Spain, among others. Thus the timing of the emergence of ETA is, at best, a partial explanation for the resort to and persistence in use of violence.

Other scholars highlight that violence as a theme in Basque nationalism is traceable to Arana himself. Watson argues:

> One cannot underestimate, then, the rhetorical force of violent imagery in the origins and inception of Basque nationalism. The images that Arana

> established constituted the basis of nationalist discourse, but it was a discourse understood not in an abstract way. This was an expressive discourse that was essentially performative, and relied on imagery associated with action, heroism, and sacrifice for its rhetorical force. The same images would survive and surface at regular intervals throughout the twentieth century in an increasingly real and less symbolic form of nationalist cultural expression.
>
> (Watson 2007, 88)

The central importance of a single individual to the formulation of early Basque nationalism and his embrace of violence as necessary to national liberation distinguishes the Basque movement from other neighboring movements, providing an ideological linkage between the liberationist struggle at the turn of the twentieth century and the violence of ETA decades later.

Spanish responses to the violence

In the early years of ETA under Franco the organization adopted an "action-repression-action" escalatory model of violence in which small acts would generate outsized reprisals by the quasi-fascist state, generating support for ETA and leading to larger actions (Whitfield 2015, 3). Prime Minister Admiral Carrero Blanco was the head of the intelligence service under Franco and "responsible for implementing the frequent states of emergency, the lack of guarantees to trial, systematic use of torture, shoot-to-kill policies and death squads" (Aiartza and Zabalo 2010, 15). Following his assassination by ETA, thousands were arrested in massive police raids and ETA activists, among other Spanish left-wing activists, were executed, leading to protests by other governments, a cessation of negotiations with the European Common Market, and a motion by Mexico to expel Spain from the UN (Aiartza and Zabalo 2010, 15; Molina 2010, 252).

However, the Spanish government of the Third Republic has, from the beginning and despite whichever of the main parties was in power, adopted a multifaceted approach to dealing with ETA, always premised on the rejection of ETA's actions as akin to a formal armed conflict and the conscious avoidance of using the Spanish military as part of state policy. Instead, various Spanish governments have used institutional structures to try and divide the movement; increased reliance on French cooperation to limit the use of French Basque territories as refuges for ETA leaders; outlawed political organizations directly associated with ETA while other Basque parties achieve and exercise power; and engaged in counterterrorist policies along twin paths of police action and negotiation.

Institutional structures

Political opposition among Basques to the terms of the new democratic constitution was overwhelming: only 31 percent of the region's population was in favor of the new democratic constitution (Whitfield 2015, 3). Yet the new constitution was to provide the foundation for Basque autonomy, while also providing institutional incentives that would divide the broader movement. One of the first efforts of the new regime was to separate Navarre, which is roughly 50 percent Basque, from the other three Basque provinces in the formation of the Basque Region to limit the size, population, and extensive border with France, factors that might, it was argued, contribute to secessionist sentiments under the new regime (Aiartza and Zabalo 2010, 18). At the same time that the Constitution articulated the unity of the Spanish nation, it also formally recognized the "historic nationalities" of the Basques, Catalans, and Galicians, annulled the 1839 and 1876 abolition of the *fueros*, and provided a "fast-track" mechanism for the creation of new Statutes of Autonomy for each, with the Basque Statute coming into effect in 1979 with the approval of over 90 percent of voters (Molina 2010, 254; Mees 2001, 808).

Cooperation with France

The division of the Basque Country by the border between France and Spain is often interpreted as a deep obstacle, at least by Basque nationalists. However, this division amidst the rugged terrain of the Western Pyrenees has also served as an opportunity, particularly for Basque activists in Spain, who have used the porous border to avoid Spanish authorities, with or without the tacit consent of French authorities. During the Franco years the French republic's support for anti-authoritarian efforts was perhaps tempered by Spain's importance in the strategic concerns of NATO, but with the establishment of the Third Republic in Spain, the opportunity for two democracies to cooperate on rooting out ETA appeared. In June 1984, the French government signed an agreement with Spain to begin arresting and extraditing Basque activists as part of a concerted and coordinated counterterrorism effort (Aiartza and Zabalo 2010, 23). The coordination between police on both sides of the borders, as well as between central governments, increased over the course of the 1990s, regardless of which parties were in power in Paris or Madrid, and took on additional impetus following the 9/11 terrorist attacks (Zabalo and Saratxo 2015, 372). This internationalization of the fight against Basque terrorism, while raising the profile of Basque nationalist concerns broadly, also served to increase the cost of violence for ETA while diminishing the benefits (Lecours 2008, 133–134).

Outlawing political organizations

Starting in 1998, the Spanish government began outlawing various political parties and organizations associated with the Basque Nationalist Left (*Abertzale*) movement, of which ETA was a key player. These included outlawing a number of specific political parties and electoral coalitions contesting various Basque, Spanish, and European elections. Various youth associations and *Askatasuna* and later *Herrira*, organizations supporting Basque prisoners, were also outlawed, while the newspapers *Egin* and *Egunkaria* were ordered closed (Zabalo and Saratxo 2015, 372). These actions undoubtedly hurt the Nationalist Left and its attempts to advance its claims through political means, increasing the pressure within ETA to cease violence and adopt a strategy aimed at a political settlement.

Counterterrorism

The banning of most political organizations associated with the Nationalist Left highlighted a central conceptual issue: what is the nature of ETA and its violence? Unlike the British use of military forces in Northern Ireland, Spain never deployed its military in the Basque region: arguably, such a move would construe the conflict as a "war," given the need for military intervention, providing support for a "war of national/worker liberation," which, from ETA's perspective, is the ideological foundation of their violence (Molina 2010, 252–254). The Spanish approach was to label the conflict the "Basque Problem," and in the early years of the Third Republic to emphasize criminality and rely on the police to try and end the violence. Yet the banning of political organizations made clear that the government understood the violence not to be merely criminal, but tied to a political agenda.

The framing of ETA violence as terrorism served to overcome this conceptual discontinuity: the violence was clearly both political and illegal, but could also be framed in terms of being illegitimate, particularly in a democratic context. Beginning in 1982, the Socialist government engaged in a "dirty war" through the use of para-police organizations, such as the Antiterrorist Liberation Groups in France, with 29 assassinations attributed to the group between 1983 and 1989 (Whitfield 2015, 23). Widespread human rights violations led eventually to widespread legal appeals and pressures from abroad for an end to state-based violence against Basques (Zabalo and Saratxo 2015, 372–373; Landa 2013, 12–13).

The Spanish Government and ETA have been engaged in what Barros and Gil-Alana, confirming earlier research, describe as a "cat-and-mouse" game in which a cycle of ETA attack—governmental retribution—ETA escalation appears difficult to prevent; the study concludes that proactive political policies by the government undermine this escalation and ETA violence (Barros and Gil-Alana 2009, 21–23). Violence by both sides has declined as public opinion increasingly mobilized around political, non-violent solutions to the conflict despite the "terrorism" framing of the conflict (Landa 2013, 20–21). This has served to highten the political dimension of the conflict, particularly as the 2011 ceasefire continues to hold and ETA appears, at least for now, to have decomissioned its remaining arms and disbanded. Pressure for a political solution involving institutional reforms appears stronger now, in the absence of violence, than in recent decades.

Spanish institutional reform in the Third Republic

Spanish institutional accommodations for the Basque region obviously occurs within the larger context of quasi-federalism, as various regions, and in particular those of the "historical nationalities," pressure the state for further competencies. In recent years the efforts of Basque nationalists have come to be overshadowed by Catalan demands for independence for their region, including a scheduled referendum in September 2017. Despite widespread opposition to the new constitution in the Basque region and the separation of Navarre, the Basque Country has enjoyed considerable autonomy relative to other regions in Spain and, notably, in comparison with Basques living across the border in France. However, while the iterative dynamic of "*café para todos*" has persisted in recent years, Basque efforts to realize additional autonomy have been eclipsed by Catalan nationalists: Catalonia successfully negotiated with Madrid a new regional constitution, which came into effect in 2006, while a similar proposal for the Basque region, known as the "Plan Ibarretxe" after PNV leader Juan José Ibarretxe and proposed unilaterally, served to split Basque nationalists and was overwhelmingly rejected by the Spanish parliament but without any subsequent major protests in the Basque Country (Barón 2015, 96–97). While proposals for a cross-border institutional framework that would encompass the entire Basque region (including Navarre), as well as other possible additional powers devolved to the region, continue to mobilize Basque nationalism, the process of reconciliation and the persistence of divides among various Basque parties suggest that further devolutionary reforms are likely to be politically difficult and come in the wake of reforms in Catalonia.

Of course, there is always the persistent fear in Spain that further devolution could lead to the disintegration of Spain itself; centralizing tendencies remain prominent among most national political parties, representing a significant countervailing force against further devolution. During the 2000s, the "most-favored region" legislation adopted by the Valencian region, which states that absent any constitutional reforms any further devolution to other regions should extend automatically to Valencia, has been adopted by other autonomous communities as well. In this regard the fears of the centralizers seem to have some foundation in the political realities of the Spanish state: should ongoing political conflicts in Catalonia or the Basque Country be resolved through additional devolutionary reforms, it may be the case that such reforms will then be automatically applied across the country, further weakening the central state. While the Spanish state has incorporated principles of asymmetric federalism to address regional ethnolinguistic distinctiveness, there is a clear concern that further concessions spell the end of Spain itself, and therefore are to be resisted.

Conclusion

After more than 50 years of violent resistance to the Spanish state in the name of leftist Basque nationalism, it appears that ETA has laid down its arms and disbanded. The threat that ETA posed to the early Spanish Third Republic was very real, with atrocities committed on both sides. Treating ETA as simply criminals run amok belied the clear political impetus behind its formation and persistence as an organization, yet the Spanish state was able to avoid giving credence to the movement as one of "national liberation." The state successfully undermined the value of political violence through a variety of strategies that both major parties adopted. Yet the deep wounds of the conflict, dating back to the civil war of 1936–1939, clearly remain.

The explanation for the emergence of ethno-nationalist violence in the Basque Country but not elsewhere in Spain lies in the timing of the emergence of ETA as well as the roots in the emergence of the PNV under Arana, the weakness of the Spanish state around the turn of the twentieth century, and shifting European norms regarding, in particular, linguistically distinct groups. Clearly violence was not inevitable; whether political violence was likely given the Basque, Spanish, and European contexts at the time of its emergence is, arguably, a more reasonable conclusion to draw.

Notes

1 While the importance of lineage for Arana was clear, he does not appear to have espoused any notion of biological racial superiority or racial hierarchy; rather, kinship as the basic identifier of membership in the Basque community and the need to protect the community from outside influences were the central themes.
2 This anti-capitalism should not be equated with Marxism. It was primarily a critique of economic concentration rather than of private property more generally.

References

Ager, Dennis. 1999. *Identity, Insecurity and Image: France and Language.* Philadelphia, Pennsylvania: Multilingual Matters Ltd.

Aiartza, Urko, and Julen Zabalo. 2010. *The Basque Country: The Long Walk to a Democratic Scenario.* Resistance/Liberation Movements and Transition to Politics, Berlin: Berghof Conflict Research.

Alcock, Antony E. 2000. *A History of the Protection of Regional Cultural Minorities in Europe: From the Edict of Nantes to the Present Day.* New York, New York: St. Martin's Press, LLC.

Anon. *List of ETA Attacks.* July 9. Accessed July 23, 2017. https://en.wikipedia.org/wiki/List_of_ETA_attacks.

Ansolabehere, Stephen, and M. Socorro Puy. 2016. "Identity Voting." *Public Choice* 169: 77–95.

Barón, Alejandro. 2015. "Why Public Finance Matters: Evolution of Independence Movements in Catalonia and the Basque Country during the Twenty-First Century." *SAIS Review* 35 (2): 91–103.

Barros, Carlos, and Luis Gil-Alana. 2009. "A note on the effectiveness of national anti-terrorist policies: evidence from ETA." *Working Paper No. 10/09.* 1–36.

Beramendi, Justo G. 2000. "Identity, Ethnicity, and the State in Spain: 19th and 20th Centuries." In *Identity and Territorial Autonomy in Plural Societies*, by William Safran and Ramón Máiz, 79–100. Portland, Oregon: Frank Cass.

Claude, Inis L. 1955. *National minorities: an international problem.* Cambridge, MA: Harvard University Press.

Conversi, Daniele. 1997. *The Basques, the Catalans, and Spain: Alternative Routes to Nationalist Mobilization.* Las Vegas, Nevada: University of Nevada Press.

Geary, Patrick J. 2002. *The Myth of Nations: The Medieval Origins of Europe.* Princeton, New Jersey: Princeton University Press.

Gibbons, John. 1999. *Spanish Politics Today.* New York: Manchester University Press.

Government of Spain Ministry of the Interior. 2010. *Victims of ETA.* March 16. Accessed July 23, 2017. https://web.archive.org/web/20100915224606/www.mir.es/DGRIS/Terrorismo_de_ETA/ultimas_victimas/p12b-esp.htm.

Jackson Preece, Jennifer. 1998. *National Minorities and the European Nation-States System.* Oxford: Clarendon Press.

Kymlicka, Will. 1995. *Multicultural Citizenship: A Liberal Theory of Minority Rights.* New York, New York: Oxford University Press.

Landa, Jon-M. 2013. "Human Rights and Politically-Motivated Violence in the Basque Country." *Journal on Ethnopolitics and Minority Issues in Europe* 12 (2): 7–29.

Lecours, Andre. 2008. "Violence as politics: ETA and Basque Nationalism." In *Intra-State Conflict, Governments and Security: Dilemmas of deterrence and Assurance*, edited by Steven Saideman and Marie-Joelle Zahar, 120–137. New York, New York: Routledge.

Leonisio, Rafael, and Oliver Strijbis. 2014. "Beyond Self-placement: Why Nationalism is a Better Predictor of Electoral Behaviour in the Basque Country." *Revista Española de Investigaciones Sociológicas* 146: 47–68.

Locke, John. 1988. *Second Treatise of Government.* Edited by Thomas P. Peardon. New York, New York: Macmillan Publishing Company.

MacClancy, Jeremy. 1996. "Bilingualism and Multinationalism in the Basque Country." In *Nationalism and the Nation in the Iberian Peninsula: Competing and Conflicting Identities*, edited by Clare Mar-Molinero and Angel Smith, 207–220. Washington D.C.: Berg.

Mar-Molinero, Clare. 1996. "The role of language in Spanish-nation-building." In *Nationalism and the Nation in the Iberian Peninsula: Competing and Conflicting Identities*, edited by Clare Mar-Molinero and Angel Smith, 68–89. Oxford: Berg.

Medrano, Juan Díez. 1995. *Divided Nations: Class, Politics, and Nationalism in the Basque Country and Catalonia.* Ithaca, New York: Cornell University Press.

Mees, Ludger. 2001. "Betrween Votes and Bullets: Conflicting Ethnic Identities in the Basque Country." *Ethnic and Racial Studies* 24 (5): 798–827.

Molina, Fernando. 2010. "The historical dynamics of ethnic conflicts: confrontational nationalisms, democracy and the Basques in contemporary Spain." *Nations and Nationalism* 16 (2): 240–260.

Moreno, Luis. 2001. *The Federalization of Spain.* Portland, Oregon: Frank Cass.

Muñoz, Jordi. 2009. "From National-Catholicism to Democratic Patriotism? Democratization and reconstruction of national pride: the case of Spain (1981–2000)." *Ethnic and Racial Studies* 32 (4): 616–639.

Rousseau, Jean-Jacques. 1968. *The Social Contract.* Translated by Maurice Cranston. New York, New York: Penguin Classics.

Watson, Cameron J. 2007. *Basque Nationalism and Political Violence: The Ideological and Intellectual Origins of ETA.* Reno, Nevada: Center for Basque Studies – University of Nevada, Reno.

Weber, Eugen. 1976. *Peasants into Frenchmen: The Modernization of Rural France 1870–1914.* Stanford, California: Stanford University Press.

Whitfield, Theresa. 2015. *The Basque Conflict and ETA: The Difficulties of an Ending.* Special Report 384, Washington, DC: United States Institute of Peace.

Zabalo Bilbao, Julen, and Onintza Odriozola Irizar. 2017. "The Importance of Historical Context: A New Discourse on the Nation in Basque Nationalism?" *Nationalism and Ethnic Politics* 23 (2): 134–154.

Zabalo, Julen, and Mikel Saratxo. 2015. "ETA ceasefire: Armed struggle vs. political practice in Basque nationalism." *Ethnicities* 15 (3): 362–384.

4 Surviving the Jacobin state

Separatist terrorism with Brittany's ARB and Corsica's FLNC

Liam Anderson

Introduction

The persistence and prevalence of militant ethnic minority nationalism (hereafter ethno-nationalism) into the second decade of the twenty-first century is puzzling to many scholars.[1] Specifically, it seems to cut against the optimistic expectations of many in the academy that the forces of modernization and globalization would gradually erode the significance of local identity differences as states converge around a set of shared institutional forms (free market capitalism and democracy) and that, in Walt's (2014) words, "Messy local issues like minority rights or border disputes would gradually disappear from the global policy agenda and we'd all converge into one big and mostly happy global family." Given this, it is equally perplexing that that since the 1960s, some of the most active ethno-nationalist groups have emerged in Western Europe, a region in which borders and national identities were assumed to be fixed in stone and beyond dispute. Disturbingly, there is little approaching a consensus among scholars on why militant ethno-nationalist groups emerge, and how best to address them. The academy is as paralyzed as the international community in the face of forces that defy easy explanation and resist simple solutions.

For some scholars, accommodating the demands of restive ethnic minorities is the preferable option; the formal recognition of linguistic diversity in India, for example, or the provision of territorial autonomy in Spain can serve to alleviate minority concerns and diminish secessionist tendencies. Others disagree. For critics, policies that institutionalize ethnic identity via language recognition, power-sharing, or the grant of territorial autonomy only serve to harden and deepen these divisions within society, resulting in escalating demands and heightening secessionist potential (Bunce 1999, 2004; Roeder 1991, 2007, 2009; Cornell 2002; Brubaker 1996; Gorenburg 2001; Leff 1999). For such critics, adopting policies and institutions that facilitate the integration or assimilation of minority ethnicities into the dominant ethnic majority are preferable.

As the state that invented the term "Jacobin," it is not surprising that France, among all European states, is among the least inclined to accommodate the demands of its ethnic minority groups, whether these are for official recognition of regional languages, increased territorial autonomy, or outright separation from the state (McGarry and O'Leary 2005). Over time this has created problems for the French state. Alluding to France's ethnic diversity, former President Charles de Gaulle once memorably asked, "Comment voulez-vous gouverner un pays qui a deux cent quarante-six variétés de fromage?" ("How can you govern a country which has two hundred and forty-six varieties of cheese?") Sooner or later, the almost pathological obsession of the French state to homogenize, centralize, assimilate, and thereby, eliminate diversity, was destined to meet serious resistance. In due course, from the 1960s onwards, France faced an increasingly ominous threat from terrorist groups, both domestic and international. Included in the former, were, for the first time, ethnically defined terrorist groups demanding separation from France and prepared to use violence to achieve this. The secessionist terrorist threat from Breton groups was low-intensity, almost entirely bloodless, and largely spent by the turn of the millennium; that from Corsican groups was high-intensity, much more violent, and has only recently subsided. Neither secessionist movement enjoyed widespread popular support within its respective region, and secession was never a serious possibility in either case, but both challenged the very legitimacy of the French state, and served as stark reminders to French officials that after 200 years of assimilationist pressure, some "peasants" still refused to be turned into Frenchmen. The focus of this chapter is on separatist terrorism in Brittany and Corsica. The following section provides a brief summary of the scholarly debate on how best to deal with the demands of recalcitrant ethno-nationalism. The subsequent two sections deal sequentially with each of the two cases, Brittany and Corsica, providing historical context, a synopsis of grievances, and a summary of the recent activities of the relevant separatist terrorist groups. The fourth section analyzes the responses of French governments over time to the emergence of ethno-nationalism in Brittany and Corsica and to its escalation to violent separatist terrorism. The concluding section evaluates the French approach to managing ethnic divisions in terms of efficacy. Superficially, the French approach can be deemed a success, in that violence has abated and France has yet to suffer a secession, but on a deeper level, a case can be made that it was France's consistent refusal to accommodate the demands of moderate nationalists that helped spawn the problem in the first place. Moreover, while the violence has subsided for the time being, there is little evidence that the nationalist flame has been terminally extinguished in either region.

Theoretical context

The resurgence of militant ethno-nationalism in the heart of Western Europe during the 1960s and 1970s presented a challenge to historians and social scientists because up to that point, the scholarly consensus had been that an inverse relationship existed between strength of ethnic identity and development/modernization. As scholars struggled to explain why Breton separatists, for example, would embark on a bombing campaign in one of the most advanced states in Western Europe, an equally pressing concern became how best to deal with this emerging threat or how to avoid it in the first place.[2] There is no scholarly consensus on how best to manage ethnically divided societies to prevent the rise of violent ethno-nationalism but the range of options available to liberal democratic governments can be distilled down to a basic choice; governments can either ignore ethnic difference, and design policies and institutions aimed at assimilation or integration (denial), or they can adopt institutions and polices that recognize the durable reality of ethnic identities (accommodation) (McGarry *et al.* 2008). Obviously, there are a range of possibilities and permutations both within and between these two basic approaches, but the two cannot be easily reconciled because they reflect different assumptions about the ontological status of ethnic identity. Are ethnic identities, as some contend, socially constructed, inauthentic, and manipulable, or, as others maintain, deep-rooted, durable, and meaningful for those who hold them? The latter set of assumptions lead logically to an accommodationist approach by which policies and political institutions are designed to alleviate the concerns of ethnic minorities, thereby diminishing societal tensions and avoiding an escalation to violence. Commonly proposed options here are formalized ethnic power-sharing in the central government, the proportional allocation of administrative positions in the institutions of state (including security forces), the legal or constitutional recognition of ethnic minority languages, and the provision of territorial autonomy to geographically concentrated ethnic groups.[3] The last of these has become increasingly popular as a means of preventing or ending ethnic conflict and has come in for close scrutiny among scholars (McGarry, O'Leary, and Simeon 2009; Lijphart 1977; Levy 2007; Wolff 2010; Bunce 1999; Bunce and Watts 2005; Roeder 1991, 2007; Brubaker 1996; Gorenburg 2001; Leff 1999).

For critics, the institutionalization of ethnic identity via the official recognition of minority languages or creation of autonomous ethnic units only serves to harden and deepen these divisions within society (Nordlinger 1972; Taylor 1992; Lorwin 1966). Far from diminishing demands for secession, these institutions increase the willingness and desire of autonomous ethnic units to "go it alone," and, crucially, furnish them with the institutional resources necessary to mount a successful secession bid (Cornell 2002; Roeder 2009).

The alternative to accommodating ethnicity is a strategy of denial. A range of policies and techniques can be used here; what they share is an intent to diminish the salience of (minority) ethnic identities as a source of societal division. Aggressive forms of denial include blanket prohibitions on the use of languages other than that used by the majority ethnic group, the drawing of electoral districts to dilute the voting power of ethnic minorities, or the delineation of sub unit boundaries to cut across the boundaries of ethnic minority regions. Moderately aggressive forms include a centralized, unitary system of center–periphery relations, the use of majoritarian electoral systems, and the designation of a single official national language to be used in public contexts. Also common in liberal democracies is the allocation of rights and liberties on an exclusively individual (rather than group) basis in an "ethnically blind" constitution interpreted by a neutral judiciary (Roeder 2005). Although nominally neutral, this approach often has the effect of privileging the dominant ethnic majority by failing to protect minority group rights. For example, if minority ethnic languages are not constitutionally or legally protected, then the language of the dominant majority will inevitably win out in the end.

The empirical evidence on whether strategies of accommodation or denial are more effective at managing ethnic tensions in divided societies is inconclusive (Anderson 2014, 2015). In cases such as India, where the federal system was reorganized to accommodate the country's linguistic diversity, the results have been largely positive; at the same time, France has yet to suffer a serious secessionist threat, despite its considerable ethnic diversity, and despite its consistent reluctance to accommodate the demands of ethnic groups. The following sections examine in detail the French state's efforts to manage relations with two of its ethnic minority groups, Corsicans and Bretons, with a view to establishing whether France's success in this regard is more apparent than real.

Brittany

Historical context

The history of Brittany, a region that occupies the Armorican Peninsula in Western France, and its relations with the French state, are, unsurprisingly, contested. The region has been inhabited for over 5,000 years, but acquired much of its distinctive Celtic identity (and language) from a significant in-migration of Celts from the West of the British Isles (mainly Wales and Cornwall) during the fifth century AD. Subsequently, three regularities, or patterns can be discerned with respect to the history of the region and its relations with various iterations of the French state. First, for much of its existence, Brittany enjoyed long periods of either outright independence (the fifth century–1532), or autonomy within the French state (1532–1789). Second, repeated efforts by centralizing Parisian powers to subdue the Armorican Peninsula have usually been actively, often violently, resisted by various Breton forces.[4] Third, from 1532 onwards, but especially after 1789, the French state has consistently refused to acknowledge, and often actively repressed, attempts by Breton activists to assert a distinct ethnic identity.

These historical regularities collectively form the bedrock of Breton nationalist historiographies of Breton–French relations. It was not until the late-nineteenth century, however, during what became known as the first *Emsav*, that explicitly Breton nationalist political and cultural movements began to appear on the scene to articulate coherent grievances and demands.[5] Aside from the "lethargic" (Reece 1977, 55) and ineffectual Association Bretonne (AB), the first serious organizational manifestation of Breton nationalist sentiment was the Union Regional Bretonne (URB), which formed in 1898 as a nonpartisan and nonsectarian movement "to develop by the revival of Breton sentiment all forms of Breton activity" (ibid., 54). Like the AB that preceded it, the URB was dominated by conservative (anti-republican) societal elites and it proved equally ineffective at achieving its goals. Critically, the URB was fatally hampered by internal divisions, most notably between Breton-speaking members (the activist rank and file) and Francophones and Gallo-speakers (most of the leadership). The disintegration of the URB paved the way for the emergence of the most strident and articulate Breton nationalist movement of the early era—the *Parti Nationaliste Breton* (PNB). The founding of the PNB in 1911 marked an important sea change in the evolution of the movement. Formed to "protest the French oppression that we have borne for centuries," the PNB's stated goal was to recapture the rights and liberties lost since 1532, and, ultimately, to separate completely from France. The PNB was, therefore, the first openly secessionist Breton nationalist movement to emerge.

Although lacking any coherent plan for achieving independence, the PNB paved the way for the post-war emergence of a succession of separatist movements and publications (*Breiz Atao* being the best known of these) that defined themselves in terms of "extreme ideological hostility" to the French state and considered themselves engaged in a "moral struggle to the death between two races and two civilizations" (ibid., 92). Accompanying this drift toward a more radical reconception of the Breton nationalist struggle as a clash between competing races, the 1930s witnessed a sharp rightward turn in terms of ideological orientation. The 1930s also evidenced the first attacks by a Breton group that could plausibly be defined as terrorism. The murky and mysterious group *Gwenn-ha-Du* ("White and Black" after the colors of Brittany's flag) claimed responsibility for a series of bomb attacks during the decade prior to World War II, all targeting symbols of the French state. The unfortunate, but predictable, end point of this shift towards extremism and violence was a disastrous policy of collaboration during World War II, first with the invading German forces, then with the Vichy Government. The collaborationist policy was instigated by a small cadre of extremist fringe leaders and only ever enjoyed the support of a small portion of the Breton population at large. Nonetheless, the taint of collaboration stunted the development of the Breton nationalist movement for decades after the war.

The first serious post-war manifestation of Breton political expression emerged in 1950 with the formation of the *Comite d'Etudes et de Liaison des Interest Bretons* (CELIB). The CELIB's sole purpose was to address Brittany's economic development (or lack thereof) and to this end, it focused exclusively on drafting an economic plan for the region and lobbying Paris for its adoption. Although the CELIB enjoyed the support of a broad range of the region's most influential leaders and most of its parliamentary delegation, the economic plan it proposed was eventually superseded and effectively negated by the central government's creation of regional economic development commissions (CODERS) for all economic regions in France. The failure of an organization that was so studiously apolitical, non-confrontational, and non-nationalistic to achieve even the most modest of concessions from Paris sparked something of a backlash. The groups that emerged to champion the cause during and after the 1960s were generally less moderate in their demands and more radically active in their tactics and strategies. The formation of the *Mouvement pour l'Organisation de la Bretagne* (MOB) in the late-1950s marked an important turning point in this respect. Like the CELIB, the MOB was avowedly non-partisan, but its narrative of economic exploitation based on a theory of "internal colonialism" marked a striking departure from the moderate rhetoric of the CELIB. This focus on Brittany's status as an internal colony of Paris and the economic exploitation that this necessarily engendered naturally led Breton nationalists in a more leftward direction. When the MOB fragmented in the mid-1960s, the bulk of its membership left to form the *Union Democratique Bretonne* (UDB). Building on the logic of internal colonialism thesis, the UDB's rallying cry was for Breton autonomy and, more optimistically, for the replacement of the capitalist economic system with a new system of planned social and economic democracy. Although the UDB has since suffered periodic crises and fluctuations in popularity, it survives to the present and still holds seats on Breton regional councils.

Contemporaneous with the emergence of the UDB, a secretive group of Breton nationalists that came to be known as the *Front de Liberation de la Bretagne* (FLB), announced its presence on the scene with a series of bomb attacks against inanimate targets during the late-1960s. Following a brief appearance during the 1930s, Breton secessionist terrorism had re-emerged with a vengeance by the 1970s.

Breton grievances

Historically, the grievances of Breton nationalists fall into three broad categories: threats to the structure of the prevailing Breton power structure, economic underdevelopment and, by extension, exploitation, and efforts by the French state to eradicate Breton culture and language. Early manifestations of Breton resistance to the centralizing state, such as the post-revolutionary *Chouannerie* and the various nineteenth century iterations of the Association Bretonne (AB) were driven by a desire for self-preservation rather than the preservation of a distinct Breton identity (Reece 1977, 18–20). Brittany remained overwhelmingly agrarian and retained its quasi-feudal social structures until late into the nineteenth century. The survival of Brittany's two main power structures—the landed nobility and the Church—which together wielded a virtual monopoly of social, economic and political power on the peninsula, were self-evidently threatened by the powerful secular, republican forces unleashed by the events of 1789, and then again as the French state increasingly asserted its power over the regions in the late 1800s. Reactionary forces of the right continued to dominate the Breton national movement until the post-World War II period. Subsequently, a cluster of economic grievances focused mainly on the underdevelopment of Brittany relative to other French regions (particularly Paris) began to assume increasing prominence in the Breton nationalist narrative. The de facto failure of the CELIB's moderate proposals for some degree of local control over the region's economic development had, by the 1960s, given way to a significantly more robust nationalist narrative that conceptualized Brittany as an internal colony of Paris. From this perspective, the problem was not just the economic underdevelopment of Brittany, but that Paris intentionally maintained the region in a state of underdevelopment and dependence to better exploit its natural resources and cheap labor force. In other words, Brittany's status relative to Paris was analogous to Algeria's status relative to France.[6] Ironically, the colonization thesis was gaining traction at a time when differentials in social and economic indicators between Brittany and the rest of the country were declining significantly.[7]

What remains at the heart of Breton grievances is the deep-rooted and long-standing antipathy toward the French state for its concerted efforts to eradicate Brittany's cultural, historical, and linguistic identity. The French state's dogged determination to "turn peasants into Frenchmen" has been zealously pursued since 1789 and has been largely effective at imposing a single French language on recalcitrant regions, especially Brittany. At the time of the Revolution, only one-fifth of the population of France could actually speak French and more than one-third knew no French at all (Mendel 2004, 68). This began to change after 1793 when legislation was passed requiring children to "learn to speak, read and write the French language" and mandating "French only" instruction, and gathered momentum from the 1870s onwards with the adoption of mandatory free public education throughout France. Alongside the legislative assault on regional languages, the stigmatization of those using the Breton language at school was unofficial, but brutally effective. In many Breton schools, an object—usually either an old shoe or a piece of wood (the *symbole*, as it was known)—with a piece of string attached was hung around the neck of any child caught speaking Breton. To get rid of the *symbole* required the victim to catch another student using a Breton word; after informing the teacher of the transgression, the *symbole* was transferred to the new victim. At the end of the day the student in possession of the *symbole* was punished, sometimes with a severe beating (McDonald 1989, 46–47; Reece 1977, 31). In religious schools, Bretonnants were often told that speaking Breton offended God, while in playgrounds, signs were posted which warned "it is forbidden to spit and to speak Breton" (Reece 1977, 32). The effectiveness of official state policies and these informal practices, which in some schools continued until the 1960s, can be gauged by examining the data. In 1863, 98 percent of the population of lower Brittany spoke Breton, and it was the *only* language spoken by 86 percent of the population. By the 1950s, those speaking any Breton had declined to 73 percent, and monolingual Breton speakers to 6 percent (Boomgaard 2008, 282–283). As of the 1970s, fewer than half of the population of lower Brittany spoke any Breton, and monolinguals were basically extinct. Current estimates place the number of those capable of speaking Breton at between 250,000 and 400,000. The stark decline in knowledge of the Breton language during the twentieth century was not entirely involuntary. The association of the Breton language with demeaning cultural stereotypes depicting Bretons as uncivilized simpletons (Reece 1977, 282) led many Breton parents to teach their children French in preference to Breton so that they would not have to experience the same humiliation (ibid.,

24). Indeed, despairing Breton nationalists often attribute the decline of the language, at least in part, to the "army of anti-Breton mothers" who refused to speak Breton to their children in the home (ibid., 35). Accelerating the demise of the Breton language was the massive outmigration of Bretons during the twentieth century, and their replacement by Francophones from metropolitan France, mainly Paris. In the 20-year period after 1954, for example, migration from Brittany "reached flood tide proportions" as more than half a million Bretons left their homeland to take up residence elsewhere in France (Reece 1979, 285).

The problem for nationalists was that Breton speakers have always been overwhelmingly concentrated in lower Brittany (Basse-Bretagne), whereas the dominant language of upper Brittany has been either standard French, or Gallo, a dialect closely related to French. Hence, the appeal of any nationalist group that defined Breton identity in linguistic terms, or that prioritized defense of the language over all other concerns, was necessarily limited. Nationalist appeals couched in terms of a distinct Breton culture, or even along explicitly ethnic/racial (Celtic) lines are potentially accessible to all native inhabitants of the region, but the precise content of Breton culture has always been somewhat vague; as one observer puts it, "it is easier to define what Breton identity is not than what it is" (Gemie 2002, 151). The French government has generally paid much more attention to stifling the Breton language than it has to squashing overt manifestations of Breton culture. Consequently, the suppression of Breton culture scarcely qualifies as a grievance. Since the 1970s, indeed, Breton cultural expressions, such as festivals (*festou-noz*) and performances by Breton pipe-bands (*bagadou*), have greatly increased in popularity and have become large-scale commercial ventures, in some cases attracting hundreds of thousands of attendees (Gemie 2005).

Of the three clusters of grievance identified above, the best known Breton secessionist terrorist group, the Breton Revolutionary Army/Breton Liberation Front (ARB/FLB), focused primarily on the second. To the extent that the ARB/FLB had a single, coherent ideology, it was firmly located on the left of the political spectrum (either Socialist or Marxist) with rhetoric steeped in the narrative of internal colonization. In its first manifesto, released in 1968, the FLB characterized its campaign against the French state as an anticolonial struggle and pledged to "borrow the schemes and methods that have proven their worth in anticolonialist struggles elsewhere in the world" (Reece 1977, 204). The manifesto paid lip-service to the idea of Brittany's Celtic identity but essentially skirted the divisive language issue entirely. By focusing on a narrative of internal colonization and the consequent economic exploitation of the people of Brittany, issues that affected all Bretons, the FLB's program had (in theory) potential appeal to the entire population of the peninsula.

The FLB/ARB: recent activities

Aside from *Gwenn-Ha-Du*'s sporadic bombing campaign during the 1930s, the Breton nationalist movement and its numerous constituent organizations were studiously non-violent until the mid-1960s. This changed seemingly overnight when, on June 11, 1966, the previously unknown Front de Liberation de la Bretagne (FLB) issued a communique claiming responsibility for the attempted bombing of a municipal tax office in St. Brieuc. The attack was staged, according to the communique, in protest at the arrest of three young Bretons in St. Nazaire for desecrating the French flag. Further, the note promised to conduct a campaign of violence against "the symbols of the occupying power in Brittany" and concluded with the pledge that, "our struggle will end only in victory" (Reece 1977, 201). The promised campaign began with half a dozen bombings in the latter part of 1967 and increased in intensity during 1968, with more than 20 bombing attacks, mainly targeting tax offices, recorded during the year. By the end of 1968, however, it had become evident that the FLB was not a single unified entity; rather, there appeared to be two autonomous FLBs in operation—one run from Ireland (the so-called "softs") and another (the "hards") based out of Paris. To add to the confusion, there also appeared to be two FLB armed wings, the Armee Republicanne Bretonne and the Armee Revolutionnaire Bretonne, both of which yielded the same acronym (ARB), making it all but impossible to discern which group was responsible for which attack.

Barely two years after the dramatic entry of the FLB onto the stage, French police were able to unravel much of the group's network following the arrest and questioning of Jean-Jacques Senart, the owner of a red Citroen D.S. that had been seen close to several of the FLB bombing targets. Senart quickly implicated fellow members and police eventually rounded up more than 50 alleged FLB members (including four priests) by the end of January 1969. There appears to have been a significant degree of sympathy for arrested members among the Breton population at large (Reece 1977, 208), and partly in recognition of this, President De Gaulle amnestied several FLB prisoners, including the four priests during, a visit to the region in February 1969. All remaining prisoners were subsequently amnestied by the incoming Pompidou administration in mid-1969.

Following a brief hiatus, the FLB resumed its campaign of violence in 1971, with incendiary bomb attacks on several tax offices and an unsuccessful arson attack on the customs office in St. Malmo. Also targeted were "instruments and symbols of the capitalist exploitation" of the Breton people, such as bulldozers and a milk truck owned by a Paris-based dairy company. The campaign continued into mid-1972, culminating in the bombing of a villa owned by a wealthy Parisian businessman in Rotheneuf. At this point, police arrested 10 suspected FLB terrorists and charged them with subversion. Following a brief trial in October 1972, two of the 10 were acquitted, and the remaining eight were dealt prison sentences ranging from two to five years that were suspended "due to extenuating circumstances." Although the precise nature of the "extenuating circumstances" was not revealed, the assumption was that by not imprisoning the eight, the French government would thereby avoid gifting the FLB its first real martyrs. The relative leniency of the sentences did nothing to diminish the group's activities, and the 1970s marked the highpoint of the FLB campaign, at least in terms of frequency of attacks. The most spectacular operations were probably a February 1974 attack on the radio tower of France's public broadcast corporation (ORTF) in Roc-Tredudon, which caused 5,000,000 francs worth of damage, and the detonation of an explosive device in the south wing of the Versailles Palace in 1978. In a letter claiming responsibility for the latter blast, the FLB justified the bombing by alleging that "the Breton people are oppressed: the land of Brittany is occupied by French military camps; the Breton language and culture are denied and destroyed by the imperialist French power" (*Decatur Herald*).

Following the Versailles bombing, there are no recorded details of any Breton terrorist incidents until 1985. This lull in activities appears to have been caused by several large-scale police operations to round up and imprison suspected FLB members during the latter years of the 1970s. When these members were granted amnesties by the incoming Mitterrand administration in 1981, most renounced violence and joined peaceful nationalist parties. The upshot, although details are scant, appears to have been the disintegration of the FLB itself in the early 1980s. Thereafter, the armed struggle was continued by the ARB, and a new political group—*Emgann* ("Fight")—emerged in 1982–1983 to serve as the ARB's political wing. The formation of *Emgann* and the emergence of the ARB from the ruins of the FLB did not immediately translate into increased activity; indeed, the Global Terrorism Database (GTD) records only 10 acts of terror attributable to the ARB throughout the entire 1980s, none of which resulted in casualties.[8]

The *modus operandi* of these attacks remained much the same as before, in that the weapons of choice were explosives, the targets were government offices or French-owned businesses, and the goal was property damage rather than human casualties. During the latter years of the 1990s, the intensity of the ARB's terror activities increased again. In October 1998, for example, a bomb was detonated in the town hall in Belfort, the home town of then Interior Minister Jean-Pierre Chevenement, causing damage estimated at several million francs; then in June the same year a tax collection agency was targeted in Cintegabelle, the electoral district of Prime Minister Lionel Jospin in an attack believed to be a response to the refusal of President Jacques Chirac to ratify the European Charter on Regional and Minority Languages.[9] The ARB's most spectacular operation to date, the theft of eight and a half tons of the explosive Titane 30 from a warehouse in Plevin came in September 1999. The professionalism of the theft stood in stark contrast to the reliably amateur nature of typical ARB operations and led police to suspect that the heist had been conducted with the assistance of the Basque separatist group ETA. This suspicion appeared to be confirmed when, three days later, two ETA members were arrested in Pau (in France's Basque region) driving a van containing two and a half tons of the Plevin explosive. On the face of it, the ARB's willingness to collaborate with ETA, a group responsible for hundreds of deaths and thousands of casualties, appeared to mark a dangerous departure for a group that had hitherto gone to great lengths to avoid civilian casualties. Unfortunately, the ARB's next major attack—and the one for which it is best remembered—lent weight to this interpretation. In April 2000, an explosive device detonated in a McDonald's restaurant in Quevert near the city of Dinan, killing a waitress (Laurence Turbec) in the process. Although the ARB always denied responsibility for the attack, the circumstantial evidence strongly suggested ARB involvement. Four ARB members, who were also either current or former members of *Emgann*, were eventually charged and tried for the bombings. All were eventually acquitted, but convicted and imprisoned for various terms for their involvement in the post-1993 bombing campaign. The McDonald's bombing and the backlash it provoked among the Breton population marked the end of the ARB as a terrorist threat. Two attacks attributed to the ARB by the GTD—both Molotov cocktails thrown at police stations in 2014—are the only evidence that the ARB continued to exist beyond 2000.

During its 35 year terrorist career, the FLB/ARB committed somewhere between 250 and 300 attacks, exclusively targeting property, symbols of the French occupation, and instruments of capitalist oppression. Aside from the death of the McDonald's waitress, the only human casualties of the FLB/ARB's long campaign were two members of the ARB who blew themselves up trying to diffuse one of their devices.

Corsica

Historical context

There are similarities between Corsica's experiences as part of the French state and those of Brittany, but there are also important differences. Foremost among the latter is that prior to its incorporation into France in the late-eighteenth century, Corsica had been occupied, almost continually, by a bewildering array of external actors, ranging from the Carthaginians and ancient Greeks, through the Romans and Byzantines, to the Republic of Pisa, Lombards, Tuscans and even a Genovese bank. The presence of various powers from the North of Italy explains why the closest relative of Corsica's indigenous language is Tuscan Italian, and the latter was indeed the island's "high" language until its progressive displacement by French after 1789. The longest lasting occupier—the Republic of Genoa—ruled Corsica (with some interruptions) from the mid-fourteenth century until 1755 (technically, until 1768). The harshness of Genoan rule, characterized as years of "cruelty and misery" (Ramsay 1983, 3), meant that by the time the French first became involved Corsican affairs in 1738, the Island's inhabitants welcomed the intervention if it meant the end of Genoan domination. As Ramsay (1983, 4) notes, when a French expeditionary force landed at Corsica to subdue an anti-Genoan uprising, the "benevolence" of the occupation "contrasted so vividly with the normal pattern of Genoan administration that the enthusiasm of a 'French Party' was at once engendered."

Unlike in Brittany, where incorporation into the French state was greeted with a mix of hostility and ambivalence, French influence over Corsica has generally been viewed positively, or at least, as the lesser of two evils, by a majority of the population. Partly because of this, the first stirrings of Corsican nationalism did not make themselves felt until the turn of the twentieth century, and even then, only fleetingly. At this time, a reassertion of Corsican identity occurred in the form of several journals and periodicals dedicated to the publication of Corsican language, literature, and poetry (Stephens 1978, 333). More explicitly political in orientation was *A Tramuntana*, a right-wing journal edited by Santu Casanova (the "founding father of Corsican language activism") and written entirely in Corsican, that appeared between 1896 and 1919. Also influential were a manifesto for Corsican independence *A Cispra: Antologia Annuale*, written by two school teachers in 1914, and the cultural/political weekly *A Muvra*, founded in 1920 by Petru Rocca to promote autonomous Corsican identity. Rocca also founded the island's first discernably autonomist political party—the Partitu Corsu d'Azione—in 1923, which evolved into the *Partitu Corsu Autonomista* (PCA) in 1927. As the name suggests, the PCA advocated for Corsican political autonomy and, more specifically, for official recognition of the Corsican language and the re-opening of the island's only University (at Corte) that had been shut down by the French in 1768. Rocca ultimately came unstuck during World War II through his support for Mussolini and unification with Italy and immediately after the liberation, he was tried along with a small number of like-minded nationalists and sentenced to 15 years of hard labor on Devil's Island, Guyana.

The unlikely initial trigger for a revival in Corsican nationalist sentiment was the French government's threat to dismantle the island's only railway line in 1960. That, together with the inadequacy and high cost of transport links to the mainland and a general sense of economic neglect, prompted a group of Corsican businessmen and professional to organize *Le movement du 29 novembre*. The group was an apolitical group of concerned citizens that hoped to stimulate public discussion of the island's economic plight and possible solutions. A second group, the *Defense des Interets Economiques de la Corse* (DIECO), soon followed. Although both groups had exclusively economic concerns and were avowedly non-ideological, the atmosphere of protest also spawned other groups that were more political in orientation. Among the most influential of these were *L'Union Corse l'Avenir* (UCA), founded in 1963 by Charles Santoni and Dominique Alfonsi, and the Simeoni brothers' (Max and Edmond) Committee of Studies for the Defense of Corsican Interests (CEDIC). In July 1966, these two groups organized a convention targeting young people that attracted over 500 delegates from all walks of Corsican life to discuss the island's problems. The intention was to forge a common "Corsican Regionalist Front" (FRC), but differences between the two groups soon surfaced over goals and tactics. Although the FRC never became a cohesive force because of this basic difference in opinion, these two groups, and their various subsequent iterations and splinter groups, were to dominate the nationalist movement for the following 50 years.

The shift from regionalist, to autonomist to separatist demands on the part of nationalist groups occurred rapidly, and the CEDIC's moderate regionalist position, focused primarily on economic issues, soon morphed into something more encompassing. In 1965, CEDIC reorganized itself into *l'Azzione Regionaliste Corse* (ARC) and began to link economic concerns with those relating to Corsican identity. In the preamble to its constitution, for example, the Corsican problem was characterized as a failure of the French state, through its "obtuse centralism," to recognize the basic cultural and ethnic differences that existed between Corsica and France (Ramsay 1983, 48). The solution, according to the ARC was an autonomous status for Corsica "within the framework of the French Republic" (ibid., 49). In other words, the ARC was autonomist, not separatist. To carry its message to the Corsican people, the ARC eschewed direct participation in electoral politics in favor of "direct action." This involved organized protests, sit-ins, and the like, but also actions designed to just cross the line separating legality from illegality. The goal of actions such as a 1969 boycott of road tax payments, orchestrated by the ARC was to prompt a reaction from authorities that would bring publicity to the cause.

Against a background of escalating tensions between French authorities and Corsican groups, the so-called "red mud" affair, which involved the dumping of toxic waste by an Italian chemical company Montedison some 40 miles from the Corsican coast, added fuel to the fire. The perceived reluctance of the French government to take decisive action prompted outrage in Corsica. The bombing of an Italian-owned ferry in Bastia harbor on February 1, 1973 was followed on February 17, by an organized day of protest that drew more than 10,000 Corsicans to the streets. In Bastia, clashes between protestors and riot police escalated to the use of Molotov cocktails on the part of protestors and baton charges and tear gas on the part of police. To capitalize on the trajectory of events, representatives from the ARC and FRC met in 1973 to forge a common front. The meeting yielded a declaration that was left-wing in tone and unambiguously autonomist in intent, but stopped short of calling for—outright separation from France. After name changes to both groups (the FRC to the *Partitu di u Populu Corsu* [PPC], and the ARC to the *Azzione per a Rinascita Corsa*) the stage was set for a more intense confrontation with French authorities.

At the ARC's annual congress in August 1973, Edmund Simeoni appeared to raise the stakes when he declared, "Autonomy will not be granted to us. It will have to be grasped.... The Corsican people is condemned to rebel" (Ramsay 1983, 74–75). At the same time, a low-level bombing campaign by, as yet, undeclared perpetrators was gathering momentum. The group responsible—the newly formed *Fronte Paesanu Corsu di Liberazioni* (FPCL)—announced its existence in October 1973 with a published manifesto entitled "Ultimatum to the French Government" in which it demanded, among other things, the obligatory teaching of Corsican in schools and the replacement of all French civil servants on the island with Corsican natives. The FPCL, together with its offshoot, *Ghjusttizia Paolina* (GP) were responsible for over 100 bomb attacks during 1974 against French government property and "colonial" targets.

The pivotal point at which the disruptive but mostly peaceful Corsican nationalist movement was transformed into separatist terrorism came in August 1975, when leaders of the ARC staged an occupation of a vineyard in Aleria owned by a *pieds noir* in protest at the owner's illegal financial dealings that detrimentally affected local wine producers. The occupation was entirely peaceful until the

French government opted for a display of force by dispatching 1,200 riot police to the scene, backed by helicopters and armored cars, and delivering an ultimatum to the occupiers. When they refused to comply, government forces chose to storm the complex, shots were fired, and two riot police were killed.

According to Ramsay (1983, 103), the authorities' decision to deploy massive force and issue an ultimatum represented a fatal misunderstanding of Corsican psychology. To have complied with the ultimatum would have meant a loss of face, and "the Corsican sense of honor almost inevitably dictated that such a humiliation could not be accepted" (ibid., 103). The government then compounded its error by banning the ARC and charging 10 of its members with serious crimes. The decision with met with protests, then riots on the streets of Bastia that resulted in 19 injuries and the death of another riot policeman. It is difficult to overstate the degree to which the Aleria incident radicalized the Corsican nationalist cause; suffice it to say, the best known, most violent, and longest lasting separatist terrorist group—the FLNC—began violent operations less than a year later.

Corsican grievances

Corsica's French connection was cemented early on by its most famous son. Napoleon Bonaparte's time at the helm of the French state lasted barely a decade, but during these years, Corsica was definitively integrated into the French state. By 1815, the "issue of Corsica's 'Frenchness' was ... beyond doubt," and, according to Ramsay (1983, 10), "the basic fact of Napoleon's Corsican background had been the greatest single factor in this development." The other person responsible for anchoring Corsica to France was Charles De Gaulle. During World War II, Corsica first came under Vichy control, and was then occupied by the Italians from November 1942 onwards. The Italian occupation provoked widespread resistance within Corsica that ultimately led to an uprising in September 1943. Supported by about 6,000 Free French forces and some U.S. marines, the Corsicans had driven out all occupying forces within a month, making Corsica the first piece of French territory to be liberated. The day after the last German left the island, General De Gaulle flew triumphantly into Corsica's capital, Ajaccio, and toured the island delivering speeches lionizing the patriotism and courage of the Corsican people. The visit initiated a mutual love affair that was to endure, much to the electoral benefit of De Gaulle, until De Gaulle's final retirement in 1969. Thus, while World War II tainted Breton nationalism for decades after, the same event burnished Corsica's patriotic credentials and reaffirmed its allegiance to the French state.

Another important difference between Corsican and Breton experiences with the Jacobin state was the impact of the French Revolution. The Revolution was a direct assault on the two pillars of power—the aristocracy and the church—that had dominated Brittany for centuries. In Brittany, this was strongly resisted by the institutions affected, and in many ways, the early birth of Breton nationalism can be traced to this reaction against the threat this posed to the prevailing order.

In Corsica, conversely, the existing social structure, based largely on clans (basically, extended family units) was left mostly untouched by the events of 1789. Clan leaders had dominated life on the island for centuries prior to the Revolution, and, in many ways, continue to dominate to the present day. These various differences between Corsica and Brittany's historical relations with the French state help explain why organized nationalism took longer to emerge in the latter, because, these differences aside, many of the factors that explain the rise of Breton nationalism—economic underdevelopment, inadequate infrastructure, mass emigration, depopulation and a sustained assault on linguistic and cultural identity—were also present in Corsica. The topography of Corsica, with its mountainous and largely inaccessible interior, makes the island unsuitable for most economic activities. For most of its modern existence, tourism and agriculture have been the mainstay industries, and neither sector was well-developed by the 1950s. Hence, the initial grievances of organized Corsican nationalism were apolitical and almost exclusively economic.

In an effort to address problems in both sectors, the French government issued a Regional Action Plan for Corsica in 1957 that created two agencies—SOMIVAC, to help develop agriculture, and SETCO for the development of tourism. By the end of the 1960s, however, efforts to develop these areas were merely generating new grievances. The expansion of the tourist trade was mostly accomplished with entrepreneurial management and capital from outside Corsica, and the jobs produced and available to Corsicans were mostly of the menial variety. SOMIVAC's ambitious plan to develop the Island's Eastern Plain into 50,000 hectares of flat and fertile farming land backfired when most of the land was acquired at preferential rates by so-called *pied noirs*, who began to leave Algeria for Corsica in large numbers in 1958. Hence, the French government's efforts to promote and develop these two sectors during the 1950s and 1960s were increasingly perceived by Corsicans as benefitting non-Corsicans to the detriment of the island's well-being.

Beyond tourism and agriculture there was not much else to develop. Corsica was, and is, disproportionately dependent on the French government for subsides and economic assistance, and Corsicans have also relied heavily on the mainland for employment. The traditional pattern of employment for young Corsicans was to either migrate to the French mainland to seek work, or to serve in the various colonial institutions of the French Empire. Remittances from the diaspora sent back to the island were a critical source of income, and upon retirement, many Corsicans returned to their homeland, bringing with them generous government pensions. Either directly or indirectly, therefore, the French government was responsible for the livelihoods of a significant percentage of the island's inhabitants. Corsica, as one observer describes it, is "economically passive," in that nearly 50 percent of its revenue derives from pensions, government salaries, or social security (Andereggen 1985, 68). This began to change during the 1950s as the French state progressively divested itself of empire and employment in the colonial service evaporated, leaving the island with a serious and growing unemployment problem. The upshot was greater levels of outmigration to the French mainland; at the same time, migration into Corsica increased during the 1950s and 1960s as first French Algerians (the *pieds noirs*) and then immigrants from former colonies began to flow into Corsica. The chronic depopulation of Corsica was revealed in 1965 when figures were published indicating that the island's population had shrunk from 320,000 to 246,000 in fewer than 20 years (1936–1954).

Concerns over Corsica's economic problems coupled with indigenous population decline and the influx of non-Corsicans had, by the 1970s, begun to morph into claims that the survival of Corsican identity itself was under threat. Prior to the 1970s, there really was no "language issue" in Corsica. The "official" language of Corsica, in the sense of being the language of high culture, law, administration, and education, prior to the arrival of the French, was Tuscan Italian, not Corsican. Hence, the aggressive promotion of the French language post 1789 resulted in the displacement of one "high" language (Tuscan Italian) with another (French), leaving the "low" language (Corsican) basically intact (Blackwood 2004). Partly because of this, Corsican, unlike Breton, was never in serious danger of extinction. Cultural and linguistic issues began to assume greater import as a result of the publication of the French government's "Planning Document" (the *Schema*) for the Corsican economy in 1971, which outlined priorities for the development of agriculture and tourism for the next 15 years. According to the government, the effect of achieving the *Schema*'s objectives would be to increase Corsica's population from 200,000 to 320,000. On the assumption that the emigration of Corsicans would continue as previously, many Corsican activists concluded that this population increase could only be the result of immigration from the French mainland, thus further diluting the pool of native Corsicans.

The internal colonization thesis was not a significant component of the nationalist narrative until 1974. That year, the ARC published *Autonomia,* in which it defined the problem of Corsica in terms of French colonialism. According to the ARC, the French state kept Corsica in a position of dependency, the better to exploit its main export—its manpower. Moreover, efforts by the French state to develop Corsica's tourism and agricultural industries were deliberately designed to cut against Corsican interests as part of a broader strategy to exploit the island economically and to eliminate expressions of Corsican identity. As the title suggests, the ARC's chosen remedy was for the French state to recognize legally the existence of a Corsican people and to enshrine territorial autonomy for the island in the French constitution. The FLNC's original manifesto expressed a similar constellation of grievances, but argued that these could only be adequately addressed by secession from the French state.

Recent activities

The FLNC was founded in 1976 through the merger of the FPCL, GP, and renegade elements of the ARC (which re-branded itself as the APC in the same year). The FLNC announced its arrival on May 4, with a coordinated series of 21 bombing attacks targeting government buildings, the property of *pieds noir*, and the offices of estate agents (Ramsay 1983, 118). This was the first of the "blue night" operations for which the group would become famous. This opening salvo was followed on May 20 by another heavy wave of attacks and on July 17, the group attacked a police station using rockets and mortars. This upsurge in separatist violence provoked a counter-reaction from groups opposed to independence. In November 1976, a group calling itself *l'Action Corse Franciase* bombed a hotel owned by a prominent politician M. Francis Pinelli who had recently come out in favor of independence. The best organized and most violent of these groups—FRANCIA—appeared in 1977 with a virtual declaration of war against the FLNC and a promise to execute "severe reprisals" against anyone openly advocating independence. The threat was backed up with a bombing attack on the pro-autonomy periodical *Arritti* that destroyed its printing presses. Predictably, the FLNC retaliated with an attack on a military installation, the explosive destruction of the waiting room at Bastia's railway station, a coordinated wave of 27 bomb attacks on the night of July 14, and the destruction of the television relay station at Sierra di Pigno. The high level of violence, both pro- and anti-independence continued into 1978. In January of that year, FLNC operatives stormed the NATO base at Solenzara and destroyed expensive radar equipment, and between June and July, the group conducted over 80 attacks, many against the property of French mainlanders. The following year, the group displayed its capacity to operate out of area when it struck 22 targets in Paris in one night. In 1982 alone the FNLC was believed responsible for over 800 attacks, including 99 in a single night. A similar rate of bombing attacks (between 600 and 700 per year) was sustained throughout the 1980s.

By the early 1980s, the FNLC's *modus operandi* was well-established. Most attacks targeted property, took place at night, and occurred outside the main tourist season to avoid disrupting one of the island's economic lifelines. The targets were generally symbols of "colonial occupation," such as police stations, law courts, and military installations, together with commercial and private property belonging to *pied noirs* or *pinzutti*. The FLNC went to considerable lengths to avoid "civilian" casualties, but French security forces and representatives of the French state were deemed legitimate targets by at least some of the group's numerous splinters and factions (Sanchez 2007, 656). The best-known casualty of nationalist violence was the French state's highest representative on Corsica, Claude Erignac, who was assassinated by three bullets to the back of the head in February 1998.[10] Highlighting the difficulties involved in effective police work in Corsica, it took until 2003 for the alleged perpetrator, Yvan Colonna, to be apprehended. Overall, the 10,000 or so attacks that occurred during the 40 years after the formation of the FLNC produced an estimated 220 deaths and thousands of injuries.[11] However, it is unclear how many of these deaths can be attributed to the struggle for independence and how many were the result of score-settling, infighting among terrorist groups, or basic mafia-style criminality. In 1983, for example, veterinarian Jean-Paul Lafay was shot in Corte for refusing to pay the FLNC-imposed "revolutionary tax," which was (in theory) levied to cover the costs of the group's operations, but to many resembled nothing more than naked extortion.

During the 1980s and 1990s the FLNC maintained a constant level of terrorist activity which never quite regained the intensity of the late-1970s, but it became increasingly difficult to distinguish politically motivated violence from organized crime as Corsican nationalist groups engaged in illegal acts, "like extortion, money laundering, and theft, in order, arguably, to finance their 'struggle'" (Sanchez 2007, 657). This gave rise to the perception that "at the core, Corsican nationalists are nothing but groups of criminals and gangsters, who have resorted to nationalism in an attempt to give same kind of legitimacy to some of their shady, violent operations" (ibid., 657).

Another characteristic of the FLNC was its almost pathological propensity to splinter into factions, either because of personal rivalries, or differences of opinion over tactics and strategies. Thus, in 1990, the FLNC split into two "channels" (*historique* [historic] and *habituel* [usual]) with each fronting its own political wing (respectively, A Cuncolta Naziunalista [aCN], and Mouvement pour l'autodetermination [MPA]). Elements of the FLNC–Historic Channel subsequently split away to form smaller terrorist groups, such as the *Fronte Ribellu* (1995–1999), the *Fronte Patriotu Corsu* (1999), *Clandestinu* (1997–1999), and *Armata Corsa* (1999–2001). Of these groups, the last was probably the most active during its short life-span. Headed by Michel Rossi and Francois "the Iguana" Santoni, the AC detonated 20 explosives, killing two people before its leaders were both assassinated.

In 1999, many of these groups joined with a subsequent iteration of the FLNC–Usual Channel (the FLNC–May 5th) to form the "new" FLNC, which subsequently came to be known as the FLNC–Union of Combatants (FLNC–UC). Further splits occurred in October 2002, with the formation of the appropriately named FLNC–October 22nd (FNLC–22) and again in 2004, with the appearance of *l'Armata di U Populu Corsu*. In the end, the FLNC–UC was grievously weakened by infighting, and, following an active 2012, which included a spasm of 24 attacks in one night (December 8, 2012), the group finally announced a cessation of hostilities in 2014. In a communique announcing the decision, the group pledged to initiate "a process of demilitarization" and a "progressive exit from clandestine activities," and claimed that the decision came in response to a series of resolutions passed by the Corsican Assembly. The most important of these, a five-year residency requirement prior to the purchase of land on the island, led the communique to conclude, "We think there now exists an opportunity to take a historic step in the fight for national liberation."[12] Given that none of the resolutions stood any chance of being enacted into law by the French National Assembly, some observers concluded that the communique was tantamount to a declaration of surrender by the FLNC–UC.[13]

Two years later, the last remaining Corsican terrorist group, the FLNC–22, announced it was initiating the process of decommissioning arms (though not disarming) in response to the outcome of the December 2015 elections to the Corsican Assembly. The election delivered a stunning victory (a "political earthquake" in the words of the FLNC-22) to a coalition of nationalist parties. Accordingly, and somewhat uncharacteristically, the group pledged, "We want to help them in moving towards the peaceful building of our nation."[14] In its only subsequent public communication (July 2016), the FLNC–22 proclaimed itself ready, willing, and able "without any qualms" to confront any attempt by ISIS to infiltrate Corsica and radicalize the island's Muslim population. For the present at least, therefore, the threat of Corsican separatist terrorism has abated for the first time in 40 years.

Government responses: denial and accommodation

Denial

As indicated in the previous sections, the French state has pursued a consistent policy of cultural and linguistic homogenization for most of the post-1789 period. This task kicked into high gear with the education reforms of the 1880s, which effectively banned the use of regional languages in the classroom. Subsequently, the use of French became a prerequisite for social advancement in many areas and the public use of regional languages, such as Breton, was increasingly, sometimes brutally, stigmatized. The net effect was a catastrophic decline in the numbers of people speaking regional languages, and the near extinction of several. Grim testament to the effectiveness of this drive for linguistic assimilation is the simple fact that of the 26 languages spoken in France listed by UNESCO as "in danger," eight (including Corsican) are categorized as "definitely endangered," and 13 (including Breton) as "severely endangered."[15] The backlash against the French state's "linguistic warfare" has, at times, produced some grudging concessions, such as the "Loi Deixonne" in 1951, which was aimed at favoring "the instruction of the local language and dialects in the regions where they are spoken" (Mendel 2004, 71). The 1951 law together with subsequent legislation permits the teaching of regional languages in schools for a limited numbers of hours per week and provides some limited resources for this. Some degree of constitutional recognition for the status of regional languages was also provided in 2008 via an amendment to the French Constitution that stated "Les langues régionales appartiennent au patrimoine de la France" ("Regional languages belong to the patrimony of France"). However, the French government's uncompromising stance on the supremacy of the French language was reaffirmed in 1992, with an amendment to Article II of the French Constitution, which stated "La lingue de la Republique est le francais." Then in 1994, the government enacted the Toubon Law, which mandated the use of French in all government publications, government-funded schools, and a range of commercial activities. Ironically, the purpose of the Law was to protect a minority language (French) against being overwhelmed by the global spread of a more powerful language (English). Likewise, no regional language enjoys "official" status, even in the region in which it is spoken, and the French government had yet to ratify the European Charter for Regional or Minority Languages.

The history of the French state's responses to demands for territorial autonomy follows a similar trajectory. For most of the period following the Revolution, the primary subnational unit of governance was the department. Originally, the boundaries of these were drawn intentionally to avoid coinciding with the boundaries of traditional regions, the better to fragment regional identities. Even with the restoration of regions during and after World War II, first as economic units, then as recognized governing entities (although with very limited powers), the goal has generally been to draw boundaries that de-emphasize established regional identities. Thus, when Brittany was restored as a region during World War II, the Breton department of Loire-Inferieure (now Loire-Atlantique) which contains Brittany's ancient capital of Nantes, was detached from the rest of Brittany and attached to the Pays de la Loire region. The restoration of Brittany's lost department is a cause that still animates nationalists to the present day. During the most recent round of reforms to France's territorial administration in 2014, which reduced the number of regions to 18, the French government refused to restore Loire Atlantique to its rightful historic homeland (as Bretons see it) and completely eliminated another ethnic region, Alsace, by drowning it in the new, much larger, Grand Est region. According to Tran (2014), the government's refusal to reunify Brittany, and its choice to "dilute" Alsace was designed "to weaken any regional or cultural identities that are not explicitly "French."

The reforms to the system of subnational governance that have been conceded by the government have been grudging and miserly. For example, reforms in 1982, 1986, 2003, and 2014 created elected regional councils and presidents, and granted these regions some administrative competence over areas such as education and transportation and the power to levy taxes (Loughlin 2008); however, Councils are not empowered to legislate, the powers they do possess can be changed at the whim of the national government because they are not embedded in the constitution, and entire regions can be, and have been created or eliminated by national government fiat, as happened to Alsace in 2014. Thus, France remains among the most unitary and centralized of states in Western Europe.

Accommodation

With respect to the *accommodation* of Breton nationalist demands, the French government has moved only minimally and grudgingly to address the core concerns of Breton nationalists. The historic region of Brittany was originally carved up into five departments after 1789, four of which were then rejoined in 1941 to recreate a Breton region during the Vichy years. As noted above, the various reforms to the French system of territorial administration mean that Brittany now enjoys more autonomy than at any time since 1789, but this autonomy is heavily circumscribed and stops some way short of the autonomy provided to, say, Catalonia in Spain. On the issue of language, the pattern is similar. After nearly two centuries of state-sponsored hostility to regional languages, the French government appeared to signal a change of heart with the passage of the "Loi Deixonne" in

1951. Further, in 1978, the French Government signed a "Cultural Charter" unique to Brittany that recognized "the cultural personality of Brittany," and established a number of cultural institutions in the region to promote Breton language and culture (Mendel 2004). However, the Breton language survives to the present day *despite*, rather than because of, French government actions. Its survival is largely a result of the activities of the *Diwan* movement, which runs a network of schools in which the Breton language is passed on to the region's children (Boomgaard 2008).

Since the 1970s, the French government has been more willing to accommodate the demands of Corsican nationalists than those of mainland regional movements. With respect to territorial autonomy, for example, the decentralization reforms of the Socialist government of François Mitterrand in the early 1980s began with a "special statute" for Corsica. Although the deal on offer stopped some way short of real autonomy, it was more than the French state had offered over the preceding 200 years. There are several reasons why this process began with Corsica, but the immediate goal, according to Henders (2010, 98) was to "co-opt moderate nationalists…encouraging them to compete for seats in a new directly elected territorial assembly, thereby weakening both radical nationalists linked with clandestine groups and traditional politicians." Officially, the purpose of the 1982 Statute was to acknowledge Corsica's distinct geographic and historical character by granting special status to the "territorial community of Corsica." The use of the term "the Corsican people," in line with the demands of many nationalists, was included in an earlier version of the Statute but omitted from the final document. The reform created a directly elected regional assembly superimposed on the existing department structure with a range of administrative and regulatory competences, and the vague power to "settle through its deliberations the affairs of the Corsican region" (Daftary 2008, 286). The assembly was denied legislative powers but could propose (non-binding) amendments to national legislation affecting Corsica. Although generous by French standards, this reform was primarily cosmetic, and the application of the Statute across all regions of the French mainland over the 1982–1986 period undermined any claim that it was "special" to Corsica. The predictable failure of the Statute to stem the tide of nationalist violence led in May 1991 to the promulgation of a second "Special Statute" for Corsica (the *loi Joxe*). Among other things, this expanded the range of areas over which the Assembly could exercise administrative authority, and created a new Executive Council to implement policy. However, a critical article of the Statute (Article 1) that referred specifically to the "Corsican people, component of the French people" was ruled unconstitutional by France's Constitutional Council, undercutting the political impact the Statute might otherwise have had (Daftary 2008, 290).

A final effort to find common ground on the issue of Corsica's autonomy commenced in 1999 in what became known as the "Matignon Process." The resultant "Matignon Proposals" were overwhelmingly approved by the Corsican Assembly in July 2000. In terms of process, the idea was for a two-phased implantation, leaving the more controversial proposals, such as allowing the Corsican Assembly to derogate from national laws, and measures potentially requiring amendments to the French constitution, to the second phase. The phase one reforms were introduced in the form of amendments to the 1991 Statute and mainly involved the grant of additional areas of administrative competence to Corsica, a series of measures to promote economic development, and the power for the Assembly to modify the application of national decrees (although not laws). In place of the phase two, the newly elected (2002) conservative government packaged a number of institutional reforms that would have enhanced Corsica's autonomy into a "third statute," and put the proposal to a popular vote in Corsica. In a referendum on July 6, 2003, the Corsican people rejected the proposals by a 51 to 49 percent vote.

The upshot of this slow and painful process is a status for Corsica that does not differ much from any other French region. Nonetheless, it should be recognized that the French government's efforts to accommodate Corsican nationalist demands have taken the French state further down the path towards decentralization than at any point in its modern history. In other words, the degree of autonomy now enjoyed by mainland regions, such as Brittany, is mainly the result of the government's efforts to answer the vexatious Corsican question.

In terms of cultural and linguistic issues, Corsica has fared better than Brittany, at least when measured in terms of language retention. As noted above, the imposition of French on the Corsican people came at the expense of Tuscan Italian and left the indigenous vernacular language largely intact. Having said this, when the French government did step in to offer some protection to regional languages, via the 1951 *loi Deixonne*, Corsican was one of languages *excluded* from the terms of the law because it was deemed to be a dialect of Italian rather than a separate language. This situation was not rectified until the 1970s, when the protection of language and cultural identity began to seep into the Corsican nationalist narrative. The first organized body to agitate on behalf of the Corsican language was *Scola Corsa*, which mounted an active campaign to re-open the university at Corte and to extend the *loi Deixonne* to include Corsican. Subsequently, the university was re-opened in 1981 (as the University of Corsica Pasquale Paoli) and the *loi Deixonne* was amended to include Corsican in 1974. During the 1990s, two French state *circulaires* (similar to decrees) were adapted by the Corsican authorities to permit bilingual teaching in Corsican schools, and by the end of the decade, the *Acadamie de Corse* was claiming that all secondary school students were receiving three hours of teaching in Corsican per week (Blackwood 2004, 28). By the 2000s, the mandatory teaching of Corsican in the island's school was still de jure unconstitutional, but had become "all but obligatory" in practice. The upshot is that, in Blackwood's (2007, 29) words "Having been overlooked during the passing of the *loi Deixonne*, Corsican, at the end of the 20th century, was emerging as the most defended and privileged regional languages in France."

Analysis and conclusion

On the face of it, the French state's campaign to eliminate rival ethnic identities and impose a single, homogenous "French" identity on an extremely diverse population has been highly successful. At the time of the French Revolution, only a minority of the population spoke or even understood the French language; fast forward 200 years, and standard French is the universal first language of almost the entire population. Casualties of the process have been the regional languages of ethnic groups such as the Bretons, Catalans, Occitans, and Corsicans, some of which have declined to the point of near extinction. Moreover, the French state's stubborn insistence on adhering to the principle of *egalite* has mitigated against distinctive treatment for the country's ethnic regions. Unlike other states, such as Spain and Italy, which acknowledge ethnic regions as "special" or "historic" and, therefore, worthy of privileged treatment, France's glacial moves towards decentralization have been applied equally across all regions. While the relentless process of assimilation has been resisted by some, Bretons and Corsicans most notably, the level of violence used has never escalated to the level experienced in Northern Ireland or the Basque country. Violent ethno-nationalist groups in Brittany and Corsica never enjoyed the support of majorities of their respective populations, were never especially violent in any case, and appear to have run their natural course. The end of terrorist violence in Brittany and Corsica is at least partly because of the generally acknowledged effectiveness of France's revamped counterterrorist apparatus, and was achieved without the sort of brutal crackdowns that have characterized counterterrorist campaigns in states such as Turkey and Sri Lanka and that run the risk of provoking a backlash.[16] Viewed from this perspective, the French approach to ethnic management—non-accommodation, minimal concessions, and effective, but limited coercion—has undoubtedly triumphed.

A more nuanced evaluation of the French approach would recognize at least three caveats to this conclusion. First, the failure of militant nationalism in Brittany and Corsica to achieve much in the way of tangible concessions from the French state is as much a symptom of the internal weaknesses of these movements as it is testament to the wisdom of the French approach. The Breton nationalist movement has always been deeply fragmented along lines of class, left-right ideology, priorities, strategies, and goals. As one contemporary participant in the nationalist movement wryly observes

> The situation in Breizh has not been helped by the continued existence of a number of different nationalist political parties—with broadly similar aims—who clamber and compete against each other for the vote of a relatively small minority.... Breton nationalists, it seems, are content to work against each other in their frustrating attempt to gain greater recognition for their nation, language and culture.[17]

What the movement has always lacked is a single unified organization with a unified leadership and a clear-cut agenda to galvanize the widespread sympathy that exists in Brittany for many of the nationalists' goals. The Corsican movement is, if anything, even more fatally fragmented than its Breton counterpart. Separatist terrorist groups like the FLNC never gelled well with the existing clan-based power structure on the island; indeed clan bosses have been among the staunchest opponents of the FLNC and the goals of greater autonomy or independence, because the status quo favors the preservation of the existing power structure (Ramsay 1983, 212–214). The FLNC was also perpetually riven with internal feuds and vendettas that escalated during the first half of the 2000s to the extent that most of the violence perpetrated over this period involved one or other faction of the FLNC attacking another. Basically, the FLNC consumed itself.

Second, while separatist terrorist groups in both Brittany and Corsica were only ever actively supported by a small minority of their respective populations, this level of support was still significantly higher over the 1960–2000 period than it had been at any time since 1789. The pertinent question to ask, therefore, is what created this problem in the 1960s that was previously non-existent? Experts on the evolution of separatist terrorism in both regions are in agreement on this. With respect to Brittany, Reece (1977, 40) observes "It became clear very early in the twentieth century … that Parisian central authorities had no sympathy for regionalist ideas," and that by "refusing to concede even the more innocuous demands of the regionalists, the authorities stood more and more in a militantly antagonistic relationship to them." The failure of moderate groups to extract concessions invariably led to the emergence of groups prepared to use more violent means in pursuit of more radical ends. Thus, the failed moderation of the first *emsav* paved the way for the emergence of organizations such as the separatist (and fascist) PNB and the terrorist group *Gwenn-ha-Du* during the second *emsav*. A similar pattern evolved during the third *emsav*. The failure of the studiously moderate CELIB to secure meaningful cooperation from Paris over the design of an economic development plan for Brittany helped, in turn, to spawn more violent groups with separatist demands, like the FLB. A similar pattern can be observed in Corsica. According to Ramsay (183, 225), "the fact remains that the essential nature of the centralized Jacobin state and the unwillingness of Pompidou and Giscard d'Estaing fundamentally to alter the pattern of its institutions, was the source from which much conflict flowed."

This brings to mind the assessments of many experts on ethnic conflict/terrorism; namely that it is better for a government to make generous concessions at an early stage when demands are still moderate (Horowitz 1985; Byman 1998). As Horowitz (1985, 625) notes, "An early, generous offer of autonomy, made before extreme separatist organizations outflank moderate leaders," may be enough prevent an escalation to violent separatism. Invariably, the failure to make early concessions leads to more radical demands and more violent tactics. In this respect, what stands out about the French state's approach to ethnic management is not that it eventually succeeded in taming separatist terrorist groups, but that it was also largely responsible for their emergence in the first place.

Finally, separatist terrorism may be dead and buried in Brittany, and on life support in Corsica, but nationalist sentiment and ethnic identity are very much alive and kicking in both regions. In the former, both the language and the culture are undergoing something of a renaissance, and a 2014 opinion poll indicated that as many as 25 percent of the Breton population favor independence from France—a figure that greatly exceeds anything previously recorded. In Corsica, both language and culture are, by now, highly protected by regional institutions and activists, and the 2014 regional election produced a victory for a coalition of nationalist parties (*Femu a Corsica* and *Corsica Libera*) for the first time since the introduction of reginal elections in Corsica in the 1980s. Strikingly, *Corsica Libera* is an openly separatist party. Hence, while the French state may be in no imminent danger of secession, it seems reasonable to conclude that the final chapter in the history of separatism in France has yet to be written.

Notes

1 Ethnicity is a notoriously slippery concept. For current purposes we rely on Van Dyke's (1977, 344) definition of an "ethnic community" as "a group of persons, predominantly of common descent, who think of themselves as collectively possessing a separate identity based on race, or shared cultural characteristics, usually language or religion."

2 For a sample of the various proffered explanations for the revival of ethno-nationalism in Western Europe, see, Enloe (1972); Hechter (1974, 1999); Simon (1975); Zariski (1989).

3 The best known advocate of these so-called "consociational" institutions is Arend Lijphart. See, Lijphart (1969, 1975, 1977, 1979).

4 For example, the sudden and decisive revocation of Brittany's autonomy by the post-revolutionary National Assembly in August 1789 sparked a counter-revolutionary insurgency (the *Chouannerie*) centered on Brittany that was not definitively subdued until 1804 (Reece 1977, 20).

5 The history of the Breton nationalist movement is traditionally divided into three periods, or *Emsavs* (meaning revival). The first *Emsav* lasted from the second half of the nineteenth century to 1914; the second, from 1914 to 1945; and the third from 1945 onwards.

6 See Reece (1979) for a detailed, and convincing, exposition of the internal colonization thesis applied to Brittany.

7 However, the inward flow of central government investment to the region was focused on modernizing the agricultural sector (in part in response to the demands of the CELIB), which in turn disrupted the traditional pattern of small-scale farming that had existed for centuries in Brittany, thus fueling further grievances.

8 See, www.start.umd.edu/gtd/.

9 "Les autonomistes soufflent sur la Breizh." *L'Express*, February 17, 2000 (available at: www.lexpress.fr/informations/les-autonomistes-soufflent-sur-la-breizh_636806.html).

10 Although Colanna was known in nationalist circles, there was no evidence that he was an active member of either of the FLNCs at the time of the murder, and neither channel claimed responsibility.

11 For example, the FLNC claimed responsibility for only about 40 percent of these attacks.

12 Quoted in: Lambroschini, C. (2014) "Corsica's Separatist Retreat." *New York Times*, August 4 (available at: www.nytimes.com/2014/08/05/opinion/corsicas-separatist-retreat.html?_r=1).

13 For example, Lambroschini (2014) concludes that "the FLNC has lost the war: Corsica wants to stay French."
14 Moloney, M. (2016) "Corsica's last major armed group to decommission to 'boost peace process'" *Anphblacht*, May 3 (available at: www.anphoblacht.com/contents/25978).
15 See, UNESCO database at www.unesco.org/languages-atlas/index.php
16 The French are generally acknowledged to have a highly successful counterterrorism apparatus as a result of reforms during the 1980s, and a dramatic change in approach that prioritizes prevention rather than post hoc punishment. For details, see, Gregory (2003); Shapiro and Suzan (2003); Wieviorka (1991).
17 "At Home Amongst the Bretons," *An Sionnach Fionn*, August 11, 2011 (available at: https://ansionnachfionn.com/2011/08/18/at-home-amongst-the-bretons/).

References

Andereggen, A. (1985). Corsica's "New Deal." *International Social Science Review*, 67–71.

Anderson, L (2014) Ethnofederalism: The Worst Form of Institutional Arrangement …?. *International Security*, *39*(1), 165–204.

Anderson, L (2015) Ethnofederalism and the Management of Ethnic Conflict: Assessing the Alternatives. *Publius: The Journal of Federalism*: pjv019.

Blackwood, R.J. (2004). The Gallicisation of Corsica: the imposition of the French language from 1768 to 1945. *Language Policy*, *3*(2), 133–152.

Boomgaard, M.C. (2008). The rise of militant Bretonité. *National Identities*, *10*(3), 281–293.

Brubaker, R. (1996) *Nationalism Reframed: Nationhood and the National Question in the New Europe*. Cambridge: Cambridge University Press.

Bunce, V. (1999) *Subversive Institutions: The Design and the Destruction of Socialism and the State*. Cambridge: Cambridge University Press.

Bunce, Valerie. (2004) Federalism, nationalism, and secession. In Amoretti, Ugo M., and Nancy Gina Bermeo, eds., *Federalism and territorial cleavages*. Washington D.C.: Johns Hopkins University Press: 417–440.

Bunce, V. and S. Watts. (2005) Managing diversity and sustaining democracy: ethnofederal versus unitary states in the postcommmunist world. In Philip G. Roeder and Donald Rothchild, eds., *Sustainable Peace: Power and Democracy after Civil Wars*. Ithaca: Cornell University Press: 133–158.

Byman, D. (1998). The logic of ethnic terrorism. *Studies in Conflict & Terrorism*, *21*(2), 149–169.

Cornell, S.E. (2002) Autonomy as a source of conflict: Caucasian conflicts in theoretical perspective. *World Politics*, *54*, 245–276.

Daftary, F. (2008). Experimenting with territorial administrative autonomy in Corsica: exception or pilot region?. *International Journal on Minority and Group Rights*, *15*(2), 273–312.

Decatur Herald (The) (1978) Breton nationalists being sought in Versailles bombing. June 28, page 4.

Enloe, C.H. (1972). *Ethnic conflict and political development*. New York: Little, Brown.

Gemie, S. (2002). The politics of language: debates and identities in contemporary Brittany. *French Cultural Studies*, *13*(38), 145–164.

Gemie, S. (2005). Roots, rock, Breizh: music and the politics of nationhood in contemporary Brittany. *Nations and Nationalism*, *11*(1), 103–120.

Gorenburg, D. (2001). Nationalism for the masses: Popular support for nationalism in Russia's ethnic republics. *Europe-Asia Studies*, *53*(1), 73–104.

Gregory, S. (2003). France and the War on Terrorism. *Terrorism and Political Violence*, *15*(1), 124–147.

Hechter, M. (1974). The political economy of ethnic change. *American Journal of Sociology*, *79*(5), 1151–1178.

Hechter, M. (1999). *Internal Colonialism: The Celtic Fringe in Bristish National Development*. Piscataway, NY: Transaction Publishers.

Henders, S. (2010). *Territoriality, Asymmetry, and Autonomy: Catalonia, Corsica, Hong Kong, and Tibet*. New York: Springer, 2010.

Horowitz, D.L. (1985). *Ethnic groups in conflict*. Berkeley, CA: University of California Press.

Leff, C.S. (1999). Democratization and distintegration in multinatinoal states: the breakup of the communist federations. *World Politics 51*, 205–235.

Levy, J.T. (2007). Federalism, liberalism, and the separation of loyalties. *American Political Science Review 101*(3), 459–477.

Lijphart, A. (1969). Consociational democracy. *World politics*, *21*(02), 207–225.

Lijphart, A. (1975). *The politics of accommodation: Pluralism and democracy in the Netherlands* (Vol. 142). Berkeley, CA: University of California Press.

Lijphart, A. (1977). *Democracy in plural societies: A comparative exploration*. Ithaca, NY: Yale University Press.

Lijphart, A. (1979). Consociation and federation: conceptual and empirical links. *Canadian Journal of Political Science*, *12*(03), 499–516.

Lorwin, V.R. (1966). Belgium: religion, class and language in national politics. In Robert A. Dahl, *Political oppositions in western democracies*: 147–187.

Loughlin, J. (2008). The slow emergence of the French regions. *Policy & Politics*, *36*(4), 559–571.

McDonald, M. (1989). *" We are Not French!": Language, Culture, and Identity in Brittany* (p. 84). London: Routledge.

McGarry, J., and O'Leary, B. (2005). Federation as a method of ethnic conflict regulation. *From Power Sharing to Democracy: Post-Conflict Institutions in Ethnically Divided Societies*, 286–287.

McGarry, J., O'Leary, B., and Simeon, R. (2008). Integration or accommodation? The enduring debate in conflict regulation. *Constitutional Design for Divided Societies: Integration or Accommodation*, 41–88.

Mendel, K. (2004). Regional Languages in France: the case of Breton. *LSO Working Papers in Linguistics*, *4*, 65–75.

Nordlinger, E.A. (1972). *Conflict regulation in divided societies*. No. 29. Cambridge, Mass.: Center for International Affairs, Harvard University.

Ramsay, R. (1983). *The Corsican time-bomb*. Manchester: Manchester University Press.

Reece, J.E. (1977). *The Bretons against France: Ethnic minority nationalism in twentieth-century Brittany*. Chapel Hill: University of North Carolina Press.

Reece, Jack E. (1979). Internal colonialism: the case of Brittany. *Ethnic and Racial Studies*, *2*(3), 275–292.

Roeder, P.G. (2007) *Where nation-states come from: Institutional change in the age of nationalism*. Princeton: Princeton University Press.

Roeder, P.G. (1991). Soviet federalism and ethnic mobilization. *World Politics*, *43*(2), 196–232.

Roeder, P.G. (2005). Power dividing as an alternative to ethnic power sharing. In Roeder, Philip G., and Donald S. Rothchild, *Sustainable peace: Power and democracy after civil wars*. Ithaca: Cornell University Press: 51–82.

Roeder, P.G. (2009). Ethnofederalism and the mismanagement of conflicting nationalism. *Regional and Federal Studies*, *19*(2), 203–219.

Sánchez, W.A. (2007). Corsica: France's Petite Security Problem. *Studies in Conflict & Terrorism*, *31*(7), 655–664.

Shapiro, J., and Suzan, B. (2003). The French Experience of Counter-terrorism. *Survival*, *45*(1), 67–98.

Simon, W.B. (1975). Occupational structure, multilingualism and social change. *Les etats multilingues: problemes et solutions. Quebec: Les presses de l'Universite Laval*, 87–108.

Stephens, M. (1978) *Linguistic minorities in western Europe*, Llandysul (Dyfed): Gomer Press 1978 333.

Taylor, R. (1992). "South Africa: A Consociational Path to Peace." *Transformation*, *17*, 1–11.

Tran, H. (2014) "Fighting for Brittany: autonomy in a centralized state, OpenDemocracy 5 December (available at: www.opendemocracy.net/can-europe-make-it/hugo-tran/fighting-for-brittany-autonomy-in-centralised-state).

Van Dyke, V. (1977). The individual, the state, and ethnic communities in political theory. *World Politics*, *29*(3), 343–369.

Walt, S. (2014). The Top 5 foreign policy lessons of the past 20 years. *Foreign Policy*. 18 November 2014 (http://foreignpolicy.com/2014/11/18/the-top-5-foreign-policy-lessons-of-the-past-20-years/).

Wieviorka, M. (1991). France faced with Terrorism. *Studies in Conflict & Terrorism*, *14*(3), 157–170.

Wolff, S. (2010). *Approaches to conflict resolution in divided societies: The many uses of territorial self-Governance*. Exeter Centre for Ethno-Political Studies 5 (November).

Zariski, R. (1989). Ethnic extremism among ethnoterritorial minorities in Western Europe: dimensions, causes, and institutional responses. *Comparative Politics*, *21*(3), 253–272.

5 From separatism to terrorism and back

The case of Kosovo and the KLA

Elena Pokalova[1]

Separatism and terrorism share a history of intricate connections. As separatists challenge the legitimacy of the state they are a part of, immediately they confront an opponent that is stronger and holds the monopoly over the use of force. While many separatist movements start as peaceful ventures, inadvertently, many of them experience the failure of peaceful advocacy and take up arms. By default, such violence against the state is illegitimate. Further, most separatist groups would not be able to withstand an open onslaught of the government's armed forces. As a result, terrorism becomes a favored tactic often employed by separatists to get their message across to the rest of the world.

Throughout history many separatists, including China's Uyghurs, Sri Lanka's Tamils, Spain's Basques, or Turkey's Kurds, have resorted to terrorist tactics. However, after World War II, while the international community condemned violence, it was sympathetic to the ethno-nationalist separatist cause. For instance, the international community encouraged Israel to negotiate directly with the PLO at Oslo. The U.S. Clinton administration was sympathetic to the Irish self-determination cause and received Gerry Adams in Washington. That was before September 11, 2001.

After the terrorist attacks on the U.S. the situation changed. Terrorism was no longer seen as legitimized by a self-determination cause. On December 4, 2001 President Bush declared: "The message is this: Those who do business with terror will do no business with the United States or anywhere else the United States can reach" (*Washington Post* 2001). PLO received a clear message: "If you harbor a terrorist, if you hide a terrorist, if you feed a terrorist, you're just as guilty as the terrorists themselves" (Bush 2002). Adams received a similar message as President Bush promised he would "never deal with Adams again" (Sherwell 2001). The IRA subsequently lost much of the U.S. sympathy and thus had more pressure to decommission. It was following September 11 that the IRA committed to the decommissioning process in earnest. As Gerry Adams explained, it was a necessary step forward "at a time when there is international calamity in the world" (BBC 2001).

Further, even before September 11, international actors were skeptical about interventions in ethno-nationalist separatist conflicts. Balancing between internationally recognized principles of the right to self-determination and the right to territorial integrity the international community has tended to issue statements of support of both and has generally abstained from interventions. In this respect Kosovo represents a unique case of ethno-nationalist separatist self-determination struggle. Not only did the conflict in Kosovo start before September 11, but it also provoked NATO air strikes against Serbia and the subsequent deployment of the Kosovo Force (KFOR) and the United Nations Mission in Kosovo (UNMIK).

Similar to other separatists, Kosovars became disillusioned in peaceful advocacy and engaged in political violence. For this Belgrade pronounced the movement terrorist. The terrorist label was approved by international actors, including Robert Gelbard, U.S. envoy to the Balkans. However, the Kosovo case demonstrates how before September 11 it was politically feasible to drop the terrorist label and to pronounce separatist militants allies. Only months after acknowledging the Kosovo Liberation Army (KLA) a terrorist organization, U.S. officials reversed the rhetoric. U.S. Senator Lieberman pronounced: "United States of America and the Kosovo Liberation Army stand for the same human values and principles.... Fighting for the KLA is fighting for human rights and American values" (Wheeler 1999).

Not only did the KLA shed the terrorist label, but it also emerged from the conflict victorious. The group reorganized and is firmly on the way to being recognized as the armed forces of Kosovo. Further, the KLA's leader Hashim Thaçi was first elected Prime Minister of Kosovo, and then President. Thaçi became the political leader who declared Kosovo's independence in 2008, a declaration that has been recognized by 114 countries. Such legitimization of a separatist militant leader who had been associated with a group called a terrorist organization is unprecedented. In this respect one can draw parallels to Xanana Gusmao of East Timor or Nelson Mandela of South Africa. Both were accused of terrorism and both were later elected leaders of their countries. However, in Gusmao's case the conflict arose from the issue of annexation, and in Mandela's case it was internationally condemned apartheid. Kosovo remains unique in the level of separatist success that was achieved.

The chapter examines the evolution of the separatist movement in Kosovo. It then traces the emergence of violence and militant attacks carried out by the KLA. International reactions to the conflict are presented in their order from recognition of terrorism to the pronouncement of the KLA as a NATO ally. The chapter analyzes the issue of legitimization of the KLA and the impact of such legitimization on the KLA's post-conflict transformations.

Separatism in Kosovo

The roots of the separatist conflict in Kosovo go back centuries (Vickers 1998; Mertus 1999; Judah 2008; Malcolm 1999). Kosovo and Serbia have shared a turbulent history with opposing views on the interpretations of the historical past. While Kosovars have viewed the Serbian rule as occupation, for Serbs, Kosovo has represented an integral part of the Serbian statehood; it has been perceived as the heart of the Serbian medieval state that unjustly fell to the Ottomans at the Battle of Kosovo Polje in 1389 (Phillips 2012). Centuries later, in April 1987, it was at the same Kosovo Polje that then President of the Serbian Communist Party Slobodan Milosevic (1987) delivered his famous speech to address the growing ethnic friction. "Yugoslavia is a nation unsettled by separatists and nationalists," Milosevic stated. Trying to address the fears of his Serbian constituents, Milosevic continued: "Yugoslavia doesn't exist without Kosovo!" He promised: "Yugoslavia and Serbia will never give up Kosovo!" Milosevic clearly indicated he was prepared to fight for Kosovo.

Ethno-nationalist tensions that necessitated Milosevic's visit intensified in Kosovo after the death of Josip Broz Tito in 1980. While Tito was able to hold the Yugoslav nationalisms together, after his death, ethno-nationalist movements started unsettling the entire country. In Kosovo, the separatist calls were initially voiced as demands for a republican status for the province. Thus, in the 1980s Kosovo Albanians did not set out to claim independence for Kosovo. Rather it was a project to elevate the autonomous status of Kosovo within Yugoslavia.

According to the 1974 constitution, Yugoslavia consisted of six republics (Bosnia and Herzegovina, Croatia, Macedonia, Montenegro, Serbia, and Slovenia) and included two autonomous provinces of Kosovo and Vojvodina (Krieger 2001). As an autonomous province with sovereign rights, Kosovo was entitled to have its own administration and judicial system, and could pass province-specific legislation (Vickers 1998). Kosovars enjoyed the constitutional protections of their language, culture, and history, and the Kosovo government was able to operate with minimal interference from the federal center in Belgrade. At the same time, according to the 1974 constitution, unlike republics, autonomous provinces of Yugoslavia did not have the right to secede. As a result, to set out legal claims to secession, Kosovo first had to gain the status of a republic.

With the rise of nationalism after Tito's death, tensions grew in Kosovo, where out of the population of 1,584,558, 77.5 percent were ethnic Albanians (Howe 1982). Riots and demonstrations broke out in Pristina with slogans demanding a status of a republic for Kosovo. In 1981 nationalist disturbances were significant enough for Belgrade to send in tanks and troops, ban public gatherings, and impose a curfew in Pristina. The ethnic unrest put much pressure on the Serbian community of Kosovo who started departing for Serbia. As one local party official explained, Serbs viewed the agenda of Kosovo Albanians as a two-step process: "first to establish what they call an ethnically clean Albanian republic and then the merger with Albania to form a greater Albania" (Howe 1982). As a result, Serbs in Kosovo staged counterprotests demanding an end to "the terror of the Albanians" (Petrovic 1987). Serbian rioters demanded better treatment appealing to Belgrade for protection.

Belgrade's response was re-centralization of Yugoslavia. In 1989, the Serb parliament amended the Serb constitution curbing Kosovo's autonomy. The constitutional amendments that were endorsed by the pro-Serb Kosovo Parliament granted Belgrade more direct control over the province. In July 1990, Serbia suspended the Assembly and the Executive Council of Kosovo and the Serbian

Parliament and Executive Council assumed legislative and administrative powers over the province. Subsequently, on September 28, 1990, Serbia enacted a new constitution that stripped Kosovo of the autonomy provisions defined under the 1974 constitution. Finally, the new Yugoslav constitution of 1992 effectively terminated Kosovo's autonomy.

These sweeping changes in the status of Kosovo provoked an explosive reaction from Kosovo Albanians. In response to the curbing of Kosovo's autonomy, in July 1990 the Kosovo parliament adopted a declaration of sovereignty that pronounced Kosovo independent of Serbia. In this move the Kosovo leadership did not seek full independence but envisioned Kosovo "an independent and equal unit within the Yugoslav federation with the same constitutional status as the other republics" (Gustincic 1990). Subsequently, Kosovo Albanians boycotted the Serbian constitutional referendum.

When Belgrade disbanded the Kosovo legislature, Kosovo separatists responded with another declaration of independence and proceeded to build a parallel government. The Democratic League of Kosovo (LDK) founded in 1989 and headed by Ibrahim Rugova boycotted the 1990 Serbian general election. "To participate in these elections would mean that we accept the conditions the Serbians have imposed upon us," Rugova said. "By calling this boycott, we are telling the Serbs to stop this repression. We are saying we want our autonomy back. We want to be equal partners in the future of Yugoslavia," he explained (Harden 1990). In defiance of Serbian rule, on September 22, 1991 the dissolved Assembly of Kosovo issued a declaration pronouncing Kosovo independent from Serbia. The LDK further held an unauthorized referendum, in which 87 percent of the population voted, and 99 percent of voters supported independence from Serbia (Horne 1991). A year later Rugova was elected president of the self-proclaimed Republic of Kosovo and since then headed the parallel government that Belgrade denounced as illegal.

Rugova's political agenda relied on peaceful resistance. He staunchly opposed violence as an illegitimate route to political independence. As he explained, "We can only offer peaceful resistance because any other tactic would give Serbia an excuse to attack" (Chazan 1992). This approach manifested itself in non-violent strategies of countering Serbia's policies (Caplan 1998; Clark 2000). Rugova believed in the power of "political means and dialogue, despite the fact that the Serbian government and the federal government won't talk" (Traynor 1990).

In line with the diplomatic approach, in September 1996 Rugova signed an agreement with Milosevic that promised to restore education in the Albanian language and put an end to a six-year boycott of the Serbian school system in Kosovo. The agreement, however, failed to bring concrete results but instead highlighted the problematic nature of diplomatic empty promises (Kostovicova 2005). The failure to implement the agreement provoked more student riots in Pristina in 1997. Belgrade's use of riot police with tear gas and clubs against the protesters forebode violence.

Kosovo Albanians began to grow impatient with Rugova's approach. For instance, Rugova's Prime Minister Bujar Bukoshi was openly critical of Rugova's inaction, and other political figures inside and outside the LDK expressed frustration with the lack of progress (Roberts and Ash 2009). Further, the signing of the Dayton agreement on Bosnia in 1995 and the subsequent lifting of sanctions against the Federal Republic of Yugoslavia (FRY) precipitated the turn to violence in Kosovo. The failure of the agreement to mention the existing situation in Kosovo demonstrated to the separatists that a political settlement of the Kosovo crisis was highly unlikely. LDK Vice President Fehmi Agani described the disappointment with the Dayton agreement as follows: "We put a lot of hope into the Dayton peace negotiations. The feeling is growing among Albanians that we have to struggle with the most aggressive means" (Uselac 1996).

By the mid-1990s it became apparent that the peaceful separatist movement was stymied. Opposition to Rugova's camp grew and many former LDK supporters started taking up arms. Rugova's opponents realized that "high goals like freedom could not come at a cheap price like patience" (Mulaj 2008, 1107). Sporadic self-defense units started appearing across Kosovo. Terrorism and political violence emerged as a powerful alternative to peaceful resistance. The KLA arose as a significant player on the Kosovo separatist arena.

Kosovo terrorism: the KLA

The signs for the explosive potential of the Kosovo conflict were present back in 1989. Back then, in response to Serbia's removal of Kosovo's autonomy, bombs were thrown at a troop truck and a newspaper office (Humphrey 1989). While the bombings indicated that a terrorist campaign in the name of Kosovo independence was possible, political violence did not become the separatist modus operandi until the mid-1990s. At that time, militant groups developed on the Kosovo scene similar to many insurgencies around the globe: when peaceful separatist advocacy failed, the separatists took up arms. As the KLA leader Hashim Thaçi explained the process:

> The Kosovo Liberation Army was created in accordance with the already-existing organizational structures of that time. Later, the resistance only got more powerful and stronger, so that it could transform from the peaceful "active" resistance into an armed resistance.
>
> (Frontline 2000)

The Kosovo Liberation Army (KLA or Ushtria Clirimtare e Kosoves, UCK) first made Belgrade aware of its existence through IRA-style car bombings, ambushes, and attacks on the Serb police and military forces. On April 22, 1996, the KLA was implicated in the assassinations of several Serbs including policeman Miljenko Bucic. On June 16, 1996, Serb policeman Goran Mitrovic was wounded in Podujevo. On June 17, an attack in Sipolje left policeman Predrag Georgovic dead. On August 2, a series of attacks on police stations followed in Podujevo and Pristina. The KLA claimed responsibility for the attacks (Human Rights Watch 2001, 32).

In 1996, the KLA made its first public claim of responsibility for an attack on the Serb police through a letter to the BBC. In the letter the KLA described the attack as an "assault against Serbian aggressors" and warned that the armed struggle in the name of Kosovo liberation "would continue until complete victory" (quoted in Vickers 1998, 293). In 1997, the KLA staged their first public appearance at a funeral of an Albanian teacher shot by the Serbian police. At the funeral the speakers declared the KLA to be the leader of the separatist movement: "Serbia is massacring Albanians. The Kosovo Liberation army is the only force fighting for the freedom of Kosovo" (quoted in Pavcovic 2000, 190).

The KLA's public relations campaign was successful. The KLA's messages resonated with individuals disillusioned with the lack of progress resulting from Rugova's efforts. As one KLA recruit explained:

> When I heard of the news about the UCK in November 1996, I thought that only they can solve the situation in Kosova. I tried to contact them and, when I succeeded in doing so, I went into the mountains in early 1997 without saying anything to my parents and friends.
>
> (Quoted in Kubo 2010, 1145)

Many more followed, with the KLA force reaching anywhere between 10,000 and 30,000 in the course of the conflict (Bekaj 2010, 22; Seper 1999).

The KLA positioned itself as an insurgency waging a guerilla war. To have the best chances for success, the KLA leadership carefully "considered and then rejected the IRA, PLO, and ETA models" (Perritt 2008, 154). The KLA's objectives were to resist the Serbs while defending civilians and fostering international sympathy. As a result, the group made concerted efforts to distance itself from terrorism. "We are not a terrorist organization," one KLA member explained

> We are not like the Irish Republican Army or the Basque separatists. These groups represent minority populations and carry out random attacks against civilians. We have the support of nearly all Albanians. The only attacks we carry out are against the representatives of Serbian regime.
>
> (Hedges 1997a)

Accordingly, KLA members wore uniforms, avoided armed attacks outside Kosovo, and drew a hard line between combatants and noncombatants. In one of the group's founding documents the KLA mandated to "commit liberation acts with a just character, and not attack socio-cultural monuments, civilian population and subjects of importance for the life of the people" (quoted in Bekaj 2010, 17). According to the document, the KLA targets included military and police combatants. Attacks in public places that could endanger civilian lives were to be avoided.

Indeed, as the KLA started emerging from the shadows in 1997–1998, its hit-and-run attacks mainly targeted the Serbian police stations and patrols. Such attacks often involved explosives being thrown at military installations or gunfire aimed at police stations. According to official counts, the KLA was responsible for 42 deaths between 1990 and 1997 (Brown 1997). Such numbers are in line with other estimates as well. According to the Global Terrorism Database, between 1996 and 1999 the KLA carried out or was suspected of carrying out 53 terrorist attacks that claimed 45 lives and injured 104 individuals (National Consortium for the Study of Terrorism and Responses to Terrorism 2017). Thus, the KLA attacks were relatively small in scale and the numbers of casualties were relatively low.

As Ambassador William Walker who headed the Kosovo Verification Mission pointed out, KLA attacks were "usually limited in scale. One, two, or three people might be targeted, usually policemen, or military – there was some reason they could point to as to why they had done it" (*Frontline* 2000). The KLA did not stage Al Qaeda-style mass casualty attacks, but instead was very discriminate with its targets. As the group matured and came to resemble regular armed forces, it started engaging in positional confrontations with the Serbs (Perritt 2008).

However, despite the KLA's public stance against attacks on civilians, civilians inadvertently became impacted. This way, on January 16, 1997, Radivoje Papovic, rector of the University of Pristina, was severely wounded in a car bombing claimed by the KLA. In this case a bomb was detonated in a parked vehicle when the rector's car was passing by. On January 29, 1999, a hand grenade was thrown at a Serb-owned café in Pristina. The café was popular among the Serb minority. The KLA claimed responsibility for the bombing (*Hamilton Spectator* 1999). The KLA justified such attacks that left Serb and Albanian civilians dead as attacks against Serbian "collaborators" (Hedges 1997b). It was such attacks and the KLA's violent means that gave the Serbian government justifications for calling the KLA a terrorist organization.

Ever since the upheaval of ethnic tensions in Kosovo in the 1980s, the Serbian press made references to Albanian "heavily armed terrorists" (Harden 1990). Early in the conflict Slobodan Milosevic talked of terrorism in Kosovo. "Every man in Serbia is ready to head for Kosovo if the terror is continued there" Milosevic promised in 1990 (*New York Times* 1990). The emergence of the KLA and its attacks provided the Serbian authorities with more justifications for such references. Describing the KLA, Bosko Drobnjak, chief of information for the Serbs in Kosovo stated: "They claim to be some national liberation army, but they are a classical terrorist group" (Coleman 1997). Drobnjak later explained the growing concerns of terrorism among the Serbs: "These terrorists [KLA] used to target state bodies and their representatives, first of all the police. They then started to murder prominent Serbs and ethnic Albanians who remained loyal to the state. Now they are killing ordinary Serb civilians" (Hedges 1998).

In response to the 1981 ethnic unrest in Kosovo, Belgrade deployed riot police and used security services to seal off areas of Pristina. Troops were sent in to crush the rebellion. In 1989, troops were deployed once again and anti-terrorist federal police was sent to Kosovo to deal with the protests (Petrovic 1989). Bans on public gatherings and ethnic protests followed. By the 1990s

Kosovo Albanians reported repeated harassment at police checkpoints (Moore 1993). Clashes with the police became common. And while the KLA contributed to some of the violence to provoke the Serbian response, the Serb authorities did not distinguish between the KLA and ethnic rioters. Serb Commander Nebojsa Pavkovic defended the actions of the Serb forces: "There was only the fight against the terrorists" (*Frontline* 2000).

The presence of foreign fighters in Kosovo also helped the government use the terrorist label. In 2002 at his war crimes trial in The Hague, Slobodan Milosevic cited an alleged FBI report and argued that the KLA was connected to Al Qaeda (BBC 2002). While Milosevic's testimony was disputed, other accounts indicate foreign fighters were making their ways to Kosovo. For instance, Robert Gelbard expressed concerns over mujahedeen forces targeting Kosovo. "It's quite clear that there are some elements of radical Islamic groups that are making overtures to the Kosovo Liberation Army and to other groups," he warned in 1998 (Sisk 1998). James Bissett, former Canadian ambassador to Yugoslavia further indicated that the KLA received training in "terrorist camps in Afghanistan" (*National Post* 2002).

Participation of foreign fighters in the Bosnia conflict is well documented (Kohlmann 2004; Schindler 2007; Malet 2013). Afghan Arab Mujahedeen Battalion was spotted there in 1992. Alija Izetbegovic awarded such mujahedeen with citizenship, and many of them stayed in Bosnia after the signing of the Dayton agreement. However, some of the Afghan Arabs were later spotted in Kosovo (Walker 1998). One Western official confirmed the presence of foreign fighters in Kosovo who "were financed by Saudi and United Arab Emirates money" (Vincent 2000). "They were mercenaries who were not running the show in Kosovo, but were used by the KLA to do their dirty work," the official explained. Expulsion of all foreign fighters even became one of the conditions of the KLA-NATO agreement of June 20, 1999.

The KLA attacks that involved civilians, the presence of foreign fighters in Kosovo, and the use of the terrorist label by the Serbian government, meant that, initially, international reactions affirmed the terrorist nature of the group. In February 1998, Robert Gelbard publicly called the KLA "without any questions, a terrorist group" (Shenon 1998). In a statement on Kosovo on March 9, 1998, the Contact Group for the former Yugoslavia condemned "terrorist actions by the Kosovo Liberation Army or any other group or individual" in Kosovo. In Resolution 1160 of March 31, 1998, the UN Security Council also referred to the KLA as a terrorist organization by condemning "all acts of terrorism by the Kosovo Liberation Army or any other group or individual and all external support for terrorist activity in Kosovo, including finance, arms and training."

For the Serbian government such condemnations signified a green light to continue with its onslaught on Kosovo. Subsequently, in the spring-summer of 1998, Milosevic stepped up crackdowns in Kosovo and repression escalated. The Serb police and the KLA engaged in open confrontations. What followed closely resembled the ethnic cleansing scenario from Bosnia: forced expulsions, massacres, retaliation killings, and overall excessive use of force. In July 1998, the

Yugoslav Army and the Serb police undertook a major offensive against the KLA that culminated in an attack on the Drenica region. In response to these actions, on September 23, 1998 the UN Security Council issued Resolution 1199 demanding a ceasefire. The next day NATO issued an ultimatum to Milosevic demanding an end to hostilities. In the absence of Milosevic's compliance, hostilities continued to escalate leading to NATO air strikes in March 1999 on the side of the KLA.

Legitimization

As a result of the international involvement in Bosnia, the Serbian government was already under close scrutiny. When hostilities sparked in Kosovo, reactions from international actors were swift. The fear of allowing a repeat of Bosnia motivated international actors to pay close attention to Belgrade's actions in Kosovo. Consequently, in 1993, UN Security Council issued Resolution 855 (August 9, 1993) in which it warned Belgrade that it was "determined to avoid any extension of the conflict in Yugoslavia." In 1997, the Contact Group for the former Yugoslavia that had first convened to resolve the conflict in Bosnia voiced deep concerns over the situation in Kosovo. When hostilities escalated in 1998, UN Security Council responded with Resolution 1160, and NATO issued a statement on May 28, 1998 encouraging Milosevic to peacefully resolve the crisis. As fighting escalated, so did international concerns, eventually leading to the international intervention in Kosovo.

As discussed in the previous section, initially international actors concurred with Milosevic in viewing the KLA as a terrorist organization. However, as Milosevic stepped up his response in Kosovo, the international community started viewing the KLA actions as proportionate to the actions of the Serbian government. This way, in disapproval of the bloodshed in Kosovo, U.S. Secretary of State Madeleine Albright warned that the United States was not "going to stand by and watch the Serbian authorities do in Kosovo what they can no longer get away with doing in Bosnia" (Erlanger 1998). When asked about the nature of the group, Albright did not call the KLA a terrorist group but instead justified its actions as provoked by the Serbs:

> We were concerned by some of the activities of the KLA. We did know that they were involved in some provocative activity. But it was also evident that what the Serbs were doing to the Kosovars was enough to provoke anything.
>
> (*Frontline* 2000)

What followed legitimized the KLA as an official party to the conflict. Moreover, the KLA not only received international recognition, but it also emerged as the leader of the Kosovo separatist movement, surpassing Rugova. In the eyes of international audiences, Ibrahim Rugova, the elected president of the self-proclaimed Republic of Kosovo, was a representative of the self-determination struggle of the Kosovo Albanians. International actors widely engaged with Rugova in his diplomatic efforts to secure international recognition for the separatist cause. For instance, in 1991 Rugova traveled to Tirana to seek endorsement of Kosovo's independence, and Albania subsequently recognized Kosovo as a sovereign and independent state. While other states were more skeptical of recognizing Kosovo's independence, Rugova still engaged in extensive diplomatic contacts.

However, as Rugova started losing domestic popularity, and as the KLA gained more followers, international actors recognized the KLA as the vanguard of the separatist movement. In 1998, Rugova still traveled to Washington to meet with President Clinton and visited New York to meet with UN Secretary General Kofi Annan. At the same time, Rugova was no longer seen as the only legitimate representative of Kosovo separatists. Ivo Daalder (*Frontline* 2000), director for European Affairs at the U.S. National Security Council, explained the transformations as follows:

> What happens in the summer of 1998 is an interesting change in the dynamics. The KLA moves out and becomes stronger and stronger militarily. In fact, they gain territory from the Serbs. By July, they claim control of about 40% of all of Kosovo … the KLA becomes the political leadership of Kosovo. It displaces Rugova, and demonstrates to the Kosovars that a policy of non-violent resistance is not working—that violence, and threats, and force are what would get Kosovo what it wants—autonomy and independence.

With that, given the level of international disapproval for Milosevic's actions, the KLA was well positioned for international legitimization.

International recognition of the KLA was marked by the U.S. approaching the group for talks. In May 1998, Robert Gelbard who had previously called the KLA a terrorist organization, met with the KLA officials in Switzerland. The U.S. dispatched Dayton agreement negotiator Richard Holbrooke to directly talk to the KLA. In June 1998, Holbrooke and the KLA leaders appeared in their first public contact. Holbrooke (*Frontline* 2000), who had been meeting with the KLA in secret, explained such transformation in the treatment of the group:

> Well, it was obvious to me from early on. I had already met with senior KLA representatives in secret, with no publicity, weeks and weeks earlier. And I had been in steady contact with them, because they were a legitimate part of the process. Whether they espoused a violent solution or not, you couldn't ignore them, because they were imposing their presence on the relationship.

This way, in the pre-9/11 environment, U.S. officials dropped the terrorist label applied to the KLA, legitimizing the violent means employed by the group as actions of Kosovo Albanian guerillas defending themselves from the Serb atrocities. Other international actors followed suite and dropped the terrorist label in reference to the KLA. Thus, while the UN Security Council Resolution 1160 referred to terrorist actions committed by the KLA, subsequent resolutions 1199 (September 23, 1998), 1203 (October 24, 1998), and 1244 (June 10, 1999) do not specifically reference the KLA in connection to terrorist activities.

Legitimization of the KLA culminated with the role the group played at the Rambouillet peace talks. The British Foreign Secretary Robin Cook and U.S. envoy Christopher Hill invited ethnic Albanians including KLA rebels to the Rambouillet conference to be held in February 1999 (see Bellamy 2002). To everyone's surprise the Kosovo Albanian delegation appointed as its head the KLA's Hashim Thaçi and not Ibrahim Rugova (Weller 1999). Ivo Daalder (*Frontline* 2000) recalls:

> They [Kosovo Albanians] pick a 29-year-old nobody called Hashim Thaçi, who is a political leader in the KLA, rather than their own elected president, Ibrahim Rugova. The surprise here even for the United States, which had put together this whole delegation, is that Thaçi becomes the leader of the game. It signals that the Albanians in Rambouillet will not be as easy to maneuver into the situation that we want as we had thought. Thaci was close to the hard-liners in the KLA. He'd talk over the mobile phones that they all carried with those hard-liners day in and day out, to make sure that Kosovo was not going to be sold down the tubes for a success of American diplomacy at Rambouillet.

This way the KLA was not only formally included in the peace talks, but also became the official leader of the Kosovo separatists and had to be recognized as such by the international community supporting the Rambouillet initiative.

At Rambouillet the KLA demonstrated to the world it was a significant player that had to be taken seriously. A key demand the KLA insisted on including in the agreement was a provision for a referendum on Kosovo's independence. To the surprise of major sponsors of the peace conference, it was Hashim Thaçi and not the Serbian side who initially refused to sign the agreement that did not include such a clause. While the U.S. and allies were taken aback by Thaçi's demands, they had to take his position into consideration. Eventually the KLA gave in and agreed to sign the Rambouillet plan according to which Kosovo would remain a nominal part of Yugoslavia yet with self-government for three more years. While the Rambouillet agreement was not a complete success as Serbia refused to sign, the KLA demonstrated its full potential as a legitimate party to the peace process. The KLA publicly laid claims to Kosovo independence and the international community stood by the group expecting Serbia to accede.

Participation in the Rambouillet talks increased the authority of the KLA and the group officially emerged as NATO's ally. While the Serbian delegation kept insisting that the KLA was a terrorist organization, labels reversed. In the NATO statement on Kosovo of April 23, 1999, it was Milosevic's actions that were described as a "campaign of terror." NATO and the KLA now had the same enemy. NATO air strikes allowed the KLA to carry out effective attacks against the Serb positions (Mulaj 2008). The KLA in turn became NATO's de facto ground force supporting air strikes.

From terrorists to politicians

The KLA emerged from the conflict victorious. Domestically, the KLA was celebrated as a heroic armed force. Internationally, it was legitimized as an official party to the conflict and a NATO ally. The KLA success has been even more apparent as Serbia has defied international support for Kosovo independence and has continued to insist on recognizing Kosovo as an integral part of its territory. Serbia has rejected Kosovo's declaration of independence and Belgrade has insisted on calling the territory "Kosovo and Metohija"—the name of the Serbian autonomous republic (Baumgartner 2016). Despite Serbia's uncompromising stance on Kosovo, the KLA firmly committed to the peace process.

International actors continued to be involved in Kosovo's post-conflict transformations. Their presence impacted the post-war trajectory of the KLA and prevented a slide back to violence. In the absence of international support securing guarantees of a peace process, many militant separatist groups go back to violence after signing a peace agreement. For instance, the LTTE went through multiple Eelam Wars interspersed with rounds of peace talks. In the case of the KLA, however, international actors managed the group's expectations, maintaining control over its transformations.

On June 9, 1999, NATO and the FRY signed a Military Technical Agreement that effectively terminated the NATO air campaign. The next day UN Security Council adopted Resolution 1244 that mandated a complete withdrawal of Serbian troops from Kosovo, approved the deployment of an international security force, and authorized an international interim administration for Kosovo. KFOR entered Kosovo in a peace enforcement operation under Chapter VII of the UN Charter. UNMIK became the interim governing authority. Both organizations, although with adjusted mandates and structures, still remain active almost 20 years after the end of the conflict.

The expectation for the KLA, as laid out by Madeleine Albright, was that it "will demilitarize and enter into a process of transformation" (Wright 1999). Transitioning requirements for the KLA were laid out in Resolution 1244 that demanded the group's demilitarization. On June 20, 1999, NATO and the KLA signed an agreement that further stipulated conditions for demilitarization and decommissioning. The KLA accepted the demilitarization requirement. "We have co-operated and will continue to work together closely with the international community, both on the military aspect and the political aspect," Thaçi promised (Wright 1999). However, while the KLA was ready to demilitarize, or reduce the size of its force, the issue of disarmament became contentious.

Disarming insurgents is usually a challenging undertaking and the KLA's transitioning into the civilian realm was not an exception. Similar to other non-state armed groups, the KLA was suspicious towards completely giving up weapons. As one U.S. diplomat explained, "nobody [knew] exactly how the KLA [would] behave" (Schork 1999). It took days of intense talks to agree on the number of weapons the KLA was allowed to retain: 200 small arms to guard their sites—half the number that was initially requested by the KLA. Finally, NATO commander Wesley Clark and the KLA's Agim Çeku and Hashim Thaçi came to an agreement on replacing the guerilla armed forces with a lightly armed civilian emergency relief agency—Kosovo Protection Corps (KPC). Hashim Thaci bid farewell to the KLA: "the KLA is transforming. It won't be called KLA but will be a defense force of the citizens and territory of Kosovo" (Reid 1999). On September 21, 1999, the KLA chief of staff Agim Çeku handed over to KFOR a written confirmation of demilitarization of the KLA.

As can be seen from Thaci's words, for the KLA, the KPC presented a way to eventually transition into Kosovo's defense force. Agim Çeku who headed the KPC promised: "We will build a new army in the future, and the Kosovo Corps will be one part of it" (Gall 1999). True to his promise, in the mid-2000s Çeku initiated reforms of the KPC to transition it into a fully operational armed force. In March 2006, Çeku himself became Prime Minister of Kosovo. After Kosovo's declaration of independence, the KPC transformed into a Kosovo Security Force (KSF). Çeku again stressed that the KSF "provid[ed] a sufficient basis for us to build a genuine military system or genuine armed forces in Kosovo in the near future" (BBC Monitoring Europe 2009). In 2014, Kosovo authorities pressed ahead to build Kosovo Armed Forces on the basis of the KSF. Seeking the approval of NATO and the U.S., in 2017 Thaci pledged to make the conversion through constitutional amendments. This way, under the guidance of the international community, the KLA has been firmly on its way to transition into armed forces of Kosovo.

The success of the KLA's demilitarization and disarmament was supported by the political transformation of the group. Often, violent wings of separatist movements undermine peace efforts spearheaded by political wings. For instance, the ETA-Batasuna or IRA-Sinn Féin relations often complicated peace efforts. In the KLA case, however, the post-conflict transition went through without resorting back to terrorist tactics because of Hashim Thaçi's transformation into a politician. While Thaçi initially failed to convert his military success into a political victory and did not win the first post-war elections, with international support and acknowledgement he and his Democratic Party of Kosovo (PDK) became firmly anchored in politics.

In April 1999, Hashim Thaçi unilaterally announced the formation of an interim government. However, because of his lack of political experience and renewed resurgence of Ibrahim Rugova, Thaçi's government was not recognized either domestically or internationally. Thaçi's political inexperience and KLA background presented a particular concern for Kosovo elites (Perritt 2010). Rugova in turn denounced Thaçi's move as illegitimate:

> At Rambouillet an agreement only in principal was reached, that the provisional government be formed in Pristina when they got back. And when

> they got back, the UCK and the LBD formed a government on their own, and they reserved a place for the LDK, but that should have been a consensual agreement on the composition of the government, and that was not the case.
>
> (Bransten 1999)

For the international community, Rugova, who was reelected president in 1998 seemed a much more logical choice to head the political transformation of Kosovo. UNMIK was skeptical about endorsing Thaci's government (Brand 2003).

And yet, the Rugova–Thaçi standoff did not result in renewed violence. For Thaçi, a confrontation with UNMIK would have terminated his political prospects. Cooperation with UNMIK, on the other hand, bore a promise of a complete transformation from a separatist militant to a legitimized politician. As a result, Thaci cooperated with UNMIK's Joint Interim Administrative Structure for Kosovo and chose to participate in the elections in November 2001. In this first post-war national election, the LDK received the largest number of votes, or 45.65 percent (OSCE 2001). Thaçi's PDK came out second receiving 25.7 percent of the votes. The next highest number went to Return Coalition (KP) at 11.34 percent. Rugova claimed electoral victory reminding the world: "We take this opportunity once again to call for the formal recognition of the independence of Kosovo as soon as possible" (CNN 2001). Thaci conceded defeat and continued to develop his political career.

Thaçi's choice to support the peaceful transformation of Kosovo paid off. After Rugova's death in 2006, he emerged as an unrivaled leader of Kosovo. In the 2007 election his PDK received 34.3 percent of votes while LDK got 22.6 percent (CEC 2007). Thaçi claimed the post of prime minister claiming: "We will make our dream and our right come true soon." "Kosovo will be independent," Thaçi promised (*New York Times* 2008a). Staying true to his promise, Thaçi declared Kosovo independence on February 17, 2008. "We are getting our independence," Thaçi stated, "Everything is a done deal. The world's map is changing" (*New York Times* 2008b). Thaçi's political success continued. On February 26, 2016, Thaçi became president of Kosovo, one of the very few former separatist guerillas to claim presidency.

Separatism, terrorism, and designations

The KLA's case stands unique because of the unprecedented level of international support. International involvement meant that Kosovo separatists were able to successfully withstand the Serb forces, receive support in the self-determination cause, and eventually declare independence that has been internationally recognized by 114 states. In 2010, the International Court of Justice ruled that Kosovo's unilateral declaration of independence did not violate international law. The World Bank and the International Monetary Fund granted Kosovo membership. Despite strong Serbian opposition, Kosovo was granted

UEFA and FIFA membership. In this gradual process of international recognition, the KLA's Hashim Thaci transformed from a guerilla fighter called a terrorist, to the Prime Minister of Kosovo, to its President. Such success among separatist movements remains rare. While parallels can be drawn between Kosovo Albanians and many other separatist movements, few separatist militants can boast of successes that would rival those of the KLA.

Similar to other ethno-nationalist separatist groups, the KLA emerged in response to the lack of progress achieved by peaceful resistance. Militant Uyghur fighters or Basque nationalists emerged under similar conditions where peaceful movements failed to achieve results and consequently embraced violence. Similar to other movements, in the Kosovo case the Serbian government pronounced separatists as terrorists. The terrorist label has been applied to Uyghur separatists and Kurdish nationalists. Just as in other cases, the Serbian government attempted to solve the problem of separatism with crackdowns. Similarly, the Sri Lankan, British, and Chinese governments have used disproportionate force in efforts to pacify ethno-nationalist militants. However, it was only in the KLA case that the movement not only shed the terrorist label, but also succeeded in achieving its objective and gaining political independence.

Unlike in many other cases of separatist conflicts, in Kosovo, Albanian separatists received acknowledgment and support from the international community. What was unique in the Kosovo case was the international presence in Bosnia. The experiences in Bosnia and the fear of a repeat of the Bosnian scenario meant that in Kosovo the international community was more committed to restraining the Serbian repression of separatists. In most other cases while the international community is often sympathetic to the self-determination rights of ethno-nationalist groups, rarely do international actors decide to intervene in domestic affairs of states trying to defend their territorial integrity.

Further, the fact that the Kosovo conflict took place before September 11 significantly impacted the ability of the KLA to achieve success. After September 11, tolerance for terrorism decreased drastically regardless of the reasons pushing groups to use terrorist tactics. Thus, sympathy for separatist groups resorting to terrorism diminished greatly. As a result, after September 11 separatist terrorist groups such as the IRA, ETA, or LTTE lost their chance to transition into politics because of their associations with terrorism. Subsequently, the IRA has decommissioned so that it can negotiate, and ETA has announced a similar intent to lay down weapons. The LTTE has been defeated militarily as the Sri Lankan government escalated its response against the group as part of the war on terror.

The KLA, on the other hand, was able to negotiate its own terms of demilitarization, represented the separatist side at Rambouillet, and was legitimized through cooperation with heads of states and international organizations. The terrorist label was abandoned before NATO's intervention, and the KLA did not face the challenges of collaborating with international actors as a designated terrorist group. The involvement of international actors in the KLA's post-war transformations ensured its complete transition into the political realm and prevented the return of violence. This way, the Kosovo case illustrates how before September 11 it was feasible for a separatist group using terrorist tactics to become legitimized and receive international acceptance.

Note

1 The views expressed in this chapter are those of the author and do not reflect the official policy or position of the National Defense University, the Department of Defense, or the U.S. Government.

References

Baumgartner, Pete. 2016. "Serbian PM: Relations with Kosovo Must Be Normalized." *RFERL*, January 6.

BBC Monitoring Europe. 2009. "Ex-PM Hopes Kosovo to Participate in NATO Peacekeeping Operations." March 29.

BBC. 2001. "IRA Begins Decommissioning Weapons." October 23.

BBC. 2002. "Al-Qaeda 'Helped Kosovo rebels.'" March 8.

Bekaj, Armend R. 2010. *The KLA and the Kosovo War: From Intra-State Conflict to Independent Country*. Berlin, Germany: Berghof Conflict Research.

Bellamy, Alex. 2002. *Kosovo and International Society*. New York: Palgrave Macmillan.

Brand, Marcus. 2003. *The Development of Kosovo Institutions and the Transition of Authority from UNMIK to Local Self-Government*. Geneva: CASIN.

Bransten, Jeremy. 1999. "Yugoslavia: Rugova Returns to Pristina Amid Muted Welcome." *RFERL*, July 9.

Brown, Justin. 1997. "Do Serbs 'Invent' Terrorists?" *Christian Science Monitor*, November 26.

Bush, George W. 2002. Speech in El Paso, TX. March 21. www.cnn.com/TRANSCRIPTS/0203/21/se.05.html.

Caplan, Richard. 1998. "International Diplomacy and the Crisis in Kosovo." *International Affairs* 74(4): 745–761.

CEC. 2007. C&RC Election Results. www.osce.org/kosovo/38260?download=true.

Chazan, Yigal. 1992. "Eyewitnesses: Kosovo Puts Faith in Latter-Day Gandhi." *Guardian*, May 25.

Clark, Howard. 2000. *Civil Resistance in Kosovo*. London: Pluto Press.

CNN. 2001. "Rugova Claims Victory in Kosovo." November 19.

Coleman, Karen. 1997. "Rebel Insurgency Looms in Kosovo." *Guardian*, December 27.

Erlanger, Steven. 1998. "Albright Warns Serbs on Kosovo Violence." *New York Times*, March 8.

Frontline. 2000. "War in Europe." Interviews with Policy Makers, Military Leaders, Negotiators, Serbs and Kosovar Albanians. www.pbs.org/wgbh/pages/frontline/shows/kosovo/interviews/.

Gall, Charlotta. 1999. "NATO and U.N. in Kosovo Agree on K.L.A. Role in Civilian Force." *New York Times*, September 3.

Gustincic, Andrei. 1990. "Sovereignty Votes Shake Yugoslavia." *Independent*, July 3.

Hamilton Spectator. 1999. "Kosovo Given Ultimatum to End Strife or Face Force." January 30.

Harden, Blaine. 1990. "Ethnic Albanians Boycott Key Election in Yugoslav Province." *Washington Post*, December 10.

Hedges, Chris. 1997a. "Notes from the Underground on Another Balkan Rift." *New York Times*, May 11.

Hedges, Chris. 1997b. "Resistance to Serbia Turns Violent in Kosovo." *New York Times*, February 17.

Hedges, Chris. 1998. "Gun Battles in Serbia Raise Fear of 'Another Bosnia.'" *New York Times*, March 6.

Horne, A.D. 1991. "Ethnic Albanians in Yugoslavia Reportedly Vote for Sovereignty." *Washington Post*, October 26.

Howe, Marvine. 1982. "Exodus of Serbians Stirs Province in Yugoslavia." *New York Times*, July 12.

Human Rights Watch. 2001. Under Orders: War Crimes in Kosovo.

Humphrey, Peter. 1989. "Bomb Attacks Fuel Fears of Albanian Terrorist Campaign." *Independent*, April 3.

Judah, Tim. 2008. *Kosovo: What Everyone Needs to Know*. New York: Oxford University Press.

Kohlmann, Evan. 2004. *Al-Qaida's Jihad in Europe: The Afghan-Bosnian Network*. Oxford: Berg.

Kostovicova, Denisa. 2005. *Kosovo: The Politics of Identity and Space*. New York: Routledge.

Krieger, Heike. 2001. *The Kosovo Conflict and International Law: An Analytical Documentation 1974–1999*. Cambridge: Cambridge University Press.

Kubo, Keiichi. 2010. "Why Kosovar Albanians Took up Arms against Serbian Regime: The Genesis and Expansion of the UCK in Kosovo." *Europe-Asia Studies* 62(7): 1135–1152.

Malcolm, Noel. 1999. *Kosovo: A Short History*. New York: HarperPerennial.

Malet, David. 2013. *Foreign Fighters: Transnational Identity in Civil Conflicts*. New York: Oxford University Press.

Mertus, Julie A. 1999. *How Myths and Truths Started a War*. Berkley: University of California Press.

Milosevic, Slobodan. 1987. Speech at Kosovo Polje, April 24–25. www.slobodan-milosevic.org/news/milosevic-1987–3-eng.htm.

Moore, Kathy. 1993. "Serbian Military Activity Raises Tension." *Irish Times*, May 11.

Mulaj, Klejda. 2008. "Resisting an Oppressive Regime: The Case of Kosovo Liberation Army." *Studies in Conflict and Terrorism* 31: 1103–1119.

National Consortium for the Study of Terrorism and Responses to Terrorism (START). 2017. Global Terrorism Database. www.start.umd.edu/gtd/search/Results.aspx?expanded=no&casualties_type=&casualties_max=&success=yes&perpetrator=720&ob=GTDID&od=desc&page=1&count=100.

National Post. 2002. "U.S. Supported Al-Qaeda Cells during Balkan Wars." March 15.

New York Times. 1990. "Upheaval in the East: Yugoslavia." February 6.

New York Times. 2008a. "Kosovo Leader Promises Independence in Weeks." January 9.

New York Times. 2008b. "Kosovo Prepares Declaration of Independence." February 17.

OSCE. 2001. Election 2001 Certified Results. www.osce.org/kosovo/20466?download=true.

Pavcovic, Aleksandar. 2000. *The Fragmentation of Yugoslavia: Nationalism and War in the Balkans*. New York: St. Martin's Press, LLC.

Perritt, Henry H. 2008. *Kosovo Liberation Army: The Inside Story of an Insurgency*. Chicago: University of Illinois Press.

Perritt, Henry H. 2010. *The Road to Independence for Kosovo: A Chronicle of the Atisaari Plan*. New York: Cambridge University Press.

Petrovic, Barney. 1987. "Serbs March on Belgrade to Demand End to Terror." *Guardian*, June 27.

Petrovic, Barney. 1989. "Troops Tighten their Hold on Kosovo." *Guardian*, February 27.

Phillips, David L. 2012. *Liberating Kosovo: Coercive Diplomacy and U.S. Intervention*. Cambridge, MA: The MIT Press.

Reid, Robert H. 1999. "Demilitarization of KLA Postponed." *Washington Post*, September 20.

Roberts, Adam., and Ash, Timothy Garton. (Eds.). 2009. *Civil Resistance and Power Politics: The Experience of Non-Violent Action from Gandhi to the Present*. Oxford: Oxford University Press.

Schindler, John R. 2007. *Unholy Terror: Bosnia, Al-Qa'ida, and the Rise of Global Jihad*. St.Paul: Zenith Press.

Schork, Kurt. 1999. "KLA Remains Dangerous Wildcard in Push for Yugoslavian Peace." *Vancouver Sun*, June 5.

Seper, Jerry. 1999. "KLA Rebels Train in Terrorist Camps." *Washington Times*, May 4.

Shenon, Philip. 1998. "U.S. Says It Might Consider Attacking Serbs." *New York Times*, March 13.

Sherwell, Philip. 2001. "I'll Never Deal with Adams Again, says Bush." *Telegraph*, March 13.

Sisk, Richard. 1998. "Islam's Looking at Kosovo." *Daily News*, June 18.

Traynor, Ian. 1990. "Denizens of Kosovo Cafe Plot Next Republican Step." *Guardian*, July 20.

Uselac, Ana. 1996. "Some Unfinished Business in the Shadow State of Kosovo." *Guardian*, July 10.

Vickers, Miranda. 1998. *Between Serb and Albanian: A History of Kosovo*. New York: Columbia University Press.

Walker, Tom. 1998. "US Alarmed as Mujahidin Join Kosovo Rebels." *Times*, November 26.

Washington Post. 2001. "White House Freezes Suspected Assets." December 4.

Weller, Marc. 1999. "The Rambouillet Conference on Kosovo." *International Affairs* 75(2): 211–251.

Wheeler, Lina. 1999. "Marchers Strut Support for Independent Kosovo." *Washington Post*, April 28.

Wright, Jonathan. 1999. "KLA Pledges not to Attack Retreating Forces." *Birmingham Post*, June 9.

6 Terrorism and counterterrorism on Europe's edge

Turkey, the PKK, and the TAK

Vaughn Shannon

Introduction

This chapter addresses the secessionist political violence of Turkey's Kurdistan Workers' Party (*Partiya Karkeren Kurdistane*, or PKK), and the response from the government of the Republic of Turkey, a nation that geographically, culturally, and psychologically straddles Europe and Asia. The broad questions to address in this chapter are (1) what caused Kurdish separatist terrorism and political violence to start and persist, and (2) what has the Turkish government done in response, and with what effect?

In terms of the scope of this chapter and volume, we elide discussion of terrorism and political violence that is not ethno-separatist. Not all terrorism is ethnic based, and not all terrorism is secessionist. Turkey itself is prone to terrorism of a variety of types: ideological (Marxist) and Islamist, among them. As noted in Chapter 1, Separatism is defined by Pokalova (2010, 430) as "a self-determination movement on the basis of an ethno-nationalist identity that encompasses claims ranging from increased cultural and political rights to struggles for territorial independence." It by definition is a relational political challenge between a group and one or more states. The "challenge of separatism" for states, notes Pokalova (2010, 430), is that it undermines the state's legitimacy, authority and territorial integrity.

The Kurds of Turkey have expressed myriad forms of secessionist sentiment and practice, violent and non-violent. This chapter examines one Turkish secessionist movement, the PKK, that resorted to political violence, including terrorism and even suicide terrorism, in pursuit of its dreams of separatism. When the PKK vowed to give up political violence at the turn of the twenty-first century, the group and the dreams they harbored splintered. One faction, the TAK, took up the mantle of separatist violence, reigniting the cycle of violence between Turkey and the PKK. As of this writing in early 2017, the conflict dynamic continues and a permanent solution remains elusive.

Why the violence and the failure of a permanent peace? Different perspectives will be addressed in this chapter, from strategic dimensions of power and physical security to ideational theories relating to identity and ontological security. In terms of the former, opportunistic actors push their agendas so long as they have the power to do so; they yield only when faced with deterrent or defeating capabilities that make their goals unrealizable. From this viewpoint, the Turkish government seeks to maintain the territorial integrity of the state and has the power to do so, denying Kurdish aspirations for not only independence but even autonomy. The Kurds from this vantage point, rise when opportunity arises, and yield under threat or coercion. Shifting regional and local circumstances, then, shape the calculus of ethnic separatist war.

The latter, ideational, view, argues that conflict and peace are about the boundaries of identity (us and them), and the feelings of security and trust those communities harbor given their defined identities. In such a rendering, Turkey's identity politics about "who is a Turk" and what the boundaries of the state are, can change and can affect the course of conflict. Refusing Kurdish identity rights and insisting on geographic contiguity and assimilation is a recipe for Kurdish frustrations and insecurity. Peace comes when Turks and Kurds change their mutual perceptions of us/them, and empathize with each other enough to legitimate each other's needs.

From either perspective, the "Kurdish Issue" continues because the Turks fear Kurdish challenges to the state's integrity, and Kurds resent the lack of political power in Turkey or in an autonomous Kurdish entity. Whether force can solve the problem, and whether the two sides can reshape perceptions for an enduring peace, is the subject of the following analysis.

The rise of Kurdish separatism in Turkey

The Kurdish people, linguistic and cultural descendants of Indo-European tribes, number some estimated 35 million strong worldwide, largely concentrated in modern Turkey (18 million), Iran (eight million), Iraq (five million), and Syria (two million).[1] Physically separated across the four Middle Eastern states, Kurds are not homogenous culturally, politically, or even linguistically—with four major dialects (Kurmanji, Sorani, Zazaki, and Gorani) predominating the region. Everywhere they reside, then, they are a minority; yet in the mountainous region of southeast Turkey, northeast Syria, northern Iraq and northwest Iran that many call "Kurdistan," they are a historic, long-standing majority.

Given the regional dispersion of Kurds, clearly not all separatist Kurds are from Turkey. Kurdish groups in Iraq, Syria, and Iran operate independently with their own agendas (Table 6.1), creating for Turkish Kurds shifting opportunities and, for the Turkish government, shifting threats. The Iranian group, The Society for the Revival of Kurdistan, Mahabad, Iran, morphed into the KDP and declared a Kurdish Republic in 1946. Initially backed by the Soviet Union in an early test of the Cold War, eventual Soviet withdrawal permitted the Persian government to suppress the Kurdish fledgling state and drive the opposition into the hills (Hassanpour 1994).

Kurds in Iraq faced repression especially after the 1975 Algiers Agreement with Iran, ending state support for factions. With the Iran-Iraq war, Kurdish groups became proxies for other regional governments' interests, and exploited

Table 6.1 Select regional Kurdish political organizations

Organization acronym	*English translation*	*Country of origin*
KDP	Kurdistan Democratic Party	Iraq
KNC	Kurdish National Council	Syria
PAK	Kurdistan Freedom Party (formerly Revolutionary Union of Kurdistan)—HAK-R (Kurdistan Freedom Eagles for East Kurdistan)	Iran
PCDK	Kurdistan Democratic Solution Party	Iraq
PDKI	Democratic Party of Iranian Kurdistan	Iran
PJAK	Kurdistan Free Life Party	Iran
PKK	Kurdistan Workers Party	Turkey
PUK	Patriotic Union of Kurdistan	Iraq
PYD	Democratic Union Party	Syria
TAK	Freedom Falcons	Turkey
YPG	People's Protection Units	Syria

the situation for their own agendas. Intra-Kurdish rivalry between Iraqi PUK and KDP allowed Saddam Hussein to play one off the other. A 1987 united Kurdistan Front, bringing the two parties together under Iran's urging, led Iraq's regime to conduct the infamous and brutal Anfal campaign, gassing Kurdish villages of rebels and civilians alike (Hassanpour 1994). The contagion, spillover, and demonstration effects of neighboring Kurdish nationalist movements can create actual or perceived hope in Turkish Kurd movements, to the fear of Ankara's officials. We return to this dynamic later in the analysis.

The modern history of Kurdish secessionism dates to World War I and the "peace to end all peace" which followed. Inhabitants of the sprawling multiethnic Ottoman Empire, Kurds lived under Turkish rule but thrived largely unattended in the areas of modern Iraq, Iran, Syria, and Turkey. Like other ethnic minorities, self-determination was stoked by the Great War. But with the vanquishing of the Ottomans at the end of the Great War in 1918, the future of Kurds, as well as Arabs, Armenians, Jews, and Turks of the caliphate, was thrown into uncertainty. The Allied themes of self-determination, emphasized particularly by U.S. President Woodrow Wilson upon America's late entry into the war, raised moral and political salience for the autonomy or independence of peoples long under the thumb of imperial or colonial design.

The Treaty of Sevres attempted to manage multiple nationalist ambitions in the wake of Ottoman dismemberment. Article 62 explicitly called for a Commission to draft "a scheme of local autonomy for the predominantly Kurdish areas" and, if "Kurdish peoples … show that a majority of the population … desires independence," Turkey shall "renounce all rights and title over these areas" (Treaty of Sevres, Articles 62, 64). The British plan to take Mosul province (in modern Iraq) included the opportunity for Kurds to vote on their future, suggesting "no objection" to the "voluntary adhesion to such an independent Kurdish State" by those in the Mosul province (Treaty of Sevres, Article 64).

Whatever the merits and promises of the Treaty of Sevres, it did not come to pass. Nationalist Turks rallied behind war hero Mustafa Kemal Ataturk to undo the Ottoman treatise, warring across the Anatolian peninsula against occupying Greeks and other allies of World War I. After successful engagements and skirmishes around the countryside to retake lost ground, Ataturk's forces compelled a new Treaty of Lausanne in 1923. Lost in the newly inked map of the Middle East was any notion of ethnic autonomy or independence for Kurds, Armenians, or other national minorities. The resulting Republic of Turkey had set its borders and demanded a national unity under a secular, Turkish nationalist vision.

So, what makes Turkish Kurds separatist? Political and cultural repression is a standard cause, denying people the right to expression and access to power (Braithwaite 2014). Discrimination, or perception of discrimination of a minority by the privileged majority (relative deprivation) constitutes another classic formula for discontented ethnic groups (Gurr 1993). With both of these variables, there is reason for cause in the denial of Kurdish autonomy before and after World War I in the new Turkish Republic. There is evidence of Kurdish cultural distinction and deprivation in the early writings of Ahmad-e Khani, whose 1694–1695 rewrite of the Kurdish ballad "Mem u Zin" asks "Why have the Kurds been deprived, why have they all been subjugated?" (Hassanpour 1994). In the late 1800s, Haji Qadiri Koyi advocated the use of the Kurdish language for publishing magazines and newspapers (Hassanpour 1994). After the Lausanne settlement ended Kurdish aspirations, rebellions in Turkey popped up over a 20-year period, to no avail, in 1920, 1924, 1930, and 1937–1938 (Bloom 2005, 103).

Then, as now, not all Kurds perceived discrimination and not all Kurds are separatist. Separatism broadly concerns increased power and authority in the hands of the ethnic group in question, but can vary from calls for mere autonomy to the more drastic demand of independence. Sarigil and Karakoc (2016) tested the hypothesis that those with a perception of discrimination by the state are more likely to support separatism, which they found to be statistically supported in multiple models of Turkish Kurd public opinion. Turkish Kurds polled in 2011 and 2013 largely support the former over the latter, with autonomy support between 55 percent and 66 percent and independence support between 23 percent and 32 percent (Sarigil and Karakoc 2016). Many Kurds have found political expression within the Turkish framework of politics, in which Kurdish parties and language is banned and ethnic minorities are not recognized. In the 1950s, many supported the center-right Democratic Party against Ataturk's nationalist Republican People's Party, while many younger Kurds of the 1960s moved leftward in support of the Turkish Labor Party (Barkey 2007, 346). The People's Democratic Party (HDP), is a prominent pro-Kurdish opposition party attracting many Kurdish politicians and voters.

Some argue that political violence in secessionist Kurdish movements was caused by the lack of legitimate political opportunities. Leftist parties banned or unwilling to support the cause in the 1960s-1970s fueled leftist approaches to the nationalist cause, such as the Revolutionary Youth in Ankara (1974) and, shortly after, the PKK, merging the nationalist cause with socialist, populist appeals. Studies show that Turkish Kurd support for Kurdish separatism decreases with socio-economic status and religiosity, and increases with perception of state discrimination (Sarigil 2010; Saragil and Karakoc 2016). One implication is that religious Kurds have different identity priorities than ethno-national, perhaps accepting the Turkish call for unity under "Islamic brotherhood" (Sarigil 2010).

Some ask not why the rise of Kurdish nationalism but why the rise of the PKK specifically, as a violent and hegemonic group in Turkish Kurd politics? If we ask, what factors explain the timing and ability of the PKK's rise as the hegemonic Kurdish nationalist organization in Turkey, Tezcur (2014) argues that the rise of the PKK was primarily a function of its ability to gain support among the peasantry in deeply unequal rural areas through its strategic employment of violence. PKK recruitment played off sentiments of revenge, social mobility, and gender emancipation, and the organization found a legitimate, credible voice for this agenda at the right time (Tezcur 2014). Founded in 1978 by Abdullah Öcalan, his following at university in Ankara spread through the countryside under the rubric of "apoism," which criticized the treatment of Kurds at the hands of the Turkish government while espousing a Marxist-infused vision of a "separate Kurdish state," with even "pan-Kurdish aspirations" (Drott 2014; Ince 2016). To the extent that the socialist appeal fell on deaf ears, especially after the end of the Cold War, the meaning and message of the PKK adapted, evolving from its Marxist roots and its draconian separatist ambitions to more modest calls for democratic participation and local autonomy. The PKK also would evolve in strategy and tactics to achieve their goals, including militarizing their cause in the 1980s and delving Turkey into civil war. Before turning to the PKK-led era of Kurdish violence in Turkey, we turn to the Turkish government's perspective on the "Kurdish Question" (Barkey and Fuller 1998).

The Turkish government perspective

As for the government in Ankara, the PKK is not an isolated organization and problem, but part of the broader "Kurdish question" (Barkey and Fuller 1998), a web of linked Kurdish threats to the territorial integrity of the country. PKK and all Kurdish secessionist and separatist movements are viewed as part of a network threatening Turkey's territorial integrity with their ideas of autonomy. The willingness to resort to political violence adds a dimension of urgency to Turkey's perceptions of danger, but the concern for national unity and territorial integrity is the primary and original concern.

Emblematic of the regional focus and long history of the problem, in 1937, Turkey, Iran, Iraq, and Afghanistan signed the Saadabad Pact, calling for "complete abstention from any interference in each other's internal affairs," including the "formation or activities of armed bands" that would "disturb the order or security … of the territory of another Party" (Treaty of Non-Aggression, 1937). These governments, aimed at preserving their governments and borders, agreed to coordinate policy and actions preventing and countering insurrection groups,

Kurdish or otherwise. Iran and Iraq would famously break from this agreement, arming and aiding Kurdish and other groups against each other before and during the Iran-Iraq war, and Turkey itself would find inconsistent help from its neighbors, especially Syria (noticeably absent from the pact).

Beyond physical threats to territorial integrity, ideational theories discuss identity as a motivator and source of psychological and ontological security. Much has been made of Turkey's identity issues, pitting its East versus West as a "Bridge civilization" (Huntington 1993). Secular nationalists facing West seek to join the European Union and modernize from Turkey's Islamist past, while Islamic Turkey seeks to return to tradition and greatness in its Eastern, Muslim context.

These identity contests play out in the political sphere, and spill into foreign policy (Hintz 2016). Öktem (2004) notes the ethno-nationalist core in Turkey in the nineteenth-twentieth centuries, in which Kurds and other ethnies have been considered the "Other." The Kemalist Turkey following Sevres refuses to acknowledge ethnic minorities in the political sphere. Kurds and others, under Turkish nationalism, could "become Turkish" under the assimilating banner of secular Kemalist nationalism (Yeğen 2007). This is all despite the fact that, as Totten (2015) observes, Turkey, constructed out of a 500-year multiethnic Ottoman empire, "with its Kurdish, Arab, Zaza, and Alevi minorities, is no more homogeneous than the rump state of the Soviet empire with the Tatars, Ingush, Sakha, Chechens, and other large numbers of non-Russian peoples on its periphery." Perhaps because of the diversity of peoples, the Turks have felt insecure and compelled to assert a Turkish identity over a more inclusive conception of state and nation. According to Cirakman (2011), Turkish self-image has recently moved away from the modernist secular vision to a more xenophobic, ethnocentric, nationalist conception, which will not likely assist in the resolving of the Kurdish Question.

Turkey's behavior towards the Kurds reflects both identity and territorial concerns. Totten (2014) calls the government's response to the Kurds tantamount to attempted cultural genocide. Ethnic Kurds were forcibly relocated from the eastern parts of the country, and speaking the Kurdish language was forbidden in schools, government offices, and in public places. Within the backdrop of cultural and political exclusion, some Turkish Kurds were likely to be frustrated. Some of those were willing to take up arms.

The PKK record of terrorism and political violence

This section reviews the record of political violence since 1984, which has been long and bloody, estimating 30,000–40,000 casualties in all.[2] According to the Global Terrorism Database, as of 2015, PKK incidents of political violence number 1,817. Of those, 799 are classified armed assault, 474 bombings, and 113 assassinations. Targets have been predominantly military (558 incidents), but attacks on private citizens (332), journalists (10), and government officials (127) show that the PKK is not above assaults on civilians. Most of their actions have led to either zero fatalities (800) or 1–10 (893), with 74 attacks leading to 11–50 fatalities and six episodes killing over 50.

Notable to the examination of PKK political violence is the ebb and flow. As shown in Figure 6.1, the insurgent war began in 1984, spiked in the late 1980s and early 1990s, then disappeared at the turn of the century. After a brief lull, episodes of violence resume. We thus can discern and discuss two broad phases, 1984–1999 and 2004–present, analyzing the rise and fall of violence therein. We explore both phases in this section, examining both Kurdish terrorism and Turkish counterterrorist efforts. The first phase discussed below is 1984–1999, from the start of the PKK insurgency to the capture of its leader, Abdullah Öcalan. The second phase, a series of flare-ups associated with splinter groups, the Iraq War, and the Arab Spring, addresses the conflict dynamic from 2004 to 2017.

1984–2000

By 1982, the PKK had decided to resort to armed warfare on the Turkish state, training and preparing in Syria and Lebanon. Starting August 15, 1984, the PKK's military wing commenced attacks against police and soldier outposts in the Turkish Kurd towns of Eruh and Hakkari. With only a few minor assaults at first, operations escalated and spread from 1986 to 1989, from the heavily Kurdish southeast of Turkey to major metropolitan areas in Ankara and Istanbul.

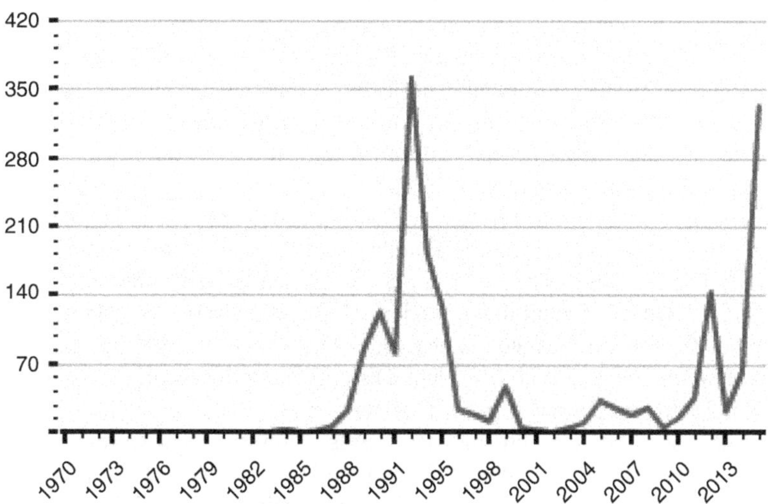

Figure 6.1 PKK terrorist incidents, 1984–2015.

Source: The Global Terrorism Database (START) www.start.umd.edu/gtd/search/Results.aspx?chart=overtime&search=pkk.

The PKK drew support from the poorer parts of Kurdish society, where its Marxist class appeals resonated (Bloom 2005, 105; Barkey and Fuller 1998). What began as unconventional warfare turned quickly to terrorism, however, targeting civilians—even Kurdish ones. The PKK targeted Kurdish landlords and "village guard units" hired by the Turkish government and thus considered traitorous to the Kurdish cause (Bloom 2005, 105). PKK operations also spread geographically to Europe, in pursuit of recruitment and financing as well as targeting opposition there (Bloom 2005, 104). The PKK also took up the practice of suicide terrorism, a notable case to remind observers that not only "Islamists" and religious groups but also secular, nationalist groups engaged in the craft. PKK also became famous for use of female suicide terrorism, with 11 of the 15 documented cases carried out by women (Bloom 2005, 102). By one account, the PKK would use the tactic to invite Turkish overreaction after being criticized by the EU for Turkey's human rights (Bloom 2005, 107).

While successful in baiting the Turks into heavy-handed counterterror measures (see below), Bloom (2005, 101) assesses that the PKK abandoned the practice of suicide terrorism when it was found to be counterproductive to recruitment and popular support. In fact, the broad problem for the PKK was the failure to win the hearts and minds of their own constituency. Barkey (2007, 348) concludes that the PKK terrorized "the very population it wanted to free."

Turkey's response: repression and reform in the EU's shadow

What has Turkey's response been to Kurdish secessionist violence, and why has Turkey been unable to end the Kurdish rebellion? The response of the Turkish government, like most in the quandary of confronting terrorism and ethnic insurgency, is a combination of repression and reform. The perennial dilemma is finding the right balance to degrade and deter militants while dissuading rather than inflaming the broader population. Turkey opted for a hard line first, before turning to political solutions and reform to buy the moderates and alienate fighters under shifting contexts. The Turkish response, also like many other states, is shaped by broader international politics, including their long-standing desire to be accepted by the west as a modern, secular state. The specific goal of membership in the European Union, for economic and prestige purposes, meant that Turkey's war was fought in the shadow of EU norms and perceptions.

For the Turkish governments since the 1970s, Kurdish PKK are terrorists threatening the unity of the Turkish state. Distrust of Kurds in Turkey and abroad led to policies to root out threat in both theaters. In the 1980s, the "village guards" program sought to "divide and rule" the Kurds, co-opting local Kurds to patrol their own neighborhoods. "Decree 413" laid the legal groundwork for press censorship and the exile of those charged with being "against the state" (Bloom 2005, 106). In 1987, Turkey put 11 provinces under a state of emergency rule, increasing military presence and operations in the southeast. Into the 1990s, frustrated Turkish authorities granted "carte blanche" authority to the military and security services, leading to extrajudicial killings and disappearances, and the equating of "all things

Kurdish with the PKK" (Bloom 2005; Barkey 2007). Population transfers and burned, evacuated villages punished Kurds beyond the PKK itself, which "eliminated the PKK's room to maneuver" but also had the result of "driving more … civilians into the arms of the PKK" (Bloom 2005, 106–109; Barkey 2007).

Abroad, the Gulf War internationalized Turkey's Kurd problem. After Saddam Hussein's repression of a Kurd uprising in 1991, the U.S. led a process to establish a no-fly zone in northern Iraq and help establish a de facto Kurdish autonomous region there. PKK bases in northern Iraq combined with the fear of contagion of the autonomy process, led Turkish forces to conduct air and land operations against PKK bases in northern Iraq. This was followed in 1995 by an invasion of 30,000 Turkish troops into Iraq.

Pusane (2015) argues that Turkish governments failed to realize that "the PKK is not just a group of armed militants," but rather a complex organization that appeals to a large number of Kurds. There were efforts of outreach and reform, to appeal to the broader Kurdish population, however. Prime Minister Özal "added carrots" to the mix in the early 1990s, by decriminalizing Kurdish culture and starting to permit Kurdish language use (Bloom 2005, 109). The southeast became flooded not just with security and military forces but economic aid packages, although nothing near the promises of Prime Minister Ecevit in 1999 (Bloom 2005, 109–110).

Repression and reform both came up short in finishing off the PKK, but arguably the most successful counterterrorism tactic employed by the Turkish authorities was leadership decapitation. Through capture or killing, leadership decapitation removes organizational leaders to deflate the morale and effectiveness of groups (Price 2012). Freeman (2014) argues that a leader's inspirational and operational position helps determine the success of leadership targeting on the effectiveness of a terror group. Abdullah Öcalan was both inspirational and operationally vital for the PKK, so targeting him was a priority for the Turks. After threatening Syria with war over its protection of the exiled PKK leaders, Öcalan was sent away in 1999, and captured in Kenya shortly thereafter. Öcalan was sentenced to death for treason, but in 2002, his death sentence was commuted to life imprisonment after Turkey abolished the death penalty in response to EU pressure.

Whether having a charismatic group leader alive is good or not has been debated (Price 2012); alive, Öcalan is a source of intelligence and leverage over PKK operations. When Öcalan encouraged his group to cease the war, they responded. Sparing his life also deflated revenge operations that were prepared over the leader's imminent demise. Importantly, while alive the Turkish government and the PKK have Öcalan to mediate and negotiate the future of the dynamic.

For a time, then, there was peace and a normalization of Kurdish politics. The PKK rolled back its demands for an independent Kurdish state, calling instead for more autonomy. In fact, the PKK technically disbanded, creating successor groups to carry the banner of Kurdish nationalism in Turkey. Hoping to work within the system, PKK members morphed into the Kurdistan Freedom and

Democracy Congress (KADEK), and again morphed into the Kurdistan People's Congress (KONGRA-GEL) by the end of 2003 (Barkey 2007, 345–346). Eventually, the Group of Communities in Kurdistan (KCK) was established, serving as an umbrella organization for regional Kurdish parties—including PKK, PYD, PJAK, and PCDK—who rally behind the Öcalan plan for what is called "democratic confederalism," stressing coordinated efforts at achieving autonomy and political rights in the region's nations. Ultimately, in Turkey, Kurdish parties and ex-PKK elements were still blocked from participating in the system. Distrust remained and a bias against recognizing ethnic minorities persisted. If Öcalan had the power to bring about ceasefires, he was also positioned to inspire a return to conflict under the right conditions.

Changing regional dynamics upset the new peace between Turkey and the PKK established in 1999–2000. The U.S. invasion of Iraq created both new threats and opportunities for Kurdish separatism in Iraq, spilling over into Turkish Kurd struggles. The instability in Iraq, coupled with the regional instability resulting from the so-called Arab Spring, fueled new bouts of Kurdish secessionism in Syria and Iraq. The growth of "pro-secessionist groups in Syria" and Iraq were viewed as a threat to the long-held view of Turkey's borders dating back to the Treaty of Lausanne (Phillips 2016, 32–36).

2004–present: resurgent insurgency

In a *Washington Post* study of insurgent activity in Turkey from 2011 to 2017, 1,173 of 1,500 deaths were attributed to "pro-Kurdish groups," versus 224 attributed to Islamic State (and 124 unattributed or attributed to other). The PKK represents a portion of this activity, but other groups emerged as well in this era. How independent these groups are is a matter of debate, but it signals a proliferation of the Kurdish problem for Turkey either way.

In the new phase of PKK politics, the group has moved away not just from its Marxist roots but also away from the strictly secular approach of the original organization and platform. Dalay (2015) speaks of a "rapprochement between religious and nationalist Kurds" in general, with estimates that at least 10–11 percent of the HDP's share of the vote come from the Kurds. HDP's outreach to the Islamist Kurds reflects the trend to find a resonating message at a time where "almost all the adversaries that the Kurds are facing in the region are disciples of one or another strand of Islamism" (Dalay 2015). PKK has likely felt the need to court a broader base to compete against the proliferating Islamist groups.

Beyond the official PKK, there has also been a rise in terrorism from other Kurdish separatist groups, raising the specter of splintering, a phenomenon when younger or more radical elements of a group part with the mainstream and parent organization out of disagreements about goals, means, or strategy (Bueno de Mesquita 2008). The concept of splinters captures the result of when governments "buy the moderates" that end major, large-scale terrorist operations. When a group and its leader agree to talks and even solutions that legitimate the enemy and its demands, some disaffected, frustrated members may splinter off the main organization, militarize and act independently of the former leader. It reflects, in essence, a legitimacy crisis within the group or movement. For examples, when Yasser Arafat's PLO disavowed terrorism and went to the negotiating table in the Oslo process, HAMAS was a rival spoiler, but Al Aqsa Martyrs Brigade was a splinter, playing spoiler in the second intifada. When the IRA sat down with the British and yielded the Good Friday Accords, The "Real" IRA (RIRA) and Continuity IRA (CIRA) splintered, and their 1998 Omagh bombing reflected this attempt to spoil the fresh peace achieved in the Good Friday Accords.

Included among splinter groups of Turkish Kurds is the Apoist Youngsters Revenge Brigade (AGIT), which has conducted protests and is responsible for vehicle fires in Istanbul (Gurcan). But the chief new group in Turkish Kurd nationalist politics is an entity calling itself the *Teyrenbazen Azadiya Kurdistan* (TAK), or Freedom Falcons (aka Freedom Hawks). Kurdistan Freedom Falcons, formed in 2004, is a breakaway militant faction of the Kurdish PKK, who aim to establish an independent Kurdish state in southeastern Turkey. The group declares the "methods of struggle" of the PKK and the Kurdistan People's Congress as "too feeble" (Porter 2016). The TAK's first public operation was in 2005. In April 2006, it attacked the police headquarters in Malatya. In June 2010, the TAK killed four military personnel and a civilian in an Istanbul suburb using a roadside bomb. Other notable operations included a mortar attack the TAK launched December 23, 2015, "retaliating for Turkish military operations" in the southeast of the country (Gurcan 2016). As of 2015, a Global Terror Database search of the Freedom Hawks and Freedom Falcons yielded 15 attacks likely linked to the group (START). The preferred method of attack is bombings, including suicide bombing. Beyond 2015, with the end of yet another peace process, things have become bloodier still. A February 17, 2016, suicide bombing in Ankara killed 29 people, leading to accusations of ISIS or YPG culpability before the TAK claimed responsibility (Bozarslan 2016). A June 2016, suicide bombing in central Istanbul killed 11, a December 10, 2016, attack at a football stadium killed 44, followed shortly after by a December 17 attacking killing 13 (*Al Araby*, December 12, 2016 and December 17, 2016).

The question of TAK independence from PKK has been much debated. For some, TAK "has adopted the PKK's ideology and philosophy, but diverges from it in actions;" and "if the PKK agrees to cease hostilities, the TAK will follow that line" (Bozarslan 2016). A 2016 analysis suggested operational differences, in that "the PKK frequently targets security forces and politicians, while TAK has claimed responsibility for several attacks including a car bombing that killed 37 people in Ankara in March" (Dearden 2016). Others doubt the independence of TAK from PKK. Journalist Aliza Marcus summarizes the skeptical view about TAK's autonomy, noting "It would be the first time in the history of the PKK that they allow the existence of any other group representing the Kurds than themselves," and citing its history of taking on rival Kurd groups and dissidents in its bid for dominance within the Turkish Kurd resistance (Porter 2016). Gurcan (2016, 24–25) concurs that the TAK is "best understood as a terrorist proxy of the PKK," in that there are "attacks during periods of mounting Turkish military pressure … without tarnishing the brand of the PKK," arguing that attacks time with Turkey's pressure on the PKK in SE Turkey.

All told, nearly continuous Kurdish political violence has been directed at the government and peoples of Turkey since 1984. Coordinated or not, periodic Kurdish groups have chosen coercive measures to achieve their shifting goals between autonomy and independence. Whether the TAK and PKK are separate or not, the official Turkish position, right or wrong, is that TAK and PKK are one and the same. To explain how the Turkish government responds, and thus itself influences the contours of the conflict, is the purpose of the next section. Turkey's decision reflects calculations of their own interests and threat perceptions, but also the broader geopolitics of the region and international patron whom they sought—for a time at least—to appease: namely, the EU and United States. As we shall see, outside forces play a role in the Turkey–PKK conflict dynamic, shaping opportunities and limiting responses.

Turkey's response: reform and repression

The changing regional environment brought Turkey back to the existential crisis that has plagued its borders for decades. But in a post-9/11 environment, Turkey felt emboldened to use force against "terrorists" without as much concern about US and EU pushback. Jacoby (2010) argues that Turkey's reform efforts of the 1990s were halted in the post-9/11 environment that emphasized security and was more permissive of the heavy-handed tactics and institutions that claimed to pursue security. By framing separatist violence as terrorism, Pokalova (2010) argues, the attention goes to the threat and the bloodshed rather than the underlying causes and nuanced distinctions among different separatist means and motives. Moreover, a terror frame "justifies" a military counteroffensive as a response strategy (Pokalova 2010, 429). This militarized response included cross-border raids on suspected PKK and affiliated sites in Iraq (2007) and, eventually, Syria.

Conflict resolution is difficult between groups engaged in long-standing history of violence, such as that between a state and secessionist rebel movement. Even after changing their names and disavowing violence, PKK successor group made little headway in mainstream politics because of persisting "out-group trust" of Kurdish intentions and power (Celebi *et al.* 2014).

Beyond repressive tactics, Turkey under the AKP and Prime Minister Erdoğan, did reengage in a "new direction" of reform to try to quell or mute the PKK resurgence (Efegil 2008). In 2002, bending to EU pressures and still interested in accession to the organization, Turkey stopped using the death penalty, commuting Öcalan's death sentence to life in prison. Operating under the constraints of international and EU norms, Turkey has sought to balance its coercive counterterrorist activities with moderation. But acquiescing to such expectations is premised at least in part on the motive to court or maintain Western support generally, and EU accession specifically. Turkey applied to join the EU in 1987, was deemed "eligible" in 1997, and began negotiations with the EU in 2005. By 2015 a joint EU–Turkey Action Plan was created (European Commission).

If the two sources of Kurdish discontent are cultural and political power, Turkey has been progressive on the first of these, while progressively ruthless resisting change in the latter. Regarding the cultural rights of language use and education (Celik 2015, 54), the Turkish government since 2002 has permitted limited Kurdish language education and legalized broadcasts in Kurdish. In 2009, Turkish Interior Minister Besir Atalay promulgated the "Kurdish Opening," modest reforms that included a Kurdish television channel, the use of Kurdish in prison, and rehabilitation law reforms for minors prosecuted for acts of terrorism (Celik 2015, 56). Turkey allows the use of the Kurdish language in court. Dialog workshops attempted to bridge divides and build consensus. Secret talks were opened between Turkish officials, PKK leadership, and their European counterparts in Oslo. In April of 2011, Turkish Prime Minister Recep Tayyip Erdoğan paid a landmark trip to Iraqi Kurdistan. Kurdish politicians have also been granted rights to visit Öcalan in prison.

Spoilers on both sides have made any progress in de-escalation an uneven endeavor. In October 2011, Kurdish rebels killed 24 Turkish soldiers. In December 2011, Turkish forces mistakenly killed 34 Kurdish civilians in an airstrike meant for rebel forces. But secret peace talks persisted, publicly acknowledged in 2012, that led to a 2013 ceasefire and release of Kurdish prisoners as a good faith confidence-building measure. At the same time, a 2017 referendum on the constitutional transfer of powers to the President (Erdoğan in this case) itself was being affected by Kurdish politics. The referendum vote in southeast Kurdish-populated Turkey, by one analysis, could be the deciding factor in the closely contested vote (update: the referendum passed narrowly with 51 percent of the vote). Appealing to Kurdish sympathies, then, for political gain, drives Erdoğan's moderation toward the region (Pamuk 2017). While from mid-2013 to mid-2015, the Turkish state and the PKK enjoyed a period of relative calm under a ceasefire, by late July 2015 the army bombed PKK positions in northern Iraq, and the PKK in Turkey declared the ceasefire void. A wave of attacks against police stations swept over the country in August (Totten 2015).

But regarding political party organization and political autonomy, the Turkish government has resisted and become harsher toward politicians inclined toward Kurdish political power tied to more Kurdish rights and autonomy. It did not help that word of the Oslo talks was leaked, raising accusations that the Turkish government was "negotiating with terrorists" (Celik 2015, 58). A combination of PKK attacks killing 13 soldiers, coupled with the declaration of "democratic autonomy" by the Kurdish umbrella group, the DTK (Democratic Society Congress), rekindled Turkish fears of physical and ontological insecurity about the integrity of the state in the face of internal Kurdish political forces (Celik 2015, 58).

If Turkey seeks Western support, the reception is mixed to say the least. A UN report on alleged human rights violations committed by Turkish military and security forces in southeast Turkey, urged the Turkish authorities to give independent investigators, including UN staff, unimpeded access to the area to verify the veracity of such reports. The report also condemned violence committed by groups and actors allegedly affiliated with the PKK, and conceded "Turkey has a duty to protect its population from acts of violence," but also noting the need to "respect human rights at all times while undertaking security or counter-terrorism operations" ("'Alarming' Reports" 2016).

Increasingly frustrated with Europe, Erdoğan has threatened to hold a popular referendum on EU accession (*Reuters*, March 25, 2017). Germany and the Netherlands canceled planned campaign rallies "by Turkish officials seeking to drum up support among expatriate Turks" for a referendum, citing security concerns. Erdoğan saw the European efforts as an affront, accusing the countries of using "Nazi methods" and revealing the frustration with Europe over waiting "at the door (of the EU) for 54 years," referring to the time since the Turks sought to further integrate into European economic union.

Erdoğan is also showing impatience at home politically. After his AKP party lost a majority in Parliament for the first time in almost 15 years, Erdoğan used the lack of a governing coalition to call a second general election in November 2015. In the followup election, the AKP won a majority again (317 of 550), while the pro-Kurdish HDP got 21 fewer MPs than in June's election and the nationalist MHP's share of the vote dropped to 11.9 percent. Clashes were reported in the Kurdish city of Diyarbakir as the results came in, as Kurds saw the process and results as tainted. Since elections in June, a ceasefire between the Turkish army and militants from the Kurdistan Workers Party (PKK) has collapsed. Ignacio Sanchez Amor, head of the OSCE observer mission, said: "Physical attacks on party members, as well as the significant security concerns, particularly in the south-east ... imposed restrictions on the ability to campaign" ("Turkey Election"). Turkey has also taken a hard line on formerly mainstream politicians and parties, arresting Kurdish politicians and closing down a pro-Kurd party, the Demokratik Toplum Partisi, or DSP (Celik 2015, 59). Twenty-six HDP ministers have been detained since November 2016—after parliament lifted immunity from parliamentary prosecution—for being accused of ties to the banned PKK (Rudaw, March 1, 2017). Thirteen HDP lawmakers were detained and 10 of them, including co-leaders Selahattin Demirtaş and Figen Yüksekdağ, for terrorism-related charges (*Hurriyet*, February 8, 2017). HDP (Peoples' Democratic Party) parliamentarian Leyla Zana of the Turkish Assembly, faced up to 20 years for terrorism-related charges of arming a terrorist group, praising crime and criminal activity, and opposing the law on meetings and demonstrations.

Beyond Turkey: the regional conundrum

Kurdish nationalist politics are fraught not just with geographic divisions, but also political divisions. In Iraq, the PKK "has dramatically increased its presence [in Sinjar] since August 2014," and has recruited a "local branch" of fighters there. Barzani's Peshmerga abandoned the Yazidis to ISIS, leading Yazidis to feel indebted to the PKK and the PYD and distrustful of the KRG. Olson and Davison call the Iraqi region of Sinjar "vital for both the KRG and the PYD, because it is the geographical and strategic link between the Syrian Kurds and the Iraqi Kurds." While the KRG has called for PKK forces to leave, the PKK leader in Sinjar, Agid Civan, said the

PKK would leave only after "all of Sinjar is liberated and Yazidis still in IS captivity are rescued" (Olson and Davison 2016). General Joseph Dunford, Chairman of the U.S. Joint Chiefs of Staff, met with Turkish counterpart, General Hulusi Akar, and agreed that Turkey "had a right to intervene against the PKK if the PKK establishes a permanent base [in Sinjar]" (Olson and Davison 2016).

Political and military events in neighboring Iraq, Syria, and Iran have made the already complex Turkish "Kurd Issue" virtually intractable. Kurdish groups affiliated with the PKK operate in all three neighboring states, adding to Turkey's anxieties about spillover and contagion effects. What's more, there are other Kurdish actors in Iraq and Syria at odds with the PKK affiliates, creating intra-Kurdish rivalry and complicating Kurd efforts at unity and U.S. efforts to counter ISIS in the region.

In Iraq, Turkey's fears of the spillover and demonstration effects of Kurdish regional autonomy shaped policy toward the post-Saddam regime after 2003. Turkey both occupied northern Iraq and forged ties with the KRG's leadership in Barzani, which "squeezed the Turkish Kurdish separatists who had always seen themselves as the leaders of region-wide Kurdish nationalism" (Phillips 2016, 22). Kurdish factions jockeyed for power in northern Iraq for years, and experienced a full-blown civil war from 1994 to 1997 between the KDP and the PKK-ally, the PUK. In the case of the Iraqi Kurd civil war, as today, the Turkish government sided with the KDP against anything related to the PKK, showing that the Turks do have a nuanced sense of threat from the Kurdish corner of the region. The Turkish, and American, governments have picked sides, and the PKK and PUK are not it. More fundamentally, any Kurdish move toward independence in Iraq is a precedent the Turkish regime does not seem willing to tolerate. A September 2017 referendum in Kurdish Iraq, in which 92 percent of voters endorsed Iraqi Kurdish independence, led Erdoğan to threaten to close borders (cutting trade) with Kurdistan and sparked speculation of intervention should the Kurds try to make their dream a reality (Chulov 2017).

Turkey's PKK has associates in Syria, namely the Democratic Union Party (PYD). Iraq's Kurdistan Regional Government (KRG), headed by the KDP leader, Massoud Barzani, assert themselves as the example of autonomous Kurdish authority and have their own Syrian counterpart in the Kurdish National Council (KNC) (Olson and Davison 2016). Recent skirmishes, protests, and arrests between competing PYD and KNC factions in northern Syria reveal the disunity of Kurdish nationalism in Syria and abroad.

For the U.S., the desire to defeat ISIS complicates its Kurdish politics. The KNC aligns with the U.S.-supported opposition Syrian National Council (SNC), while the PYD operates independently, at times even siding with the Syrian government. But the PYD's military arm, the People's Protection Units (YPG), is a chief component of a group called the Syrian Democratic Forces (SDF), which is the most viable opposition to march on Raqqa, the ISIS de facto capital. Turkey opposes U.S. President Trump's decision to arm and aid these forces, and in fact occupied northern Syria under Operation Euphrates Shield in part to degrade the YPG and prevent them from achieving a unified foothold for a future autonomous region for the Kurds.

In short, Totten (2015) summarizes the Turkish government threat perception thus: "alarmed by the existence of an autonomous Kurdish region in Iraq since the day it was founded," "doubly alarmed now that the Kurds of Syria have cobbled together their own autonomous region," and "*triply* alarmed because the Kurdish militias in Syria—the YPG, or People's Protection Units—are aligned with the PKK." Turkey is trying to dampen the flames of Kurdish nationalism in Syria's north, so as to keep the PKK's aspirations contained. A tripartite negotiation process involving Turkey, Iran, and Russia has aimed to set the parameters of the Syrian civil war's endgame, with U.S. Presidents Obama and Trump acquiescing to the local powers to solve the Syrian puzzle. A report in March 2017 claimed that Russia was setting up a "reconciliation center" in northwest Syria that some considered a training ground for Kurdish YPG militia, no doubt against Turkey's interests (Perry 2017).

Even in Iran, Kurdish insurrection has resumed. Iran blames "external powers" for the renewed mayhem (Entekhabi-Fard 2016), a likely reference to the United States, among others. The Kurdistan Freedom Party (PAK), has received military training from both American and European advisers, as part of the fight against the ISIS, but it also has carried out attacks inside Iran (Szlanko 2016). Another Iranian Kurdish rebel group based in Iraqi Kurdistan, the Kurdistan Democratic Party of Iran (KDPI, aka PDKI), has declared "armed action" after over 20 years of peace (Entekhabi-Fard 2016).

Conclusion

After 30 years of overt political violence, and a century of unfulfilled Kurdish aspirations of statehood or separatism, things have changed yet remained the same. The PKK is not what it used to be, says Totten (2015), morphing from the Marxist group seeking independence to a group that "first and foremost" is "fighting against the fascists of ISIS, and second for Kurdish independence, a secular system of government, and equality between men and women (Totten 2015).

The situation for the Kurds has changed over the years, yet fundamental obstacles remain: namely, the local, regional, and international hesitancy to permit successful secession in a world of pre-existing nation-states, no matter how questionable the origins of that state order happen to be. In Iraq, President Erdoğan vows not to permit a "new Qandil" in the Sinjar Mountains, alluding to the PKK presence and operations in the Turkish border regions (Frantzman 2017, 14).

U.S. or other international sympathy waxes and wanes, especially when Kurdish fighters help them remove tyrants (Iraq 2003) or combat common foes (ISIS 2013–), but American interests likely will never be strong enough to compel recognition of an independent state. De facto autonomy is already present, and ethno-federal solutions in Syria and Iraq may satiate Kurdish nationalist desires for local autonomy while preserving the existing borders of the modern state system.

More dire views point to problems in Syria, Iraq, and Turkey itself. Syria and Iraq are far from stable. While the Kurds dig in on de facto self-governance in each state, the future of de jure autonomy is unclear. Some in Syria embrace a model of federalism (*World News*, March 27, 2017), while others insist it would not work (*Syria Direct*). Cagaptay (2015) argues "Turkey faces a toxic combination of political polarization, government instability, economic slowdown, and threats of violence—from both inside and outside Turkey—that could soon add up to a catastrophe." Arguing that "Turkey's Kurdish problem has changed," Cagaptay (2015) claims the Kurdish community is more unified than before. While conservative Kurds, have tended to vote for the governing, pro-Islamist Justice and Development Party (AKP), he argues that the dynamic changed during Turkey's 2015 election, when liberal, conservative, and nationalist Kurds "coalesced around the Kurdish-nationalist Peoples' Democratic Party (HDP)" (Cagaptay 2015). When the government launched airstrikes against the PKK in the summer of 2015, ending the tenuous ceasefire, it included collective punishment against the Turkish Kurd community: a week-long curfew; shut down electricity, Internet, and phone access; and sent in thousands of troops and police. For Cagaptay (2015), "the source of Turkey's dangerous polarization is Erdoğan himself," for having "successfully targeted and politically brutalized the secular Turkish military, businesses, liberals, the media, Jews, left-wing voters, Alevis, and now the Kurds."

The problem is surely bigger than Erdoğan or any one leader, but if the Turkish perennial ruler continues to distance from, and alienate himself from, Europe and the U.S., the notion of external assistance to a permanent solution also would fade. For Turkey, the Kurdish question is not going away. A 2017 referendum on the constitutional transfer of powers to President (Erdoğan in this case) itself was being affected by Kurdish politics. The referendum vote in southeast Kurdish-populated Turkey, by one analysis, could be the deciding factor in the closely contested vote. Appealing to Kurdish sympathies, then, for political gain, drives Erdoğan's moderation toward the region (Pamuk 2017). The future of Kurdish political power may still be decided by Kurds, perhaps voting instead of fighting.

Notes

1 Exact numbers are difficult to obtain, partly because Turkey bars census-taking on the ethnic identity.

2 This analysis uses the Global Terrorism Database (START), which tracks incidents, attack types, weapon types, casualties, and location of attacks. The latest data were culled May 27, 2017. See www.start.umd.edu/gtd/search/Results.aspx?chart=overtime&search=pkk; www.start.umd.edu/gtd/search/Results.aspx?search=freedom+falcons&sa.x=0&sa.y=0&sa=Search.

References

"'Alarming' reports of major violations in south-east Turkey – UN rights chief." UN News Centre, May 10, 2016 www.un.org/apps/news/story.asp?NewsID=53895#.WSnUHOvyuUl

Barkey, Henri. 2007. "Turkey and the PKK: A Pyrrhic Victory?" In *Democracy and Counterterrorism: Lessons from the Past*, edited by Robert Art and Louise Richardson, 343–382. Washington, DC: USIP Press.

Barkey, Henri, and Graham Fuller. 1998. *Turkey's Kurdish Question.* Lanham, MD: Rowman and Littlefield.

"Blast kills thirteen off-duty soldiers in Central Turkish City." Al Araby, December 17, 2016: www.alaraby.co.uk/english/news/2016/12/17/blast-kills-thirteen-off-duty-soldiers-in-central-turkish-city

Bloom, Mia. 2005. *Dying to Kill.* New York: Columbia University Press.

Bozarslan, Mahmut. 2016 February 29. "Who is TAK and why did it attack Ankara?" *Al-Monitor.* www.al-monitor.com/pulse/originals/2016/02/turkey-outlawed-tak-will-not-deviate-line-of-ocalan.html#ixzz4DqAW1CNM

Braithwaite, Kirstin. 2014. "Repression and the Spread of Ethnic Conflict in Kurdistan." *Studies in Conflict and Terrorism* 37: 473–491.

Bueno de Mesquita, Ethan. 2008. "Terrorist Factions." *Quarterly Journal of Political Science* 3: 399–418.

Cagaptay, Soner. 2015 October 5. "Turkey is in Serious Trouble." *The Atlantic* www.theatlantic.com/international/archive/2015/10/turkey-isis-russia-pkk/408988/

Celebi, Elif, Maykel Verkuyten, Talha Kose, and Mieke Maliepaard. 2014. "Out-group Trust and Conflict Understandings: The Perspective of Turks and Kurds in Turkey." *International Journal of Intercultural Relations* 40: 64–75.

Celik, Ayse Betul. 2015. "The Kurdish Issue and Levels of Ontological Security." In *Conflict Resolution and Ontological Security*, edited by Bahar Rumelili, 52–70, London and New York: Routledge Press.

Chulov, Martin. 2017 September 27. "More than 92% of voters in Iraqi Kurdistan back Independence." *Guardian* www.theguardian.com/world/2017/sep/27/over-92-of-iraqs-kurds-vote-for-independence

Dalay, Galip. 2015. "Kurdish nationalism will shape the region's future." *Al Jazeera* www.aljazeera.com/indepth/opinion/2015/07/kurdish-nationalism-shape-region-future-150708082641707.html

Dearden, Lizzie. 2016 October 8. "Ankara terror plot: suicide bombers blow themselves up after refusing to give themselves up to police." www.independent.co.uk/news/world/europe/ankara-turkey-suicide-bombers-plot-woman-man-blow-themselves-up-haymana-pkk-kurdish-a7351471.html

Drott, Carl. 2014, May 20. "The Syrian Experiment with 'Apoism'". Carnegie Middle East Center http://carnegie-mec.org/diwan/55650

Efegil, Ertan. 2008. "Turkey's New Approaches toward the PKK, Iraqi Kurds and the Kurdish Question." *Insight Turkey* 10(3): 53–73.

Entekhabi-Fard, Camelia. 2016 July 19. "Iran's Kurdish Party and the Challenge of Ethnicity." *Al-Arabiya.* http://english.alarabiya.net/en/views/2016/07/19/Iran-s-Kurdish-party-and-the-challenge-of-ethnicity.html

European Commission. https://ec.europa.eu/neighbourhood-enlargement/countries/detailed-country-information/turkey_en

Frantzman, Seth. 2017. "Kurdistan after Islamic State: Six Crises Facing the Kurds in Iraq." *Middle East Review of International Affairs* 20(3): 12–23.

Freeman, Michael. 2014. "A Theory of Terrorist Leadership and its consequences for Leadership Targeting." *Terrorism and Political Violence* 26(4):

Gurcan, Metin. 2016. "The Kurdistan Freedom Falcons: A Profile of the Arm's-Length Proxy of the Kurdistan Workers' Party." *CTC Sentinel* (July): 24–27. www.ctc.usma.

edu/posts/the-kurdistan-freedom-falcons-a-profile-of-the-arms-length-proxy-of-the-kurdistan-workers-party

Gurr, Ted. 1993. *A Global View of Ethnopolitical Conflicts*. United States Institute of Peace, Washington, DC.

Hassanpour, Amir. 1994. "The Kurdish Experience." *MERIP* #189 www.merip.org/mer/mer189/kurdish-experience

"HDP MP Leyla Zana Released after Detention in Turkey." *Hurriyet Daily News*, February 8, 2017 www.hurriyetdailynews.com/hdp-mp-leyla-zana-released-after-detention-in-turkeys-diyarbakir.aspx?pageID=238&nID=109493&NewsCatID=338

Hintz, Lisel. 2016. " 'Take it outside!' National identity contestation in the foreign policy arena." *European Journal of International Relations* 22(2): 335–361.

Huntington, Samuel. 1993. "The clash of civilizations?" *Foreign Affairs*, 22–49.

Ince, Adem. 2016, February 24. "What Might Secular Kurdish Nationalism Produce?" Daily Sabah www.dailysabah.com/op-ed/2016/02/24/what-might-secular-kurdish-nationalism-promise

Jacoby, Tim. 2010. "Political Violence, the 'War on Terror' and the Turkish Military." *Critical Studies on Terrorism* 3(1): 99–118.

Olson, Robert, and Derek Davison. 2016. "Kurdish Rivalries Create New Challenges for Islamic State Fight." https://lobelog.com/kurdish-rivalries-create-new-challenges-for-islamic-state-fight/

Öktem, Kerem. 2004. "Incorporating the time and space of the ethnic 'other': nationalism and space in Southeast Turkey in the nineteenth and twentieth centuries." *Nations and Nationalism* 10(4): 559–578.

Pamuk, Humeyra. 2017 March 20. "Anger and Frustration in Kurdish Southeast to Shape Turkey's Referendum." *Reuters*. www.reuters.com/article/us-turkey-referendum-kurds-idUSKBN16R1IO?utm_campaign=trueAnthem:+Trending+Content&utm_content=58d027de04d3016400b6aa15&utm_medium=trueAnthem&utm_source=twitter

Perry, Tom. 2017 March 20. "US-allied Kurd Militia says Struck Syria Base Deal with Russia." *Reuters*. www.reuters.com/article/us-mideast-crisis-syria-russia-idUSKBN16R1H4?feedType=RSS&feedName=topNews&utm_source=twitter&utm_medium=Social

Phillips, Christopher. 2016. *The Battle for Syria: International Rivalry in the New Middle East*. New Haven: Yale University Press.

Pokalova, Elena. 2010. "Framing Separatism as Terrorism: Lessons from Kosovo." *Studies in Conflict and Terrorism* 33: 429–447.

Porter, Tom. 2016 March 15. "TAK: What we know about Militant PKK Offshoot allegedly responsible for Ankara attacks." *International Business Times*. www.ibtimes.co.uk/kurdistan-freedom-falcons-what-we-know-about-militant-pkk-offshoot-allegedly-responsible-ankara-1549637

Price, Bryan. 2012. "Targeting Top Terrorists: How Leadership Decapitation Contributes to Counterterrorism." *International Security* 36(4): 9–46.

Pusane, Ozlem Kayham. 2015. "Turkey's Military Victory over the PKK and its Failure to End the PKK Insurgency." *Middle East Studies* 51(5): 727–741.

Sarigil, Zeki. 2010. "Curbing Kurdish ethno-nationalism in Turkey: An empirical assessment of pro-Islamic and socio-economic approaches." *Ethnic and Racial Studies*, 33(3), 533–553.

Sarigil, Zeki, and Ekrem Karakoc. 2016. "Who Supports Secession? The Determinants of Secessionist Attitudes among Turkey's Kurds." *Nations and Nationalism* 22(2): 325–346.

Syria Direct. 2016, April 11. "Commander of Kurdish FSA Brigade: 'Federalism is not an effective system for Syria'." http://syriadirect.org/news/commander-of-kurdish-fsa-brigade-%E2%80%98federalism-is-not-an-effective-system-for-syria%E2%80%99/

Szlanko, Balint. 2016 September 8. "Iranian Faction Among Kurds Trained by U.S. against Militants." *Washington Post*. www.militarytimes.com/2016/09/08/iranian-faction-among-kurds-trained-by-u-s-against-militants/

Tezcur, Gunes Murat. 2014. "Violence and Nationalist Mobilization: The Onset of the Kurdish Insurgency." *The Journal of Nationalism and Ethnicity* 43(2): 248–266.

Totten, Michael. 2015. "The Trouble with Turkey: Erdogan, ISIS, and the Kurds." *World Affairs* www.worldaffairsjournal.org/article/trouble-turkey-erdogan-isis-and-kurds

Treaty of Non-Aggression. 1937, July 8. World Legal Information Institute www.worldlii.org/int/other/LNTSer/1938/163.html

Treaty of Sevres. 1920. www.yasa-online.org/documents/Kurds%20in%20the%20Treaty%20of%20Sevres%201920.pdf

"Turkey Election: Erdogan Calls on World to Respect Result." *BBC*, November 2, 2015 www.bbc.com/news/world-europe-34696489

"Turkish authorities recommend lengthy sentence for HDP's Leyla Zana." Rudaw, March 1, 2017 www.rudaw.net/english/middleeast/turkey/01032017

"Who is the Kurdish Group Behind Istanbul's Deadly Attack?" *Al Araby*, December 12, 2016 www.alaraby.co.uk/english/indepth/2016/12/12/who-is-the-kurdish-group-behind-istanbuls-deadly-attack?utm_campaign=magnet&utm_source=article_page&utm_medium=related_articles

World News. 2017, March 27. "Syria's Raqqa expected to join Kurdish-led federalism: Kurdish leader." *Reuters* www.reuters.com/article/us-mideast-crisis-syria-pyd-idUSKBN16Y1B0

Yeğen, Mesut. 2007. "Turkish nationalism and the Kurdish question." *Ethnic and Racial Studies* 30(1): 119–151.

7 Russia's response to IK and Chechen separatist terrorism

The surprising success of "Ramzanization"

Liam Anderson

Introduction

The violent confrontation between Russia and Chechnya has been described as "the most brutal conflict in post-war Europe" (Russell 2008, 659; Matejova 2013, 9), but this characterization is misleading in one respect. For more than 200 years, Russia's efforts to subdue the Mountaineers of the North Caucasus have been met with resistance, with Chechens, invariably, at the forefront of the fighting. As Lieven (1999, 304) puts it, "the entire period from 1785 to the present ... has been essentially one long struggle by the Chechens against Russian domination, interspersed with unstable truces and periods of sullen and unwilling submission." Viewed as a "two hundred years' war" rather than as a product of a particular constellation of events in the 1990s, helps convey some sense of the scale and nature of this struggle between a great power that refuses to relinquish conquered territory, and an ethno-nationalist group that refuses to bow down in the face of overwhelming military force.

By the early 1990s, as the Soviet Union fell apart and Russia struggled to define its newly independent identity, most ethnic groups in the North Caucasus appeared to have reconciled themselves to their Russian status, and accompanied assertions of sovereignty with declarations of loyalty to the Russian state; Chechnya was the exception. Chechnya's declaration of independence in 1991 triggered two devastating wars with Russia that killed tens, perhaps hundreds, of thousands and left the Republic in ruins, both physically and socially. By the mid-2000s, what had once been a secular, nationalist struggle for Chechen self-determination had morphed into a religiously motivated, region-wide insurgency/terror campaign aimed at establishing an Islamic state in the North Caucasus. Accordingly, most (mainly Western) experts had concluded by 2007 that "Russian policy had failed miserably," and predicted ever greater military disasters to come (Hughes 2013; Matveeva 2007; Wood 2007). That same year, 30-year-old Ramzan Kadyrov ascended to the Chechen presidency, and more than a decade on, Ramzan's effectiveness as a leader can no longer seriously be questioned. Violence is down precipitously throughout the North Caucasus region; Chechnya itself is now more secure and stable that at any time since 1991; the capital Grozny, which once resembled a "gigantic bomb crater"

(Matveeva 2007, 3) has been extensively reconstructed, as have many of Chechnya's other major cities; and, Ramzan is in the process of promoting a Chechen identity that is no longer grounded in hostility to the Russian state.

The price to pay for a pacified Chechnya—especially in terms of the loss of basic liberties and human rights—has been steep, but Russia's policy of "Chechenization" has returned Chechnya to a state of normalcy that few thought possible in the mid-2000s; the implementation of the policy may be messy and ugly, but the policy itself has been effective. The main purpose of what follows is to evaluate the Chechenization policy as a response to Chechen separatist violence, and specifically, to Chechen separatist terrorism. To this end, the next section provides a brief review of the scholarly debate regarding the effective management of ethnic separatism. Subsequent sections provide overviews and analyses of, respectively: historical context, recent Chechen separatist terrorist activity, and Russian responses to the terrorist threat emanating from the North Caucasus. In turn, these sections provide context for an informed evaluation of Russia's Chechenization policy. While not without problems, Russia's approach to its Chechen problem is more nuanced, more effective, and potentially more durable than generally acknowledged.

Theoretical context

Finding the appropriate location for the Russia–Chechnya conflict within the scholarly literature is problematic because the conflict has, at various times, been a conventional war for independence, a secular, nationalistic guerilla war/insurgency, a religiously inspired insurgency, an intra-Chechen civil war, and a separatist/religious terrorist campaign. Often, it has been more than one of these simultaneously. The most interesting aspect of the conflict for current purposes is how Russia succeeded in ending it, which leads us naturally to the literature on ethnic conflict management, and more specifically, durable solutions to ethnic conflicts. As Toft (2010) observes, civil wars, ethnic or otherwise, end either because one or other of the parties to the conflict prevails militarily, or through negotiated settlement. The problem, as Toft presents it, is that while negotiation is strongly preferred by policymakers, civil wars terminated by negotiated settlements are more likely to recur than those that end with a decisive victory by one or other side (ibid., 7). Thus, the problem is less about achieving peace than it is about "keeping the peace," in Byman's (2002) words.

The difficulty, in other words, is finding *durable* solutions to ethnic violence, as Russians have previously discovered to their cost in Chechnya. Some of the approaches Byman discusses are of limited relevance to Chechnya as solutions to the problem. Policies of control and repression on the part of the Russian state, for example, are more the cause of the problem than its solution (see below). More promising are the options of co-optation, and what Byman terms "participatory systems." The former, as the name suggests, involves "buying off elites to gain their support" (Byman 2002, 81) through access to power, bribes, or "recognition of their status in society" (82). Importantly, Byman distinguishes between authentic power-sharing and co-optation, in that with the latter, "Co-opted leaders do not have a genuine voice in the political process" (82). As Byman illustrates, co-optation has enjoyed some success in the context of the Middle East, but its long-term impact is limited because it does little to address the grievances of the broader population or the underlying causes that spawned that violence in the first place.

The term "participatory systems" basically refers to political power-sharing, ideally within a democratic framework, to provide ethnic groups with a "voice in government" (Byman 2002, 125). In societies that are deeply divided along ethnic lines, this approach leads logically to Arend Lijphart's model of consociational democracy, in which each of society's main ethnic groups enjoys a proportional share of political power at the center, and, at the extreme, veto power over central decision-making (Lijphart 1969, 1975, 1977, 1979).

As part of a negotiated solution to an ethnic civil war, power-sharing along ethnic lines may be unavoidable, but as many critics have argued, to define political institutions in ethnic terms risks strengthening and hardening ethnic identities, making future conflict all the more likely (Aitken 2007; Roeder 2009; Taylor 1992). Territorial autonomy is a variation on the ethnic power-sharing theme that has been employed extensively to diminish violent ethnic secessionist threats. What is sometimes termed "ethnofederalism" is, in essence, a compromise between a centralized, unitary system, inevitably controlled by a dominant ethnic majority group, and outright independence for the rebellious ethnic minority. Like ethnic power-sharing at the center, ethnofederalism may be difficult to avoid as part of a negotiated settlement to an ethnic civil war, but equally, critics charge, the longer-term consequences of ethnic autonomy can be recurring crises between the center and the ethnic unit, a heightened secession capacity, and even state collapse, as occurred with the ethnofederal Soviet Union (Roeder 1991, 2007, 2009; Cornell 2002; Hale 2004).

Regardless of the approach advocated, most scholars who work on issues relating to ethnic conflict caution against a "one-size fits all" prescription. Reasonably enough, they point out that the engineering of political institutions should be tailored to the specific context, and it is to this context that the analysis now turns.

Historical context

The date alluded to by Lieven above (1785), marks the first organized Chechen resistance to Russia's expansion into the North Caucasus, and helped establish the blueprint for future conflict across the centuries. Sheikh Mansur, the inspiration behind the uprising, was a Sufi imam of the Naqshbandi order and the first Chechen leader to infuse resistance to Russia with religious fervor. Mansur's movement for spiritual purification through the expulsion of "sinful" Russian influence, mobilized followers across the North Caucasus and culminated in a declaration of holy war (*gazavat*) against the Russian infidels. In an attempt to suppress the burgeoning movement, a reported 7,000 Russian troops (Gune-Yadcy

2003, 106) marched on Mansur's home village of Aldi and burned it to the ground, killing Mansur's brother in the process. In response, Mansur mobilized a force of some 12,000, ambushed the retreating Russian troops, and reportedly killed all but 100 of the 7,000-strong force. Subsequently, a string of military defeats and unsuccessful sieges eliminated Mansur's force as a serious threat to Russia's hold over the Caucasus, but a pattern had been established. The use of religion as a rallying cry to unite the diverse peoples of the North Caucasus became a mainstay of (almost) all subsequent Chechen rebellions against Russia. Likewise, Russia invariably adopted heavy-handed, sometimes brutal, tactics in response to these uprisings, with the result that any short-term gains were generally outweighed by the long-term costs of increasing anti-Russian sentiment among the targeted population (Schaefer 2010, 57).

Symptomatic of Russia's uncompromising approach to the region over the last 200 years was the subjugation campaign launched by General Aleksey Yermolov in 1817 that involved "scorched earth actions, repression, cleansing operations and punitive campaigns, deportations, and forced assimilation" (Pokalova 2015, 40). Fittingly, the Chechen "revolution" in 1991 opened with the destruction of a monument to Yermolov in Chechnya's capital Grozny, a testimony to the enduring hatred this "satanic figure in the memory of Chechens" (Gammer 2006, 35) still inspires in Chechnya (Lieven 1999, 307).

Mansur's uprising and the violence of the Russian response paved the way for a period of conflict, the Murid Wars, between the Tsarist Empire and a succession of religious leaders from the North Caucasus that would continue until 1859. Key to understanding the durability of the conflict was the figure of Imam Shamil, who transformed the nascent Caucasus Imamate (CI) (first declared in 1828) into the region's first viable statehood project. The CI initially united Chechnya and Dagestan, and from there, was progressively expanded by Shamil to encompass large parts of the North Caucasus. Unlike previous rebellions, Shamil put in place an architecture of political and military institutions to govern the CI based on the Ottoman administrative model, whereby territory was divided into *vilayets*, with each of these administered by Shamil's representatives (*naibs*). Resting atop these institutions of government, which included armed forces, secret police, and a hybrid legislative/judicial body (the *Divan-Khaneh*), was the dominant figure of Shamil himself, whose interpretation of Sharia provided CI's legal code (Pokalova 2015, 8). The dependence of this construction on a single dominant personality meant that the CI did not survive Shamil's surrender in 1859, but its broader historical significance cannot be underestimated. In many ways, Shamil's state represented "a prototype that many future generations have tried to emulate." During the turbulent years of the Russian Revolution and the civil war, Shamil's legacy provided the inspiration behind unsuccessful efforts to forge region-wide separatist entities such as the Mountainous Republic of the North Caucasus (1918), and the Emirate of the North Caucasus (1919). The victory of Bolshevik forces in the civil war temporarily put an end to these separatist initiatives, and the early years of Soviet rule were notable for the caution with which authorities approached the task of integrating the populations of the North Caucasus into the Soviet system. The initial policies of the Soviet regime were geared toward recognition and respect for cultural and religious diversity. Thus, Sharia courts were not only permitted, but institutionalized as an "inalienable right of the locals" (ibid., 12), Imam Shamil was celebrated as a hero of the anti-Tsarist resistance, and the well-known policy toward nationalities of *korenizatsiia* (nativization), was applied across the North Caucasus.[1] This kinder, gentler approach did not last for long, however. As the Soviet antireligious campaign kicked into high gear after 1923, Sharia courts were targeted, and by 1927, they had been banned throughout the North Caucasus. The assault on Islam coupled with the damaging effects of the crash industrialization program and the collectivization of agriculture prompted numerous small-scale uprisings during the 1930s, culminating in a fateful anti-Soviet rebellion during World War II led by Khasan Israilov under the banner of the unfortunately named National-Socialist Party of the Caucasus Brethren. Israilov is estimated to have assembled a 5,000-strong force to engage in the "armed struggle against Bolshevik barbarism and Russian despotism"; although Israilov's insurrection never got off the ground, his movement inspired widespread passive resistance across Chechnya. For example, of the estimated 80,000 eligible Chechen males called up to serve in the Soviet army between 1941 and 1944, 70,000 (nearly 90 percent) failed to appear (Burds 2007, 292). Evidence that Chechen rebels collaborated with invading German forces to any great degree is scant, but the lack of enthusiasm among Chechens to join the fight in defense of the "motherland" at a time when the very survival of the Soviet Union was at stake was probably enough to seal their fate. In January 1944, the Soviet State Committee on Defense issued a decree on the deportation of the Chechen and Ingush populations to Central Asia, and on February 23, 1944, the deportations began. At the same time, the Chechen–Ingush ASSR was decreed out of existence. In all, approximately 460,000 Chechens and Ingush (virtually the entire population of the Republic) were loaded onto trucks and shipped off to Kazakhstan;[2] between 1944 and 1948, official figures suggest that nearly 24 percent of these people died, although the precise number may never be known (Pokalova 2015, 16). It was not until 1956 that Khrushchev restored the status of the Chechen–Ingush ASSR and the deported populations were allowed to return home. The psychological impact of the deportations continues to be felt to the present day. As Lieven (1999, 321) notes, "More even than the wars of Shamil in the nineteenth century, the memory of the deportation became the central defining event in modern Chechen history."

Against this backdrop of enduringly troubled historical relations between Chechens and Russians, the chaos that engulfed the Soviet Union, and, subsequently, Russia, at the beginning of the 1990s provided an opportune moment for the reassertion of Chechen autonomy. Starting with Lithuania's declaration of independence in March 1991, the Soviet Union underwent a process of slow-motion disintegration that finally ended in December of that year with the union's official termination. Between March and December 1991, the majority of the Soviet Union's 53 ethnically defined administrative regions adopted declarations asserting some sort of autonomous status, either sovereignty or independence, most of which occurred after the abortive August 1991 Communist coup (Hale 2000). Chechnya's own path toward independence picked up pace in November 1990 when the newly formed National Congress of the Chechen People appointed General Dzhokar Dudayev as leader, then accelerated further with declarations of sovereignty (July 1991) and, finally, independence (November 1991). Importantly, Chechnya's separatist impulse was not widely shared by other ethnic entities in the North Caucasus region; indeed many entities, such as North Ossetia, used the collapse of the Soviet Union as an opportunity to reaffirm their loyalty to the Russian state. Meanwhile, in December 1991, the population of Ingushetia voted overwhelmingly to remain within the Russian Federation as a "sovereign" entity, a status that was finalized in June 1992 with the formation of the Ingush Republic. This meant that when the newly independent Chechen Republic of Ichkeria (ChRI) emerged, it stood in splendid isolation in its showdown with the Russian state.

Russian President Yeltsin's initial response—declaring a state of emergency in the republic and the deployment of Interior Ministry (MVD) troops—was half-hearted and short lived, and between 1992 and the onset of war in 1994, Chechnya was "governed" by Dudayev in a state of "ordered anarchy" (Lieven 1999, 76). However, as Chechnya's economy spiraled downwards in the face of a Russia-imposed trade blockade and the reduction (and eventual elimination) of state subsidies from Moscow, public services began to collapse in the republic and opposition to Dudayev's "unrule" mounted. Fueling the escalation of violence and criminality in Chechnya were two early Dudayev decrees that released inmates from the republic's prisons and legalized the possession of firearms. As Russian forces withdrew fully during 1992, in many cases leaving behind their light and heavy weapons (Pokalova 2015, 27), so the quantity of armaments in circulation multiplied exponentially with predictable consequences. Between 1991 and 1994 estimates suggest that over 10,000 people were either killed, or simply disappeared (ibid., 27). Efforts by Russian-backed opposition forces to topple Dudayev culminated in an unsuccessful effort to storm Grozny in November 1994, and this failure, coupled with a wave of hijackings conducted by Chechens against targets in Russia (Lieven 1999, 86) prompted Yeltsin to order a full-scale military intervention "to restore constitutional law and order on the territory of the Chechen Republic." (Pokalova 2015, 30). On December 11, 1994, Russian troops crossed the border with Chechnya to initiate a conflict that was scheduled to be done and dusted by December 19. In the event, the war would drag on until August 1996, costing the lives of 5,000 Russian troops and anything up to 100,000 (mainly civilian) Chechens.[3]

The First Chechen War was notable both for the tenacity of the Chechen resistance, and the shockingly poor performance of the Russian army, which was poorly equipped, ill-disciplined, and badly organized (Lieven 1999). Another notable feature was the Chechen use of terrorism for strategic purposes for the first time in the form of Shamil Basayev's infamous Budennovsk hostage-taking raid in June 1995. The success of this operation arguably turned the course of the war in that it forced the Russian government to negotiate a ceasefire, which then allowed Chechen forces to regroup and, ultimately, to retake Grozny from Russian troops in August 1996. Bereft of military options, Yeltsin signed off on the Khasavyurt Accords on August 31, 1996 that officially ended the war, withdrew of all Russian troops from Chechnya, and agreed to delay a decision on Chechnya's final status until 2001. In this way, terrorism played a pivotal role in restoring Chechnya's de facto independence.

Much like the 1991–1994 period, the inter-war years demonstrated that Chechnya is, to put it mildly, a difficult place to govern effectively. The unenviable task fell to Aslan Maskhadov, the ChRI's prime minister, Chief of Staff and Defence Minister, and the man credited with orchestrating the defeat of Russia, following his victory in a surprisingly free and fair presidential election of January 1997. Maskhadov faced all of the same problems confronted by Dudayev, but in addition, he had somehow to reconstruct a shattered economy and rebuild a physical infrastructure that had been comprehensively flattened by Russian bombardment during the war. These tasks had to be accomplished with no functioning administrative or political institutions, and in an "independent" state that was drowning in a sea of weapons and warlords. The economic crisis and endemic corruption at the heart of the Russian state meant that most of the financial aid promised by Moscow to help rebuild Chechnya did not materialize, and once again, criminality became the default survival option for the Chechens.[4] In particular, kidnapping became almost a national sport; in the first six months of 1997 alone, 76 kidnappings were reported, and by 1999, there were between 700 (officially) and 2,000 (unofficially) victims being held in captivity in Chechnya (Pokalova 2015, 70). In short, Chechnya became a "hotbed of crime and terror, as the OSCE described it (Hughes 2013, 96).

Beyond this, the greatest challenge faced by Maskhadov was how to deal with the threat posed by the spread of Wahhabi Islam—an austere, intolerant strain of Islam that took root first in Dagestan, then seeped into Chechnya during the 1990s. The arrival of Wahhabism in Chechnya was to play a fundamental role in transforming both the goals of the Chechen struggle, and the nature of the terrorism conducted in pursuit of these goals.

Grievances

To identify and explain the Chechen grievances that ultimately led to the events and the 1990s and beyond is simultaneously straightforward, and, at the same time, immensely complicated. The simplest explanation is that many Chechens have never willingly acquiesced in Russian rule. The most consistent pattern in the history of Chechen–Russian interaction is the refusal of the former to submit to the military power of the latter. As Wood (2007, 18) observes, it is the "striking depth and consistency of Chechen resistance" to external domination that separates them from the myriad other ethnic groups that inhabit the North Caucasus. Important here is the traditional structure of Chechen society, which was, and to some extent, still is, organized around clans/tribes (*teips*)—basically extended kinship units, tied to territory and with a strong sense of collective identity (Souleimanov 2015, 6).[5] Relations between and among Chechen *teips* (and lower level family units) have been organized traditionally on the basis of strict equality, guided by an elaborate code of obligations and norms (*nokhchella*), and administered according to an unwritten code of customary law (*adat*) (Souleimanov 2015, 6; Gammer 2006, 6–7). To the extent that any conquering power, Russian or otherwise, would necessarily be required to impose a hierarchical governing order on this "anarchic mode of social organization," it would likely provoke resistance. This traditional social structure was, to an extent, reinforced by religious attachment. Most Chechens adhere (however nominally) to either one or other of two orders of Sufi Islam, each of which further divided into brotherhoods that have, over time, come to be closely associated with specific geographical areas, and/or specific *teips* or families (Vatchagaev 2014, 25). The majority of rebellions against Russian rule since 1785 have been accompanied by declarations of "holy war" against the invading Russian infidel. But to conclude from this that religion has been the driving force behind Chechnya's conflicts with Russia would be to mischaracterize its significance and role. While the religious convictions of Sheikh Mansur and Imam Shamil cannot be doubted, their call for *gazavat* was also a calculated strategy to mobilize the Mountaineers (not just Chechens) around a common cause. Later declarations of holy war by the obviously secular, and thoroughly Sovietized figures of Dudayev and Maskhadov cannot be taken too literally (Walker 1998). These were not calls to mobilize around strictly religious beliefs, but rather appeals to transcendent Chechen nationalist identity, real or imagined (Janeczko 2014, 437–439). Adherence to Islam (Sufism) was part of what it meant to be Chechen and what helped to differentiate "us" (Chechens) from "the other" (Russians). At some point after 1995, the role of religion (specifically, the Wahhabi strain of Islam) in perpetuating the conflict became more authentic and more complex (see below).

Beyond this are a range of unquantifiable, but undeniably relevant and deeply rooted cultural norms and values often attributed to Chechens that make submission to any external power implausible. Foremost among these is the notion of freedom (*marsho*), which occupies "pride of place" in Chechen culture, as per the well-known Chechen adage, "free and equal like wolves," and evidenced in the range of everyday greetings in the Chechen language that include the word (Gammer 2006, 6). The importance of collective memory, stretching back at least seven generations, the lionization of military prowess, and an umbilical link between honour and revenge (via the blood feud), are also prominent cultural attributes (Souleimanov 2014, 6; Janeczko 2014, 438).

To conquer the Chechens, therefore, involves taming a people who are organized into tightly knit, mutually supportive communities that valorize equality, freedom, martial prowess, and vendetta, and who possess an elephantine collective memory for injuries suffered, real or imagined. Of course, the injuries suffered by the Chechens at the hands of Russia over the centuries are mostly very real. As noted above, Yermolov's tenure as "Proconsul of the Caucasus" was marked by an uncompromising approach toward pacifying the region; the

Chechens resisted more vigorously and for longer than other groups, and accordingly suffered the most. But even when Yermalov was dismissed from his post by Tsar Nicholas I in 1827, his successors did not notably adjust the basic strategy; the construction of imposing Russian fortresses continued, as did the felling of forests that covered much of Chechnya at that time, and "punitive expeditions" against civilians continued to be the chosen method of exacting revenge for Chechen raids on Russian forces.

The wars of the 1990s were not pre-determined by the events of the nineteenth century, but the harshness of Russian rule set in motion a vicious dynamic "that only increased in power and resonance with each subsequent round of revolt and repression" (Lieven 1999). The fundamental problem for the Russians was an inability to decisively break the will of Chechens to continue the fight. Even when the entire population was shipped off to Kazakhstan in 1944, the Chechen spirit of resistance survived. As Solzhenitsyn memorably observed of exiled Chechens, "There was one nation which would not give in, would not acquire the mental habits of submission – and not just individual rebels among them, but the whole nation to a man. These were the Chechens."[6] As a result, the deportation did nothing to break the Chechens and instead became yet one more grievance fueling the cycle of "revolt and repression." Wood (2007, 41) takes the argument a stage further, arguing that the "Chechen Revolution" of 1990–1991 was "not merely an ethnic backlash against Russian domination, but a push for sovereignty as the best means of collective self-preservation against genocide."

By the 1990s, the Russians had apparently still not learned how to break this vicious cycle. The 1994 War began with an intense and largely indiscriminate bombing of Grozny, and deteriorated from there (Williams 2001, 130). As civilian deaths mounted (both Russian and Chechen), Chechens rallied behind the nationalist cause of the previously unpopular Dudaev. As the chronic ill-discipline of Russia's predominantly conscript army began to express itself in the form of rape, looting, and wanton cruelty toward Chechen civilians, so the operation to restore constitutional order degenerated into "a horrible orgy of violence against the civilian population" (Gall and De Waal 1999, 233), which only strengthened Chechen fighters in their will to resist.[7] Russian tactics during the second war were more discriminate, but equally brutal and engendered a similar effect. Viewed historically, therefore, the resurgence of Chechen nationalist separatism in the early 1990s is the end product of 200 years (or more) of accumulated grievances on the part of an ethnic group that has never accepted its status as part of Russia. Chechen nationalism was forged by 200 years of Russian (and Soviet) reliance on military force to compel Chechen quiescence, and the collapse of the Soviet Union provided the opportunity for this to express itself in dramatic fashion.

The evolution of Chechen terrorism

The first recognizably "terroristic" act associated with the 1990s conflict occurred in November 1991 and was perpetrated by Shamil Basayev and involved hijacking a plane containing 178 passengers at an airport in Russia's Stavropol region. Basayev had the plane flown to Turkey, and from there, he demanded, and was granted, a press conference at which he drew the world's attention to the situation in Chechnya and the impending Russian military action. Basayev then negotiated safe passage back to Chechnya for his group and released the hostages unharmed. This was a classic example of "old school" terrorism, in which the goal was to maximize publicity for the cause and minimize the harm done to innocent civilians.

In was not until June 1995 that terrorism became a significant factor in the Russian-Chechen conflict. Prior to this date, the Chechens had stood toe-to-toe with Russian forces in defending Grozny and then melted away in the face of vastly superior firepower to conduct guerilla warfare. Facing imminent defeat, Basayev announced his intention to shift tactics and rely on "subversive activities," the first of which involved an assault on the town of Budennovsk in the Stavropol region by Basayev and a force of some 200 fighters.[8] Over a five-day period, the group rampaged through the streets of Budennovsk, killing bystanders, taking hostages, and staging a dramatic massacre of police officers. Events ended with the group holed up in a local hospital with approximately 2,000 hostages. After executing five hostages (all either police or military) to demonstrate his seriousness of intent, Basayev demanded a press conference at which he issued his demands—an end to the war, the immediate withdrawal of all Russian troops from Chechnya, and safe passage back to Chechnya for himself and his group. After a failed storming of the building, the Russian government agreed to negotiate and, in essence, caved into most of Basayev's demands in return for the safe release of hostages. The Budennovsk raid helped change the course of the war in two ways. First, it provided breathing space for Chechen fighters to regroup at a point in the war when defeat looked likely. Second, the raid turned the Russian public decisively against an already unpopular war. According to polls, fully 49 percent of the Russian population held the government responsible for the deaths (approximately 100) associated with the raid, compared with 32 percent who blamed the Chechen leadership (Pokalova 2015, 46). It is important to note that as of 1995, Basayev was careful to distinguish between "subversive action," a legitimate military tactic (in Basayev's view), and terrorism, which involved inflicting indiscriminate violence on innocent civilians, and was rejected by Basayev.

This initial aversion to killing innocents was also evident from Basayev's next escapade in November 1995, when a package wired up with explosives and containing radioactive cesium 137 was uncovered in Moscow's Izmailovsky Park. The existence of this dirty bomb, along with three others at undisclosed locations, was revealed by Basayev to a journalist for the purpose of sending a clear message to Russia about the capacity of Chechen force to carry the war into Russia's capital city. At the same time, the intent of the threat was clearly to end the war in Chechnya without the unnecessary killing of civilians.

The third major terrorist attack of the first war took place in January 1996 and was spearheaded by Dudayev's son-in-law Salman Raduyev. What began as an attack on a military base in Kizlyar, Dagestan, by Raduyev and a force of some 400 fighters, ended up as a copy-cat version of the Budennovsk raid. Unlike at Budennovsk, the Russian government refused to negotiate with the separatists, but agreed to grant the rebels safe passage while intending to attack and eliminate them on the way. A convoy of buses and trucks carrying the rebels and more than 150 human shield hostages came under Russian fire outside the village of Pervomaiskoe, forcing the rebels to dismount and disperse throughout the village. In response, the Russian troops stormed the village on January 15, and launched a bombardment of rockets on January 18. Despite this, Raduyev, along with most of his fighters and several hostages escaped, raising serious concerns about Russia's counterterrorism capabilities. The Raduyev operation was also notable for being less discriminate than the Budennovsk raid; indeed according to Rudayev, Dudayev had ordered him to shoot civilians and advised "There should be more casualties among women than men" (Pokalova 2015, 57). In the aftermath of the second incident, Maskhadov and Basayev called a press conference at which they promised to conduct a campaign of "mass terror" on Russian territory, an indicator that terrorism had emerged "as a permanent tool in the Chechen arsenal" (ibid., 56). In due course, Chechen terrorists launched a wave of explosions targeting transportation links in Moscow during June and July 1996 to coincide with elections in both Chechnya and Russia. The expanding threat posed by these attacks, the effects of which were now being experienced on a regular basis in Russia's capital city, together with the rebels' successful assault to reclaim Grozny from federal forces led directly to the signing of the Khasavyurt Accords in August 1996 that ended the first war.

During the first war, terrorism was initially used sparingly and relatively discriminately by Chechen forces and was born of military necessity. Each act of terrorism was accompanied by clearly articulated political demands—basically an end to the war and the removal of all Russian troops from Chechnya, with the end goal of furthering Chechen independence. Over the course of the war, the use of terrorism and its underlying rationale evolved. Explosive attacks aimed at trolley buses and the Moscow Metro in June and July 1996 were claimed by Chechen field commander Ruslan Khaikhoroev as retaliation for Russia's continued bombardment of Chechen villages, and the attacks themselves were inherently more indiscriminate in the sense of deliberately targeting civilians. Nonetheless, the clear goal of all acts of terror at this stage was to secure Chechen independence. That is, they were clear-cut acts of separatist terrorism.

Between August 1996 and late 1999, as a de facto independent Chechnya slid back into anarchy, it became increasingly difficult to determine the identity and motivation of the perpetrators of violent events in the North Caucasus. As noted above, this period was also marked by an epidemic of kidnappings. Mukhina (2005, 530) calculates that from January 1997 to August 1999, close to 1,100 civilians were kidnapped in Chechnya. Victims included Valentin Vlasov, Yeltsin's envoy to Chechnya, and an Interior Ministry General (Gennady Shpigun). In the face of this dramatic upsurge in criminality, elected President Maskhadov proved singularly incapable of controlling the various Chechen groups that had melded effectively to confront a common enemy, but that were unwilling to acknowledge his political authority when the enemy had left. More serious was the growing split in the ranks of Chechen separatists between secular nationalists, led by Maskhadov, and those driven by religious conviction, under Basayev's command. Key to this split was the spread of the Wahabbi movement, which took root in the North Caucasus in 1990, and had seeped into Chechnya via Dagestan by the mid-1990s. The face of the Wahabbi invasion in Chechnya was Samir Saleh al-Suwailem, better known as Khattab, who arrived in 1995 with a group of perhaps 100 foreign fighters and significant financial resources. Khattab allied with Basayev to fight the Russians, but his role during the first war was limited. During the post-1996 period, however, his influence expanded as he used his connections with financial backers in the Middle East to establish a network of bases in Chechnya to train fighters in unconventional warfare. Initially, the alliance between Wahabbis and Chechen separatists was one of convenience, but over time, the religious dimension came to assume greater importance, and the goals of some separatist groups became more ambitious.[9] Specifically, for some groups, the focus shifted from the national to the regional level and the goal became the creation of an Islamic state encompassing both Chechnya and Dagestan. To this end, an umbrella organization—the Congress of the Peoples of Chechnya and Dagestan (CPCD)—was convened in April 1998 under Basayev's leadership with the stated goal of resurrecting Imam Shamil's nineteenth-century Imamate (i.e., unifying Chechnya and Dagestan). At roughly the same time, Basayev and Khattab created several groups to serve as militant branches of the CPCD, the best-known of which was the multinational Islamic International Peacekeeping Brigade (IIPB).

An opportunity for Khattab and Baseaev to further their goal of a single Islamic state spanning Chechnya and Dagestan arose in August 1998 when two Wahabbi-controlled villages in Dagestan declared de facto independence from Russia. Following armed clashes between Dagestan's security forces and a number of armed formations created to defend the rebellious villages, Russia dispatched several divisions of MVD troops to Dagestan, and Dagestani Wahabbis called on Chechens for assistance. In August 1999, Basayev and Khattab answered the call, leading the IIPB across the Chechen border into Dagestan. After Basayev and Khattab retreated back into Chechnya under heavy Russian fire on August 23, Russian troops moved in to retake control of the rebellious villages. A second incursion into Dagestan by Basayev and Khattab in early September was pushed back by Russian troops, but by this point, events on the ground in Dagestan were being overshadowed by a wave of high-casualty attacks on apartment buildings throughout Russia. The first attack, a September 4 explosion in an apartment building in Buinaksk, Dagestan that killed 62 and wounded nearly 150, was followed in quick succession by explosive attacks on two apartment buildings in Moscow (killing 230 and wounding 270) and another apartment bombing in Volgodonsk that left 19 dead and over 300 wounded. Predictably, the Russian government laid blame for the attacks at the feet of Chechen terrorist groups, and specifically Basayev and Khattab, though both men vehemently denied their involvement.[10]

Russia's second Chechen war—officially classified as a counterterrorist operation—was an exercise in calculated brutality that began in September 1999 and ended officially in April 2009. The intensity and uncompromising nature of Russia's military attack prompted a shift in terror tactics. Notably, suicide bombings, many carried out by Chechen females (so-called "Black Widows"), became a key component of the Chechen struggle. The well-organized nature of suicide bombings, which commenced in June 2000, was the brainchild of Basayev, who created the Islamic Brigade of Shahids to coordinate the campaign. The large majority of suicide attacks were conducted in Chechnya and against security forces, either Russian, or Chechens tagged as collaborators, making it difficult to definitively characterize these as terrorist acts. However, no such ambiguity surrounded the suicide bombings that deliberately targeted civilians in Russia, such as the attacks on the Moscow metro of February 6, 2004 (which killed 41), or the two Black Widows who blew themselves up aboard planes in August the same year, killing 89. Alongside the tactical use of suicide bombings, Chechen forces relied on explosive attacks and occasional hostage-takings to pressurize Russia to back down. The two best-known hostage dramas of the post-2000 period took place at the Dubrovka Theater in 2002, and School No. 1 in Beslan, North Ossetia in 2004. In the first of these, a group of between 40 and 50 members of the Islamic Brigade of Shahids, roughly half of whom were Black Widows armed with suicide vests, seized control of the Dubrovka Theater during a performance on October 23, 2002, thereby taking more than 900 people hostage. After sealing off the theater and wiring it with explosives, the groups issued its demands for an end to the war in Chechnya, the withdrawal of Russian troops, and the opening of negotiations between Maskhadov and Russian authorities. After three days, during which the Russian leadership refused to negotiate, the siege ended with the FSB pumping an unidentified gas into the theater to incapacitate the terrorists, then storming the building, killing all the terrorists in the process. Also killed were 129 hostages, many of whom were assumed to be victims of exposure to the incapacitating agent which the FSB refused to identify to medical personnel on the scene.

The assault on School No. 1 in Beslan marked a critical turning point for the Chechen separatist struggle. Some 30–40 terrorists from Basayev's Islamic Brigade of Shahids carried out the attack, but many of the attackers were non-Chechens, and the operation was spearheaded by Ruslan Khuchbarov, a native Ingush. After rounding up everyone present at the school—1,128 men, women and children in all—and herding them into the gymnasium, the attackers (equipped with gas masks in case of a gas attack) wired up the gym with explosives and held the victims hostage for two days. In contrast to the Dubrovka episode, where Basayev had ordered the release of children, the Beslan attack intentionally targeted children. According to Basayev's logic, "I figured that the more brutal I could make it, the quicker they'd get the message" (Pokalova 2015, 134) To this end, the hostages were denied food, water, and medical treatment for the duration of the incident. The siege ended in confusing fashion as Russian forces responded to the detonation of a Black Widow's suicide belt with an apparent storming of the building (although the exact sequence of events is disputed). The upshot was the deaths of 331 hostages, including 186 children, and the elimination of all of the hostage-takers bar one who was captured alive.

Beyond the tragic deaths of large numbers of innocents, the Beslan attack was significant for a number of reasons. First, the identities of the group members carrying out the attack—including Ingush, ethnic Russians, and two Afghan Mujahedeen—indicated that, "terrorism in the North Caucasus was no longer limited to Chechens" (ibid., 134). Second, the decision to target children and the treatment of the hostages marked this operation out as different in kind from Basayev's previous exploits. During the Budennovsk operation, for example, Basayev had stated clearly that killing hostages, especially women and children, was morally unacceptable; as he put it at the time, "we're not maniacs" (Henkin 2006). By the time of Beslan, Basayev's forces were apparently willing to deny food and water to hostages for days, to shoot children, and allegedly to rape a group of 15-year-old schoolgirls (Henkin 2006, 194). Mainly as a result of this "sad metamorphosis," sympathy for the Chechen cause eroded rapidly, both inside Russia and internationally after Beslan. Finally, the Beslan attack was deeply unpopular within Chechnya,[11] helping to crystallize divisions between secular, pro-separatist, Chechens, such as Maskhadov, who consistently condemned terrorism and pledged to "fight in honor," those Chechens who were part of a broader, religiously inspired struggle to establish an Islamic state across the North Caucasus, and finally, Chechens who had fought for the separatist cause during the first war, but who were now loyal to Moscow. In turn, these divisions helped create the necessary space for Moscow's "Chechenization" policy that would eventually restore some semblance of normality to Chechnya.

The deaths in quick succession of Maskhadov (March 2005) and Basayev (July 2006) deprived Chechen forces of their two most effective and inspirational military leaders. As the mastermind behind the evolving Chechen separatist terrorist campaign that had, by 2006, expanded to include Wahabbi communities/cells (*jamaats*) throughout the North Caucasus, Basayev was the more important of the two commanders, and, unsurprisingly, the death of Russia's most wanted terrorist prompted the pro-Russian Chechen president Alu Alkhanov to declare an end to the war on terror in the North Caucasus (Pokalova 2015, 140). By 2006, however, the insurgency had changed shape and was no longer limited geographically, or in terms of goals. As pro-Russian security forces tightened their grip on Chechnya, groups such as *Amanat Jamaat* (in Ingushetia), *Jamaat Sharia* (Dagestan), and *Jamaat Yarmuk* (Kabardino-Balkaria), emerged elsewhere in the North Caucasus to fight jihad against their respective pro-Russian governments, often with the help of Chechen insurgent forces. A range of common factors appeared to animate these groups, with "poor socio-economic conditions, lack of effective governance, widespread corruption, and the repressive policies of local and federal authorities" (Pokalova 2015, 155–156) among the most frequently cited. However, while similar grievances inspired the emergence of these groups, this network of *jamaats* that spanned the North Caucasus comprised separate structures that lacked any form of centralized control. This changed following the death of Maskhadov in 2005. Maskahdov's replacement, Abdul-Halim Sadulayev, restructured the armed forces of the ChRI to incorporate the various *jamaats* across the North Caucasus into what Sadulayev characterized as "one unified mechanism" under Chechen command. The articulated goal of the new movement was a "national liberation struggle to decolonize the whole of the Caucasus," but in pursuit of this goal, Sadulayev declared a "unilateral rejection of terrorist acts" and pledged to target only "military objects," a tactical shift that was mostly adhered to until Sadulayev's death in June 2006 (ibid., 159). Sadulayev's successor, Doku Umarov, expanded both the geographic and ideological scope of the insurgency still further. For the first time, *jamaats* outside the North Caucasus, in Tartarstan and the Volga–Ural region, for example, were drafted into the movement, and in fall 2007, Umarov declared war on all enemies of Islam, not just Russia. To give organizational substance to this new, global perspective, Umarov created the Caucasus Emirate (IK) in October 2007, in the process effectively abolishing the ChRI. In deference to Imam Shamil's eighteenth century creation, Uramov organized the various *jamaats* under his command into *vilayets* and appointed *naibs* to each. Within this new structure, the former ChRI, now renamed Vilayet Nokhchicho, became one just among several units of equal status within the IK. The complete separation of Chechen nationalism from the IK was solidified when Umarov was killed and replaced as leader by the movement's first non-Chechen, Aliashab Kebekov, an Avar from Dagestan. Hence, what had begun as an explicitly secular, ethno-nationalist struggle for Chechen independence in 1994, had, by the late-1990s, transitioned to a Chechen-led, religiously inspired struggle to unify Chechnya and Dagestan into a single Islamic state, and from there to a Chechen-centered, but North Caucasus-wide campaign to purify and decolonize the region of Russian influence. The IK, in which Vilayet Nokhchiicho enjoys no more status than any other sub unit of the Emirate, and which espouses goals of international scope (at least rhetorically), and is headed by non-Chechens, completed the transition and, in Youngman's (2016, 1) words "formalised the victory of the insurgency's Islamist wing over nationalist-separatists in its historic Chechen core." Henceforth, the violent acts perpetrated by IK members and affiliates can no longer meaningfully be classified as acts of Chechen separatist terrorism.[12]

Russia's response

Russia has adopted a variety of different approaches over the years to address its Chechen problem, some more successful than others. It is important to note that the Chechen population has always been divided along multiple lines of cleavage and, therefore, susceptible to a policy of divide and rule/co-option. During the pacification of Chechnya in the eighteenth century, for example, the Russians recruited heavily from the indigenous population to create various militia formations to police the newly conquered territory (Gammer 2006, 73). Since then, there has always been sizeable portion of the Chechen population that has willingly cooperated/collaborated with Russian/Soviet forces.

During the early Soviet period, the official policy was one of accommodating national diversity, which translated into a policy of affirmative action toward indigenes and state-sponsored recognition of "national" culture, languages, and even religion. Although official hostility toward religion, especially Islam, soon replaced tolerance, Soviet authorities never attempted to eradicate entire languages or cultures with the intensity of the Turkish government (against Kurds), or even the French government (against all rivals to standard French). A more explicit policy of "Russification" was pursued in Chechnya during the Chechens' exile. Large numbers of Russians were encouraged to migrate to Chechnya during the Chechen absence, and two Russian dominated districts were added to the re-formed Chechen-Ingush Republic to ensure the numerical superiority of ethnic Russians. Owing to the outmigration of Russians and the higher birth rate of Chechens, ethnic Chechens had been restored to majority status by 1970, and by 1989, comprised nearly three-quarters of the population.

This is not to suggest that these Russian/Soviet efforts to address the Chechen problem enjoyed much success, but rather to acknowledge that a variety of approaches—military force, wholesale deportation, accommodation, and assimilation—had at least been attempted by the time Dudayev declared independence in 1991. Likewise, during the 1990s and 2000s, military force was clearly front and center in Russia's repertoire of responses to Chechen separatism, but other approaches were tried. During the 1991–1993 period, for example, Yeltsin made clear his willingness to negotiate a deal with Chechnya along similar lines to the deal reached with Tatarstan that would, conceivably, have been acceptable to a majority of the Chechen population. At the same time, Moscow was backing loyalist opposition forces with money and arms in their efforts to remove Dudayev from power. As the first war dragged on into 1995 and 1996, the Yeltsin Administration's approach became even less coherent. Shortly after the Russian government's shambolic response to the two hostage crises of 1995, the Kremlin appointed native Chechen, but Moscow loyalist, Doku Zavgayev as head of the Chechen Republic, then "legitimated" his appointment via rigged elections in December 1995. This ham-fisted attempt to end direct Russian involvement in the war by turning over security to indigenous Chechen forces—that is, to "Chechenize" the conflict—was a miserable failure. Simultaneously, the Russian state renewed military action against Chechen rebels *and* pursued negotiations with rebel leader Maskhadov. The excesses and widespread human rights violations committed by Russian troops during the first war owed more to the absence of a coherent war plan and the chronic ill-discipline of Russian troops than to any deliberate plan to brutalize the Chechen population. The same cannot be said of the second war. The use of indiscriminate bombings to minimize Russian casualties, the conduct of cleansing/mopping up operations (*zachistki*) in captured towns and villages, often using contracted forces (basically, state-sponsored mercenaries), and the processing of those "mopped up" through filtration camps, in which torture and summary execution were routine, all point to a war plan that was brutal by design (Felgenhauer 2002, 159). The effectiveness of this approach (to say nothing of its morality) was certainly questionable. By 2002, federal forces controlled the major population centers, as they had in 1995, but faced daily guerilla attacks from rebel forces and mounting casualties (Felgenhauer 2002).

There was no official launch of what became known as the policy of "Chechenization," but most date it to Putin's decision to appoint Akhmad Kadyrov as acting head of the Chechen administration in July 2000. As the former Chief Mufti of Chechnya, and a rebel commander in the first war against Russia, Kadyrov enjoyed a degree of credibility with the Chechen population that set him apart from the pro-Russian "stooges" that preceded him. He also strongly objected to the growing influence of Wahabbis in the North Caucasus during the inter-war period and was one of several pivotal figures who stayed loyal to Russia during the second war. The political dimension of the policy continued in 2003 with the promulgation of a new Chechen constitution, article 1 of which, somewhat dubiously, declared Chechnya to be "a democratic, social law-governed state with a Republican form of government," but more predictably to be "an inalienable part of the territory of the Russian Federation."[13] The new constitution was endorsed in a referendum by 96 percent of the voting population (which included nearly 40,000 Russian troops stationed in Chechnya) based on an 80 percent turnout, and the political deal was apparently sealed with the rigged election of Kadyrov as president in October 2003. Almost immediately, the Chechenization project came off the rails with the assassination of Kadyrov at a victory day celebration in a Grozny football stadium in May 2004. Hastily organized elections then took place in August 2004 to produce a successor to Kadyrov that resulted in the "election" of Alu Alkhanov, a Moscow-loyalist who had fought against separatists in the first war. Although Alkhanov's pro-Russian credentials were beyond question, his lack of an indigenous support base made him a potential liability as the standard bearer for Chechenization. Thus, in 2007 Alkhanov "resigned" from office and was replaced by Ramzan (son of Akhmad) Kadyrov. Ramzan's role on the separatist side in the first war is opaque, although he claims to have killed his first Russian at the age of 15; from there, he headed the *Kadyrovsky* following his father's appointment as acting president (under the official title of head of the Presidential Security Service), then moved up to Deputy Prime Minister in 2004 after his father's death, to acting Prime Minister (November 2005), Prime Minister (March 2006), and, finally, President (2007). Subsequently, Ramzan was appointed "Head of the Chechen Republic" in 2011, then overwhelmingly elected for a third term in September 2016. Ramzan's meteoric, unchecked rise through the ranks and his relative youth—he became Prime Minister at age 29—raised serious questions about Ramzan's capacity to "manage" Chechnya on Russia's behalf, but his performance in office since 2007 continues to defy critics' expectations (Mulcahy 2005).

Ramzan's success to date has little to do with the dubious legitimacy of the political process that brought him to power and everything to do with his ability to re-impose security on Chechnya. Key here was the evolution of Ramzan's eponymous militia (the *Kadyrovsky*), which was created during the first war to fight against the Russians, but became the backbone of the various pro-Russian security forces in Chechnya during the second. The *Kadyrovsky* was only one of many, mostly clan/family-based Chechen militias that stayed loyal to Moscow during the second war, but it soon emerged as the dominant force. This was largely the result of a series of amnesties—seven in all between 1999 and 2007—offered by the Russian government to attract fighters from the increasingly demoralized ranks of the rebels. The first of these, offered in December 1999, was ineffective, but subsequent amnesties served to swell the ranks of the *Kadyrovsky* because the Kadyrovs controlled the vetting process to determine which rebels were eligible for amnesty, and which were guilty of crimes or terrorism, and thus excluded from the offer. In practice, this came to mean that Akhmad or Ramzan would vouch for defecting rebels in return for a pledge of personal loyalty (Souleimanov 2015). The *Kadyrovsky* also attracted members from the ranks of uncommitted "fence sitters" who supported neither side actively in the war. By 2001, a Chechen male of fighting age faced a grim choice; join the ranks of nationalist rebels under Maskhadov, which by this point seemed increasingly like the losing side; stay out of the conflict and face the likelihood of being "mopped up" and processed through a filtration camp; or, join the *Kadyrovsky*, earn a living wage, and gain protection for oneself and family against the excesses of federal forces and rebel reprisals. Small wonder that many opted for the latter. As Souleimanov observes, "In a situation in which established *teyp* bonds failed to provide individuals with protection, the need for alternatively delineated groups that could offer real security on the basis of reciprocity became irresistibly attractive" (Souleimanov 2015, 16). The brutal effectiveness of the *Kadyrovsky* at rooting out insurgents (as well as Ramzan's personal enemies) meant that by 2009, the security of Chechnya was effectively back in the hands of native Chechens, either in the form of Ramzan's militia, or indigenously manned branches of the various Russian security forces (OMON, the FSB, *Spetsnaz*, and so on). Moreover, Chechnya is now more peaceful (if defined as the absence of violence) than it has been at any time since 1991. Aside from a few high-profile terror attacks, such as the assault on the Chechen parliament in 2010, and a botched "storming" of Grozny by Islamist militants in 2014, most of the terror attacks that have occurred in the North Caucasus region over the last ten or so years have been outside Chechen territory. In turn, an improving security situation and generous annual subsidies from Moscow have allowed for the wholesale physical reconstruction of Grozny, complete with new roads, schools, hospitals, stadiums, and the largest mosque in Europe. In short, something close to normal life has returned to Chechnya for the first time since 1991.

Russia's approach to ethnic conflict management

There is plenty to dislike about Russia's "solution" to the problem of Chechen separatist terrorism. The Chechenization (or more accurately, "Ramzanization") process has provoked searing criticism from many observers from a human rights perspective,[14] but also from critics who argue that the crackdown in

Chechnya has merely served to disperse the insurgency across the territory of the North Caucasus, thus making it potentially more dangerous (Schaefer 2010, 6–7; Campana and Ratelle 2014; Wood 2007; Hughes 2013; Dannreuther and March 2008), and others who stress the inherent fragility of a solution that lives or dies based on the quality of relationship between two unpredictable, egotistical individuals (Hughes 2013; Wood 2007; Bullough 2015; Yaffa 2016). Each of these criticisms has validity.

Ranged against the skepticism of critics, a few points are in order. On the issue of human rights, it is difficult to defend what is a truly appalling track record. That said, counterinsurgency/counterterrorist operations, whether conducted by the British in Malaya, the French in Algeria, the U.S. in Iraq, or the *Kadyrovsky* in Chechnya, are invariably relentlessly brutal experiences that routinely ignore the established "rules" of war, and always involve human rights violations on a massive scale. Kadyrov's suppression of Chechen insurgents may be different in degree, but it does not differ in kind. Moreover, any balanced assessment of the *Kadyrovsky*'s counterinsurgency tactics must factor in their effectiveness, and what this means for everyday life in Chechnya. Chechnya is now more stable and less violent than at any point during the last quarter of a century. In turn, this has allowed for the large-scale physical reconstruction of Chechnya, and Grozny in particular, and a significant improvement in the quality of life (rights and liberties aside) for ordinary Chechens. After 25 years of brutal conflict, sacrificing rights and liberties for stability and security is a trade-off that most Chechens appear more than happy to make.[15]

With respect to the spread of the insurgency beyond Chechnya's borders, it is indisputable that levels of violence have increased in neighboring republics in almost direct proportion to their decrease inside Chechnya. Far more dramatic, however, has been the decrease in violence levels *throughout* the North Caucasus since 2010. Data from *Caucasian Knot* identified 1,705 people in the North Caucasus as "victims of terrorism" in 2010; this declined to 1,225 in 2012, 525 in 2014, and just 258 in 2015.[16] Offered explanations for this precipitous decline include the outflow of militants from the North Caucasus to other battlefields, such as Syria and Iraq, but the most straightforward conclusion is that the North Caucasus insurgency has run out of steam (International Crisis Group 2016). It had jettisoned its Chechen nationalist ideology and rhetoric by the mid-2000s in favor of a Wahabbi-inspired jihad that enjoys little popular support either inside Chechnya, or elsewhere in the North Caucasus, and appears to be in terminal disarray because of factional infighting (International Crisis Group 2015). The massive escalation in violence across the region predicted by some—Hughes (2013), for example—has simply not occurred.

With respect to the potential fragility of the arrangement between Chechnya and the Russian state, meanwhile, there is little doubt that codifying Chechnya's status in treaty form would help to institutionalize what is currently little more than a personal understanding between two idiosyncratic individuals. In its current form, Chechnya's relationship with the Russian state depends on the survival (political and physical) of Ramzan and Putin, and if either departs the scene, the deal could unravel in short order. Assuming both survive, however, it is difficult to see why either has a compelling incentive to change the status quo. Putin's success at pacifying Chechnya, especially when juxtaposed against the debacles of Yeltsin years, fueled his meteoric rise to power and remains a cornerstone of his enduring popularity. Putin's image as a firm, decisive leader who achieves results—everything that Yeltsin was not, in other words—owes much to the successful implementation of the Ramzanization policy and there is no obvious reason for Putin to jeopardize this success. Meanwhile, Kadyrov's extravagant lifestyle and his status as omnipotent leader of the Chechen Republic hinges entirely on the continued support, both political and economic, of the most powerful man in Russia. To challenge Putin openly would risk plunging Chechnya back into a ruinous conflict with the Russian state that the Chechens can never win. In the process, everything that Kadyrov has achieved over the last decade or so would be destroyed.

Further enhancing the stability of the arrangement is a death of viable alternatives. For Putin, the three alternatives to the prevailing policy are: same policy, different Ramzan; granting independence; or, reasserting Russian state authority. Dropping Ramzan in favor of a less volatile partner may have its appeal, but there are no obvious successors who are still living. Based on opinion polls, granting independence might actually be a more popular option among Russians than Chechens, but successfully retaining Chechnya in the Russian fold (i.e., winning the war) is pivotal to the narrative of the Putin presidency, so this option is highly implausible. Reigniting the war, meanwhile, would be disastrous for Russia and Putin, for any number of reasons. For Ramzan, the choice is simple. He can continue to govern his own fiefdom with absolute power, or he can challenge the Russian state, either by declaring independence, or, maybe, seeking to expand his power into other North Caucasian republics, and thereby risk triggering another ruinous, unwinnable war. For both men, therefore, the current status quo represents an equilibrium of interests, which neither has an incentive to disturb. Moreover, whomever replaces either man in the future will face the same array of incentives and an equivalent lack of viable alternatives, suggesting that the arrangement may be more durable than often assumed.

Beyond these observations, there are three further points that merit mention. First, the Ramzanization policy is often dismissed as a crude solution to the Chechen problem, but its evolution was more nuanced than generally acknowledged. Many observers have characterized the policy as "co-optation" by bribery (Matejova 2013), and Putin himself has referred to it as "buying them off with autonomy and money" (International Crisis Group 2015). However, the key to the success of the policy lies in the choice of who to co-opt (and bribe), and in this respect the Russian approach was cynical, but effective. Rather than selecting a single recipient of state support, the Russian chose to back several prominent individuals (each with their own regional power base) with power and resources. As Souleimanov (2015, 13) puts it "three influential military leaders in charge of three parallel power bases were simultaneously retained in position by the Kremlin in order to counterbalance Kadyrov." The net effect of this approach was to set in motion a Darwinian struggle for power, from which the Kadyrovs emerged as the "fittest." Ramzan's emergence as the leader most adept at rooting out insurgents is by design rather than accident. This leads to a second point. Ramzan is invariably dismissed by Western media as somewhere between a homicidal maniac and a cartoon character. He has been variously described as "Putin's little Saddam," "Putin's dragon," as "somewhere between Uday Hussein and the Notorious B.I.G." and, most memorably, as "basically like a can of Monster energy drink come to life."[17] Although Ramzan may be an easy object of ridicule, his political acumen should not be underestimated.

At the age of 30, he inherited the Chechen presidency—which must be among the most challenging positions in the world of politics—and proceeded to impose his own power *vertikal* on a fiercely egalitarian society through ruthlessness, charisma, and sheer force of will. The end result is a personality cult in which Ramzan portrays himself as the embodiment of traditional Chechen values through an idiosyncratic, although potent, combination of Sufi Islamist and Chechen nationalist ideology, incongruously wedded to Putinism and Russian patriotism (International Crisis Group 2015). This highly personalized interpretation of "Chechenness" seems to resonate with the broader population, and while "fear and loathing" may be an important part of the mix, even critics acknowledge that Ramzan is genuinely popular (Dannreuther and March 2008, 98). In sum, Ramzan has (partially) reconstructed a devastated infrastructure, stifled an insurgency, and commenced construction of a Chechen national identity that, for the first time in more than 200 years, does not have hostility to Russia at its core. "Chechenness," as defined by Ramzan, is compatible with being part of the Russian state.

Finally, Russia's approach to resolving the Chechen problem is often treated as *sui generis*—indeed, the very name "Chechenization" implies its uniqueness; but at the core of a policy dismissed by many as co-optation, or "buying off elites," is accommodation. Ramzan is not a puppet of the Russian state; he is the leader of one of the very few republics in the Russian federal system that exercises a level of autonomy significantly beyond that mandated by the Russian constitution. Certainly, Chechnya depends heavily on Moscow for revenue, but how the money is dispersed within Chechnya is dictated by Ramzan; Ramzan also controls all the security institutions within the republic, even those that are branches of Russian state security forces. As Yaffa notes, "Russian federal troops are practically invisible in Chechnya, confined to a single base east of Grozny." As a constituent element of the Russian federation, Chechnya is technically subject to Russian law, but most experts would agree with statements like "Federal law does not work at all," or "Russian law does not apply in Chechnya." The reality is that, in the words of one observer, there is just one law, "which can be formulated in two words: Ramzan's order" (Bullough 2015). In the cultural domain, rates of indigenous language retention remain strikingly high (over 96 percent), and Ramzan assiduously promotes Chechen language, ethnography, and literature. Moreover, as Chechnya's Russian population has declined drastically, because of war and post-war intimidation, the remaining population is now more ethnically homogenous than at any point in its history. In sum, the key to the success of the Chechenization policy is Russia's grant of autonomy to Chechnya that comes close to the independence that Chechens have craved for hundreds of years (tantamount to "independence-lite"). In this respect, Russia's deal with Chechnya does not differ in kind from the many other cases (the Kurds in Iraq, the Achenese in Indonesia, the Nagas in India, and so on) in which a central government provides territorial autonomy to restive ethnic groups with a view to diminishing violent secessionist impulses. Accommodation, not co-optation or divide and conquer, is the cornerstone of Russia's Chechenization policy and the key to its future success.

Conclusion

It would be incongruous to contextualize the Russia–Chechnya confrontation as a 200-year conflict and then to argue that Russia has successfully solved its Chechen problem after little more than a decade of relative peace and stability. The most that can be claimed at this stage is that Russia has arrived at a formula for stability that has enabled something close to normal life to return to Chechnya. Moreover, neither party has an obviously rational reason to renege on the deal; another Chechen war would be a disaster for both sides. For as long as the deal remains dependent on the quality of the personal relationship between President Putin and Ramzan Kadyrov, however, its durability cannot be guaranteed. Neither man is especially predictable, and the death of either might derail the arrangement in short order; but the solution is not to scrap the arrangement—there are, after all, no good alternatives—but to codify the deal in a more tangible form (a treaty perhaps). Or, possibly, the deal works exactly because neither party has to spell out the precise nature of the power relationship between Chechnya and Russia, leaving both sides with a credible claim to victory. President Putin has won in the sense that the violence in Chechnya (and the North Caucasus as a whole) has abated and Chechnya remains unambiguously part of the Russia, while Ramzan can sell himself as the deliverer of peace, stability, Russian cash, and maximum autonomy to his beleaguered people.

Russia's deal with Chechnya does not fit neatly into any single one of Byman's approaches to "keeping the peace." There is more to the deal than co-optation, and a lot more to it than simply "bribery of elites." The deal works because the Russian state is prepared to grant a level of territorial autonomy to Chechnya that exceeds anything granted to other ethnic units in the Russian federal system, and in this sense, it is not different in kind from the deal offered to the Kurds of Iraq, the Gagauz of Moldova, or the Basques of Spain. In its Chechen manifestation, the use of territorial autonomy as an institutional solution to the management of ethnic conflict may be unpalatable to Western eyes, but, for the time being at least, it is proving more effective than many predicted.

Notes

1 Administratively, Chechnya's status changed multiple times between the Bolshevik victory and World War II. Initially, Chechnya was lumped together with most of the rest of the North Caucasus into the Mountain Autonomous Soviet Socialist Republic (ASSR); then in 1922, Chechnya was peeled off to create its own autonomous oblast, which was then joined together with the Ingush autonomous oblast to form the Chechen-Ingush Autonomous Oblast in 1934. Two years later, this entity's status was elevated to that of "Republic."

2 See Wood (2007, 37) for different figures (412,000 Chechens, 96,000 Ingush).

3 Estimates on the dead and wounded from the first war differ markedly. For details, see Lieven (1999, 108) and Hughes (2013, 81–82). The most detailed analysis is provided by Dunlop (2000), whose calculations yield a total of 11,500 combatant deaths and 46,500 deaths overall.

4 For example, of the trillions of rubles were allocated for the "restoration" of Chechnya during the 1994–1996 period—equivalent to one-quarter of total Russian state allocation investments—almost all was embezzled by Russian or Chechen officials (Dunlop 2000, 10–11).

5 While many scholars emphasize the importance, both past and present, of the *teip* as a basic unit of social organization in Chechnya, others are more skeptical as to their significance (see, for example, Hughes 2013, 4–5; Lieven 1999, 336–339).

6 Quoted in Lieven (1998, 347).

7 For details of serious human rights violations on both side, see Human Rights Watch (www.hrw.org/reports/1996/WR96/Helsinki-16.htm).

8 For details, see Akhmadov and Lanskoy (2010).

9 Elsewhere in the North Caucasus, Dagestan and Ingushetia most notably, the threat posed by radicalized Wahabbi communities (*jamaats*) led to an outright ban on Wahabbism as an "extremist activity." In Chechnya, Maskhadov attempted to undercut the appeal of the growing, Wahabbi-inspired opposition to his rule by issuing a decree in February 1999 that disbanded parliament, made Sharia the official law of Chechnya, and introduced a new religious constitution modelled on that of 1983 Sudan.

10 Given that Basayev was not exactly reluctant to claim credit for terror attacks, including the sinking of the Kursk submarine, his denial of responsibility for the apartment bombings is striking. Speculation as to the identity of the perpetrators of Russia's 9/11 has ranged from Dagestani terrorists (as Basayev himself suggested) to the FSB, who, so the argument goes, blew up the apartments in a false flag operation designed to provide a pretext for the second Chechen war (Satter 2003; Wood 2007); either way, nearly three-quarters of an outraged Russian public blamed Chechens and demanded tough action from the Russian government (Pokalova 2015, 101).

11 As Henkin (2006) notes, news of the Beslan attack and its consequences provoked anti-Basayev demonstrations on the streets of Grozny.

12 Under Uramov's leadership the frequency of terrorist acts associated with the North Caucasus increased significantly after 2007, peaked in 2010, then declined thereafter. Most of these attacks were explosive detonations targeting security forces and government officials in the North Caucasus, with the occasional suicide bombing thrown in for good measure. Of particular note was the suicide bombing of the Lubianka station on the Moscow metro of March 29, 2010, that killed 40 and injured more than 100.

13 Text taken from the copy of the Chechen constitution available at: www.servat.unibe.ch/icl/cc00000_.html.

14 On the use of house burnings to punish the families of insurgents, see Human Rights Watch (2009); on the range of other human rights abuses committed by forces controlled by Kadyrov, see Human Rights Watch (2011); on the recent wave of attacks on the LGBT community, see Human Rights Watch (2017).

15 Notably, in a 2003 scientific opinion poll, the first conducted in Chechnya since the onset of the conflict, nearly 80 percent of Chechens expressed a preference for remaining within Russia (Parfitt 2003). This certainly does not indicate much in the way of enthusiasm among rank and file Chechens for continuing the separatist conflict.

16 *Caucasian Knot* (available at: www.eng.kavkaz-uzel.eu/articles/34546/). To put this in perspective, Chicago, a city with about one-quarter the population of the North Caucasus, suffered more than 700 homicides in 2016 alone. "Gun Deaths In Chicago Reach Startling Number As Year Closes." www.npr.org/2016/12/28/506505382/gun-deaths-in-chicago-reach-startling-number-as-year-closes.

17 Respectively, these quotes are taken from: Franchetti (2007); Yaffa (2016); Bullough (2015); and, Walker (2016), quoting comedian John Oliver.

References

Aitken, R. (2007). Cementing divisions? An assessment of the impact of international interventions and peace-building policies on ethnic identities and divisions. *Policy Studies, 28*(3), 247–267.

Akhmadov, I., and Lanskoy, M. (2010). Raid on Budennovsk: Basayev Forces Peace. In *The Chechen Struggle Independence Won and Lost* (pp. 41–61). New York: Palgrave Macmillan US.

Bullough, O. (2015). Putin's closest ally – and his biggest liability. *Guardian*, 23 September.

Burds, J. (2007). The Soviet War against Fifth Columnists: The Case of Chechnya, 1942–4. *Journal of Contemporary History, 42*(2), 267–314.

Byman, D. (2002). *Keeping the peace: Lasting solutions to ethnic conflicts*. Washington D.C.: JHU Press.

Campana, A., and Ratelle, J.F. (2014). A political sociology approach to the diffusion of conflict from Chechnya to Dagestan and Ingushetia. *Studies in Conflict & Terrorism, 37*(2), 115–134.

Cornell, S.E. (2002). Autonomy as a source of conflict: Caucasian conflicts in theoretical perspective. *World Politics* 54, 245–276.

Dannreuther, R., and March, L. (2008). Chechnya: has Moscow won?. *Survival, 50*(4), 97–112.

Dunlop, J.B. (2000). How many soldiers and civilians died during the Russo-Chechen war of 1994–1996?. *Central Asian Survey, 19*(3–4), 328–338.

Felgenhauer, P. (2002). The Russian Army in Chechnya. *Central Asian Survey, 21*(2), 157–166.

Franchetti, M. (2007). Putin hands Chechnya to his "Little Saddam." *Sunday Times, April, 1*.

Gall, C., and De Waal, T. (1999). *Chechnya: calamity in the Caucasus*. NYU Press.

Gammer, M. (2006). *The lone wolf and the bear*. Pittsburgh: University of Pittsburgh Press.

Gune-Yadcy, Z.B. (2003). A Chechen national hero of the Caucasus in the 18th century: Sheikh Mansur. *Central Asian Survey, 22*(1), 103–115.

Hale, H.E. (2000). The parade of sovereignties: Testing theories of secession in the Soviet setting. *British Journal of Political Science, 30*(1), 31–56.

Hale, H.E. (2004). Divided we stand: Institutional sources of ethnofederal state survival and collapse. *World Politics, 56*(2), 165–193.

Henkin, Y. (2006). From tactical terrorism to Holy War: the evolution of Chechen terrorism, 1995–2004. *Central Asian Survey, 25*(1–2), 193–203.

Hughes, J. (2013). *Chechnya: From nationalism to jihad.* Philadelphia: University of Pennsylvania Press.

Human Rights Watch (2009). "What Your Children Do Will Touch Upon You" Punitive House-Burning in Chechnya" (available at: www.hrw.org/report/2009/07/02/what-your-children-do-will-touch-upon-you/punitive-house-burning-chechnya.

Human Rights Watch (2011). "Russia: Guests Should Refuse Pay for Chechnya Gala" (available at: www.hrw.org/news/2011/10/17/russia-guests-should-refuse-pay-chechnya-gala).

Human Rights Watch (2017). "Anti-LGBT Violence in Chechnya: When Filing 'Official Complaints' Isn't an Option" (available at: www.hrw.org/news/2017/04/04/anti-lgbt-violence-chechnya).

International Crisis Group (2016). *The North Caucasus Insurgency and Syria: An Exported Jihad?* Europe Report No. 238, 16 March.

International Crisis Group (2015). *Chechnya: The Inner Abroad.* Europe Report No. 236, June 30.

Janeczko, M. (2014). "Faced with death, even a mouse bites": Social and religious motivations behind terrorism in Chechnya. *Small Wars & Insurgencies, 25*(2), 428–456.

Lieven, A. (1999). *Chechnya: tombstone of Russian power.* Ithaca, NY: Yale University Press.

Lijphart, A. (1969). Consociational democracy. *World politics, 21*(02), 207–225.

Lijphart, A. (1975). *The politics of accommodation: Pluralism and democracy in the Netherlands* (Vol. 142). Berkeley, CA: University of California Press.

Lijphart, A. (1977). *Democracy in plural societies: A comparative exploration.* Ithaca, NY: Yale University Press.

Lijphart, A. (1979). Consociation and federation: conceptual and empirical links. *Canadian Journal of Political Science, 12*(03), 499–516.

Matejova, M. (2013). Russian "chechenization" and the prospects for a lasting peace in Chechnya. *International Journal on World Peace, 30*(2), 9–34.

Matveeva, A. (2007). Chechnya: dynamics of war and peace. *Problems of Post-Communism, 54*(3), 3–17.

Mukhina, I. (2005). Islamic terrorism and the question of national liberation, or problems of contemporary Chechen terrorism. *Studies in Conflict & Terrorism, 28*(6), 515–532.

Mulcahy, Conor (2005). Pre-Determined: The March 23, 2003 Constitutional Referendum in Chechnya and its Relationship to the Law of Self-Determination. *BC Int'l & Comp. L. Rev.* 28, 179–195.

Parfitt, T. (2003). "Most Chechens 'want to remain part of Russia'" September 7, 2003. www.telegraph.co.uk/news/worldnews/europe/russia/1440823/Most-Chechens-want-to-remain-part-of-Russia.html.

Pokalova, E. (2015). *Chechnya's terrorist network: the evolution of terrorism in Russia's North Caucasus.* Santa Barbara, CA: ABC-CLIO.

Roeder, P.G. (1991). Soviet federalism and ethnic mobilization. *World Politics* 43(2): 196–232.

Roeder, P.G. (2007) *Where nation-states come from: Institutional change in the age of nationalism.* Princeton: Princeton University Press.

Roeder, P.G. (2009). Ethnofederalism and the mismanagement of conflicting nationalism. *Regional and Federal Studies* 19(2), 203–219.

Russell, J. (2008). Ramzan Kadyrov: the indigenous key to success in Putin's Chechenization strategy?. *Nationalities Papers, 36*(4), 659–687.

Satter, D. (2003). *Darkness at dawn: The rise of the Russian criminal state.* Ithaca, NY: Yale University Press.

Schaefer, R.W. (2010). *The insurgency in Chechnya and the North Caucasus: From gazavat to jihad.* Santa Barbara, CA: ABC-CLIO.

Souleimanov, E. (2015). An ethnography of counterinsurgency: kadyrovtsy and Russia's policy of Chechenization. *Post-Soviet Affairs*, *31*(2), 91–114.

Taylor, R. (1992). South Africa: A Consociational Path to Peace?. *Transformation*, (17) 1–11.

Toft, M.D. (2010). Ending civil wars: A case for rebel victory?. *International Security*, *34*(4), 7–36.

Vatchagaev, M. (2014). The politicization of Sufism in Chechnya. *Caucasus Survey*, *1*(2), 25–35.

Walker, E.W. (1998). Islam in Chechnya. *Contemporary Caucasus Newsletter*, *6*, 10–15.

Walker, S. (2016). "Fur flies as Chechen leader and comedian John Oliver clash over lost cat." *Guardian*, 24 May (available at: www.theguardian.com/world/2016/may/24/fur-flies-chechen-leader-ramzan-kadyrov-comedian-john-oliver-clash-lost-cat).

Williams, B.G. (2001). The Russo-Chechen war: a threat to stability in the middle east and Eurasia? *Middle East Policy*, 8(1), 128–148.

Wood, T. (2007). *Chechnya: the case for independence*. New York: Verso Books.

Yaffa, J. (2016). "Putin's Dragon. Is the ruler of Chechnya out of control?." *The New Yorker*, February 8–15. 7

Youngman, M. (2016). Broader, vaguer, weaker: The evolving ideology of the Caucasus Emirate leadership. *Terrorism and Political Violence*, 1–23.

8 Legitimate political discourse versus terrorism

The counter cases of Quebec's FLQ, Scotland's SNLA, and Catalonia's TL

Glen M.E. Duerr

Introduction

So far, the chapters in this volume have investigated prominent cases of secessionist terrorism throughout Europe and Eurasia from the IRA in Northern Ireland, ETA in the Basque Country, FLNC and ARB in Corsica and Brittany, respectively, KLA in Kosovo, PKK and TAK in Turkish Kurdistan, and IK in Chechnya. Conclusions in the form of similarities and differences are assessed in a comparison of all six cases, which is provided in the concluding chapter. The goal of this chapter, however, is four-fold. The first goal is to investigate other prominent cases of secessionist movements in Europe and Eurasia that either (a) once had a small terrorist movement that disbanded, or (b) never had a terrorist attack such that a peaceful secessionist movement is the only type of contestation for independence. Terrorism is unfortunately a common occurrence where even peaceful countries and regions periodically experience terrorist attacks. The second goal of this chapter is to investigate various cases that fit point (a), regions that had a small terrorist movement that then disbanded, using the same seven prompts as the other chapters. The third goal of the chapter is to briefly discuss other cases that fit point (b), subnational units with growing secessionist movements that never experienced the relationship between secessionism and terrorism. The final goal of this chapter will be to present an overview of the actions of Islamic State/ISIS/ISIL/Da-esh to investigate their nascent designs on a wider caliphate including parts of Europe and Eurasia. In general, the focus of the chapter is on the first two goals, which in some ways highlight a foil between the existence of a high-profile secessionist movement and a terrorist movement. After examining these four goals, a range of tangential and philosophical questions remain: why do some groups resort to terrorism while others pursue their goals by legitimate, political means? Which groups are more successful: violent or non-violent secessionist groups?

In addition to the aforementioned cases of secessionism in Europe and Eurasia, there are several other, high-intensity regions with political parties advocating for independence. For example, Flanders in Belgium, Scotland in the UK, Catalonia in Spain, Veneto in Italy, and Greenland in Denmark, among others. In the academic literature, there are comparative works of some of the most prominent secessionist movements (Duerr 2015; Greer 2007; Keating 1996); some also investigate single cases (Guibernau 2004; McRoberts 2001) while others examine secessionism in the EU as a whole (Jolly 2015; Duerr 2015). There are many other secessionist groups in regions throughout Europe, but these are the most likely to gain independence in mature democratic states. Taking a wider geographical area, the province of Quebec in Canada is also considered to be one of the most vociferous separatist regions in well-established democratic countries.

Secessionist movements exist in virtually every country in Europe and Eurasia, yet little attention may be given to these groups, outside of their immediate state. However, when terrorist attacks occur, this is the moment when most people in the international community hear about the grievance. Thus, many pro-independence groups are not well known outside of their immediate geographic vicinity. Paradoxically, when a terrorist attack attached to a group tied to a secessionist movement occurs, this is the moment when more information is disseminated.

There is a tangential circumstance to this discussion, the idea of a "false flag" terrorist organization. A false flag terrorist organization is one that is created to smear the name of secessionists who seek to go through legitimate, peaceful political channels to obtain their maximalist goal of independence. Obviously, the idea of a "false flag" group is hard to prove because there are real people who start these organizations who face prolonged prison sentences. They also cause numerous other societal ramifications, because of their actions. There are also potentially sinister implications for a false flag group because questions such as "Why did the group start?" and "Who funds the group?" are applicable. Finding someone with the motivation and will to convince someone else to start and fund a terrorist organization usually means implicating someone within, or close to, an existing government.

General overview

In response to the six cases already outlined in this book, this chapter examines the cases of the Front du Libération du Québec (FLQ) in Quebec, the Scottish National Liberation Army (SNLA) in Scotland, and Terra Lliure (TL) in Catalonia. All of these terrorist organizations existed for a relatively brief amount of time (at least in comparison with the other groups studied in this volume), committed acts of terrorism, and then disbanded. In all of these cases, legitimate political parties seeking to influence politics through peaceful channels eventually supplanted all of these terrorist organizations. The interesting point of contention here is that Quebec, Scotland, and Catalonia all had secessionist terrorist organizations, but all disbanded much more quickly than the previous six cases. These groups are still correctly labeled as terrorist organizations that committed heinous atrocities, but the goal here is to uncover some of the reasons why terrorism was limited as a mechanism to attain the maximalist goal of independence, whereas it persisted in other cases.

The FLQ in Quebec, a nascent terrorist group in the French-speaking Canadian province existed from 1963 to 1970 (Crelinsten 1987, 59). This period in

Quebec's history saw an increase in violence, which culminated with kidnapping of James Cross, a British Trade Commissioner, and Pierre Laporte, the Quebec Labour Minister, whom the FLQ murdered in October 1970. After the two kidnapping incidents in October 1970, the Canadian government under Prime Minister, Pierre Trudeau (the father of Justin Trudeau), then responded using emergency governing measures—the War Measures Act—which heightened concerns in Quebec over civil liberties (Saywell 1977, 30), but restored security in the most populous city of the province of Quebec, Montreal.

The FLQ, ideologically, supported the independence of Quebec, but also under a Marxist-Leninist vision of the society. Thus, some of the violent tactics were inspired by the possibility of using a revolution to gain control of the government, in a mechanism advocated by Marx—violent revolution to overthrow a bourgeois government. The first attack took place on March 7, 1963, with Molotov cocktails as the weapon of choice. These were planted at military installations in Montreal and its surrounding suburbs. Included alongside the attacks were leaflets explaining the goals of the FLQ, under four broad political demands. Some of the first terrorist attacks of the FLQ resulted in deaths, including a furnace technician, William Vincent O'Neill, and a night watchman, Wilfred O'Neill, in separate attacks.

In general, the FLQ sought to conduct vandalism through terrorism, and to raise the specter of Quebec independence. The attacks were fairly low in sophistication as three homemade Molotov cocktails were used in the first attack, and 75 sticks of dynamite in another (Chilton 2008). Each cell of the FLQ reportedly consisted of five to seven members in coordinated attacks (Crelinsten 1987, 59), which suggests a higher level of coordination, even if the means of attack were fairly low-tech. Despite the low-tech aims of the FLQ, the terrorist killed innocent civilians, thus raising ire in parts of Quebec and much of Canada.

One scholar, David Charters, argues that the FLQ suffered from organizational weakness and poor strategic judgment (Charters 1997). Thus, when lives were lost as a result of the terrorist's actions, any moral high ground was lost. Ultimately, it was not until the killing of Pierre LaPorte that led the government to step in and get systematically involved. Moreover, with the kidnapping of James Cross, the FLQ invoked a major international incident, especially as a British diplomat was the clear target. The assassination of LaPorte immediately brought up tensions between English- and French-speaking communities in Canada, as well as with the UK given that the target was an agent of the queen, the formal Head of State of Canada.

The FLQ committed numerous terrorist attacks from 1963 to 1970. Most of the attacks occurred in 1963, while some spin-off, but related groups conducted small-scale attacks in 1964 and 1965. A powerful bomb on the Montreal Stock Exchange in 1969 renewed the goals of the FLQ, which culminated in the 1970 attacks. According to the Global Terrorism Database, the FLQ conducted two, formal terrorist attacks—both in 1970 including the aforementioned fatality—Pierre LaPorte, the Minister of Labour and Immigration. The murder of LaPorte proved to be a major turning point in the life of the FLQ. Public opinion turned sharply against the FLQ, and Quebec political leaders vowed to fight their battles through political means, rather than allowing terrorist organizations to advance the interests of Quebec. In the same year, 1970, the Parti Québécois (PQ)—a political party advancing the cause of Quebec independence—first contested a Quebec provincial election. As discussed in a later section, the rise of the PQ coincided with the decreased terrorist attacks by the FLQ in Quebec society. However, the connection between supporters of Quebec independence was a difficult point of contention in Canadian society.

The SNLA in Scotland was created in 1979 with varying and sometimes disparate goals (trackingterrorism.org). In general, the SNLA is also known for conducting low-level terrorist attacks into the 1980s. The SNLA was created by Adam Busby as a means for advocating for an independent Scotland (BBC "Tartan terrorists"). In total, the SNLA conducted a few dozen attacks with numerous injuries but no known fatalities. According to the Global Terrorism Database, the SNLA conducted seven attacks between 1983 and 2005, all in the city of London. The last three attacks were all suspected, not confirmed terrorist attacks by the SNLA. No fatalities were ever recorded as an outcome of an attack by the SNLA; eight people were injured across various attacks. On December 10, 1983, a military installation was attacked by the SNLA resulting in five injuries (Global Terrorism Database). The bombing of a Royal Artillery Barracks also resulted in property damage assessed at $100,000.

Similar to the FLQ in Quebec, the SNLA used a set of low-tech means to conduct terrorist attacks. Letter bombs were frequently used by the SNLA, for example. In 2002, there was an alleged renewal of the SNLA when numerous packages, containing bombs, were mailed to high-profile political leaders in the UK, including Cherie Blair, the wife of the Prime Minister, Tony Blair (Politicians 2002). Even as late as 2008, an attack was alleged to the members of the SNLA. The difficulty in this case was finding evidence to directly attribute the attacks to the SNLA, or that the organization was sufficiently strong enough to conduct terrorist attacks.

The Scottish National Party (SNP)—a political party advocating Scottish independence—began to grow in its support during the 1970s and 1980s. The advancement of the SNP also dovetails with the decrease in the number of terrorist attacks committed by the SNLA, with the exception of the attacks in the 2000s. Although no formal correlation is possible, the advancement of a legitimate means of advocating for change seems to have coincided with fewer terrorist attacks. This point is disputed in the UK, but the assessment depends on who actually committed the terrorist attacks, or foiled terrorist attacks in the 2000s. Did the perpetrator have a direct connection to the SNLA, or simply act as a "lone wolf" attacker under sympathy for the SNLA?

TL in Catalonia was founded in 1978—the same year as the ratification of the Spanish Constitution—and remained active until 1991 before the group officially disbanded in 1995. In English, TL stands for "free land," which is the maximalist goal of the organization. The first attack was conducted in March of 1981 (Global Terrorism Database). According to the Global Terrorism Database, TL was responsible for 62 terrorist attacks spanning from 1981 to 1992. The last seven attacks were all suspected to be TL; the last confirmed TL attack took place in April 1990 (Global Terrorism Database). In total, TL was responsible for one fatality, although a bombing in Barcelona in 1988 had an unknown number of fatalities in the Global Terrorism Database—there were three confirmed injuries in the explosion at the bar. TL was also responsible for 47 injuries across their 62 attacks. TL then splintered into several different, smaller groups (Bassa and Gonzàlez 2007).

During that period, political parties supportive of Catalan autonomy governed Catalonia: Convergència I Unió—a coalition of Convergència Democràtica de Catalunya (CDC) and Unió Democràtica de Catalunya (UDC). The party existed in a coalition from its founding in 1978 until 2015 (Duerr 2015). Over time, CDC gradually tilted their support towards independence, such that by 2010 the party came to support the platform of full sovereignty for Catalonia; one of the reasons the CiU coalition disbanded was that the UDC only supported autonomy for Catalonia, not outright independence. Unlike the previous two cases, there is no clear timeline that shows the growth in support for legitimate political parties with the decrease of terrorist attacks. Yet, TL also disbanded over time, with legitimate political parties taking up the cause of independence.

The terrorist organizations in Quebec, Scotland, and Catalonia collectively killed between four and nine people, injured dozens more, and committed a lot of personal and property damage. By comparison with the other cases in this volume, the scale of terrorism was more limited. This distinction raises a set of questions, particularly as to why secessionist terrorism starts and stops.

In the cases of Quebec, Scotland, and Catalonia, the violence of the terrorist organizations seems to have been tolerated by a portion of the population while the targets were inanimate objects. Yet, to those impacted by these terrorist attacks, especially those who lost loved ones, the terrorists deservedly were brought to justice. As soon as casualties were incurred, the SNLA, specifically, effectively stopped committing attacks (this point is contested depending on the source of the SNLA-related attacks in the 2000s). For the FLQ, the earliest fatalities did not dissuade the terrorists, but much opposition amounted in the rest of Canada; however, when the Quebec Labour Minister was killed, opposition even among hardcore supporters declined dramatically. The success of the counterterrorism efforts must be extended to a range of different actors including the Canadian, British, and Spanish governments, as well as regional and local law enforcement. Police and military officials in the province of Quebec, including the City of Montreal, were especially important. In the UK, existing counterterrorism measures were in place for the IRA, and were extended to stifle the SNLA. In Spain, policing measures were the primary mode of response to ETA, and these were extended to TL (Duerr 2017).

Political grievances/why terrorism is not evident in every secessionist region?

Chapters 2–7 in this volume all lay out the tactic of terrorism being used by members of a secessionist movement and the uses of said tactic in Europe and Eurasia. All of these cases represent violent reactions to the state, with the overarching objective of political divorce, or at the very least, cultural and linguistic protections with requisite autonomy for the subnational region. Political grievances, often including economic and social grievances, exist in many heterogeneous societies throughout the world. Political grievances also have cultural elements such as language or cultural norms within the society that contribute to its uniqueness. In the case of Quebec and Catalonia, in particular, language politics play a central role in the existence of an independence movement.

In the case of Catalonia, the independence movement at times has explicitly tried to make the case for Catalan culture being more pacifist in nature. For example, the Government of Catalonia recently outlawed bullfighting in Catalonia—in part for the rise for animal welfare policy, but also as a mechanism to display distinctions between Madrid and Barcelona.

Obviously, terrorism is not the only tactic for secession. Imagine a small house surrounded by a moat. Inside the house are three animals. There is a large guard dog. In this analogy, the dog is older, very well fed, and has reached full size—imagine a 50-plus pound dog. The dog is wise and experienced, but is also considered slow and takes for granted that its food bowl will be filled regularly—after all, the dog wants to make sure that its owner, represented by the state, maintains a safe environment for people to live and work. There is also a cat, which, at times, is much more nimble and aggressive than the dog. Given that subnational regions are smaller than the state, imagine a cat that is smaller in size than the guard dog. The young cat—probably in the range of five pounds—lashes out vociferously using aggressive means to try to intimidate the dog and exit the house. The final animal is a sizeable, experienced mouse. Although the mouse is quite small, it is intelligent and is much quicker than the heavy, old guard dog.

The overarching goal of the guard dog is to maintain the order of the small house. The goal of the cat and the mouse is to leave the house through the front door to gain international legitimacy via an independent state. Exiting through other means—a window or a hole—risks drowning in the moat (any region that unilaterally secedes risks being cast as an international pariah). Only by leaving through the door is there a legitimate pathway to safety across the moat.

In a sense, these cases reflect a "snarling, scratching cat" in that some secessionists resorted to violent tactics as a means of attaining their maximalist goal of independence. The "snarling, scratching cat" analogy is best described under the assumption that the guard dog is a larger breed such as a Labrador or Rottweiler, given that the cat (the subnational region) is smaller than the dog (the government of the state).

On the other hand, a "cunning mouse" is a region wherein the pro-independence party is simply trying to outsmart the state government by trying to agitate for independence. The mouse is clearly smaller in size than the cat, but has a few advantages. A mouse, for example, tends to be faster and more nimble. Both of these points reflect the advantage of being more efficient with a smaller, leaner government. The mouse is also unwilling to resort to violence to complete its mission—escape from the house.

In Canada, the UK, and Spain, there is a long-standing guard dog that protects each of the three states. A snarling cat, in the form of the FLQ, SNLA, and TL all attempted to exit the house via violent attacks on the dog. The wise, old dog, however, rebuffed all attempts—in two of the cases, the dog blocked violent attacks on multiple fronts; in the UK, both the IRA and SNLA committed attacks at the same time over grievances in Northern Ireland and Scotland; in Spain, both ETA and TL attempted to agitate for the Basque Country and Catalonia, respectively. When all three terrorist organizations—the FLQ, SNLA, and TL—disbanded, a cunning mouse opted to exit the house. In Quebec, Scotland, and Catalonia, the cunning mouse has had success in all cases, but has not yet left the house.

Across Quebec, Scotland, and Catalonia, there are a range of different grievances. First, each region once held either independence or significant autonomy within a different governing structure. Quebec, prior to the Battle of the Plains of Abraham in 1759 (part of the wider Seven Years' War), was a French colony in North America. When the British defeated the French at the Battle of the Plains of Abraham, it was a major defeat for Francophone speakers (Taras 2002, 119). Thus, under British rule, the territory that came to be known as Quebec was poor, rural, undereducated, and largely socioeconomically weaker than the growing Anglophone province of Ontario (O'Sullivan-See 1986, 134). Quebec's first experience with terrorism came in 1837 and 1838 when a group known as Les Patriotes began attacking colonial institutions (Behiels 1985, 3). Derided as a terrorist organization by the British, but upheld as a freedom fighter organization by some Francophones, Les Patriotes still has a much contested legacy in Canada (Taras 2002, 119). In the aftermath of the attacks by Les Patriotes, the Lord Durham report recommended the 1840 Act of Union that consolidated Upper (Ontario) and Lower (Quebec) Canada into one colonial province under British rule. The goal of the British government was assimilation along ethnic and linguistic lines. Of course, this new policy did not receive much support in Lower Canada. For example, the parliamentarian, Louis Hippolyte Lafontaine protested by only speaking French in the legislature—a move that was technically illegal (Richler 1992, 10). In general, Quebec remained poorer, less educated, and heavily religious (Catholic as opposed to Protestant), with a rural population that had very few upper-level economic opportunities for the next century (O'Sullivan-See 1986, 134). In the 1960s, Quebec shifted dramatically with the "Quiet Revolution" to become more urban and secular in the span of a decade (Ignatieff 1993, 182). The rise of the FLQ coincides with these tectonic shifts in Quebec society.

Scotland, prior to the 1707 Act of Union, which created the Kingdom of Great Britain, was its own independent kingdom. Like Quebec, Scotland was typically a poorer region, albeit it one with similar levels of strong cultural and religious identity that distinguished its people from the British. After the union of the English and Scottish Crowns under King James I/VI in 1603, Scotland maintained its separateness from London (Duerr 2015). However, in the aftermath of the disastrous Darien colonial campaign in Central America in the 1690s, Scotland was bankrupt, and accepted English terms for an Act of Union in 1707, thus unifying Great Britain into one, unified kingdom (McCrone and Linklater 2013). Under direct rule from London, Scotland remained relatively poor, although Edinburgh maintained significant autonomy in the legal system and the Church of Scotland, in particular. The rise of the SNLA coincided with a time when Scotland sought devolution from Westminster, but the vote failed based on its being pegged to turnout—a requirement of 40 percent of all Scots needed to be in favor of devolution. Even though 51.6 percent of voters supported the 1979 devolution referendum, only 63.7 percent of voters turned out to vote. Thus, less than 32 percent of all eligible Scottish voters cast votes in favor of devolution—enough to stifle the push for devolution.

Catalonia, prior to 1714, was the central part of the Kingdom of Aragon until its forced union with Castile. The Siege of Barcelona in the War of Spanish Succession is one that still comprises a large portion of Catalan history when the independent kingdom fell under the rule of a Castilian Spanish king (Guibernau 2004). For much of the history, the Catalan language gained some level of toleration. This all changed, however, with Francisco Franco's victory in the 1936–1939 Spanish Civil War. The Catalan language was formally outlawed in a range of different areas from the media to schools to newspapers. Only in very limited settings was the use of the Catalan language difficult to stop, such as at a football match featuring FC Barcelona in Camp Nou, their home stadium. When Franco died in 1975, many Catalans hoped that some protections for their language and culture would be restored. TL was formed in 1978, its group members might argue, for advocating for greater Catalan rights. One of TL's founders, Marti Marco was killed by Spanish police on January 30, 1979, creating the first "martyr" for the cause, and launching TL as a destructive force in Catalan society (Bassa and Gonzalez 2007).

In the three cases, all of these dates, all from the eighteenth century, form a historical grievance for lost autonomy. Although to many these events may seem like ancient history, the grievances of stateless nations remain at the forefront of politics (Keating 1996). These events are taught—from generation to generation—in the schools. Where this history is not allowed to be taught, for example, under Franco, many overt signs of Catalanism were outlawed, the discussions continue at home.

The people of both Quebec and Catalonia speak a different language from the majority of people in their respective states, Canada and Spain. In Quebec, the vast majority of the population speaks French, as opposed to the dominance of English in the rest of Canada. In Catalonia, the population speaks Catalan, a mutually unintelligible language from Spanish, albeit one with significant similarities. In Scotland, the vast majority of the population speaks English, which is the same as the vast majority of people within the rest of the UK. Language does not feature prominently in the case for Scottish independence, although Gaelic speakers, especially in the north of Scotland maintain the case for greater language protections.

In terms of culture, Quebec, Scotland, and Catalonia, supporters of independence all make a case as distinct entities with enough separation from Canada, the UK, and Spain to be thought of as different. In some ways, these cultural differences are evident in terms of major holidays, cuisine, art, and other indicators of culture; in other ways, the Canadian political scientist, Michael Ignatieff's rebuttal is apt: these movements are based on the "narcissism of minor differences" (Ignatieff 1993). Although Ignatieff would certainly concede that some distinctions are present, virtually none of them is so vast as to ascribe statehood. The caveat to this argument, however, is that Ignatieff assumes a level of federalism that protects localized customs, languages, and cultures. Ignatieff then follows up with another question: "If you are a nation with significant autonomy, why do you need a state?" (Ignatieff 1993). For supporters of an independent Quebec, Scotland, or Catalonia, they would all argue that the level of autonomy provided by the Canadian, British, and Spanish governments is not encompassing enough. Only full, de jure independence replete with membership in the UN is enough to institutionally protect each culture and language. In Quebec, there has long been a desire for some form of special status as in a federacy model wherein Quebec receives more governing powers than any other province. Many members of the Canadian government who argue that Canadian federalism should provide equality to all provinces have blocked this idea. In Scotland, Scottish nationalists seek a much more powerful Scottish Parliament replete with more extensive taxation powers. This idea has been investigated by numerous British Prime Ministers, but none have acted on the initiative. Former Prime Minister, David Cameron, proposed a "devolution max" idea in 2014 towards the end of the Scottish independence referendum campaign, but did not act on the idea; he resigned in 2016 after losing the Brexit vote. In Catalonia, Catalan supporters of independence seek commensurate fiscal and taxing powers as in the Basque Country, as well as greater rights for the Catalan language. The Spanish Constitutional Court in Madrid ruled the 2006 Statute, which was designed to provide more autonomy to Catalonia, unconstitutional. Further proposals to devolve power have yet to be fulfilled.

In terms of economics, nationalists/secessionists in all three regions argue for the ability to be "masters of their own houses." Interestingly, the three regions are in different financial positions. Catalonia is wealthier than the average autonomous community in Spain, by a significant amount, and pays a lot of money into the national government. Catalonia is not as wealthy as Madrid, but is substantially wealthier than many other regions. Scotland is on par with the average in the UK. Scotland is not as wealthy as London and the southeast of England, but is wealthier than every other region of the UK. Quebec is a "have not" province in Canada, and receives significant annual redistribution. Quebec, in terms of GDP per capita, is less wealthy than many other provinces, especially the energy-rich Alberta, Saskatchewan, and Newfoundland and Labrador, as well as the urban economic engines of Ontario and British Columbia. Quebec is marginally wealthier than the Maritime Provinces of New Brunswick, Nova Scotia, and Prince Edward Island, but not by much, and remains near the bottom in the Canadian rankings.

In terms of political position, Quebec tends to be a very difficult province to predict. The PQ has sought to develop a specific political constitution, which distinguishes the province from all others. In particular, the PQ tends to follow positions in France in terms of the separation of church and state, as well as the establishment of significant constitutional proposals making Quebec distinct. In Scotland, the citizens of the territory tend to elect, at present, center-left candidates, as opposed to center-right governments elected by "English" voters (Jolly 2015). Although this distinction is an oversimplification, it is an argument purported regularly by members of the SNP (Duerr 2015). In Catalonia, several measures have recently been passed as a means of presenting a distinctly different political culture in the region. The aforementioned example of bullfighting is apt, which has been outlawed in Catalonia, and provides a cultural and political difference with the rest of Spain. Catalan society, especially in Barcelona, is often depicted as very cosmopolitan and receptive of different peoples.

Nationalists in all three regions make the case for civic nationalism, via welcoming immigrants from elsewhere as well as people from other regions within the state. In Quebec, the case for civic nationalism is more difficult given the intensity of the French language to Quebec's independence project, and with recent leaders hedging towards ethnic nationalist positions. In Scotland, the case for civic nationalism is stronger because the independence project is based around residence, rather than language. Nonetheless, there are few members of ethnic minorities within the major ranks of the SNP (Duerr 2015). In Catalonia, internal migration, and external immigration have created a multiethnic society—the case for civic nationalism is likewise quite strong. Given the intensity of the Catalan language demands, however, there are some entanglements with Spanish speakers, which makes for contestation in some places. Nonetheless, all three of these movements are now peaceful, as opposed to the other chapters in this volume wherein violence was used as a means of projecting political independence.

In Quebec, there are several secessionist political parties, and many more organizations. The largest party—at the provincial level—the aforementioned PQ was founded in 1968, and contested their first election in 1970. Although the PQ did not win, the party rose dramatically in the first decade of its existence (the PQ was founded in 1968). The PQ contested the 1973 Quebec provincial election with a similar result to that of 1970. Then, in the 1976 Quebec provincial election, the PQ won a majority in the National Assembly, and formed the government of Quebec. At the federal level, the Bloc Québécois was founded in 1991, and first contested the 1993 federal election only running in districts in the province of Quebec.

In Scotland, like Quebec, there are several secessionist political parties, and numerous pro-independence organizations. On the political front, the aforementioned SNP—founded in 1934—has sought to advance Scottish autonomy, now independence, through the political system. For the early decades of its existence, the SNP was not a major factor in British parliamentary elections. The SNP did, however, win by-elections in 1945 and 1967, eventually catapulting the party to a legitimate contender within the society (Duerr 2015). By the 1970s and 1980s, the SNP began to win regular seats in the British House of Commons, although still a small minority. When the Scottish Parliament was formally created with the Scotland Act of 1998, the SNP came in second place in the 1999 and 2003 Scottish Parliamentary elections (Jolly 2015). The Scottish Parliament is designed to make majoritarian governance much more difficult to obtain than in the British House of Commons by using a mixed "First Past the Post" and Additional Member Proportional Representation system (Duerr 2015). When the SNP won the 2007 Scottish Parliamentary election, the party held a minority government, and had to work together with other major parties to govern. However, in 2011, the SNP accomplished the unexpected by winning an outright majority in the Scottish Parliament (Jolly 2015). This provided the SNP with the ability to pass a bill calling for an independence referendum. In tandem with British Prime Minister, David Cameron, the Edinburgh Agreement of 2012 outlined the rules and procedures of the independence referendum in September 2014, drawing many similarities with Quebec. After a long campaign, the "yes" side garnered the support of 44.7 percent of voters—thus, Scotland remains part of the UK (Duerr 2015). In 2016, the SNP again won the Scottish Parliamentary election, but with 63 of the 129 seats, two short of a majority. With some support from the Scottish Green Party, the SNP again passed a bill to hold a second independence referendum in 2017. British Prime Minister, Theresa May, however, did not provide a timetable for another independence referendum, and instead called for a British general election to gain greater support for the Brexit negotiations. The SNP was thus left in limbo.

In Catalonia, there are two major pro-independence political parties that, at the present, have formed a wide Catalan-sovereignty coalition. CDC was in an ongoing coalition with UDC from 1978 until 2015 under the name CiU. UDC long favored greater autonomy for Catalonia, so as the pro-independence wing of CDC grew, the two coalition partners eventually grew apart (Duerr 2015). CDC tends to fill the center-right of the political spectrum in Catalonia; although this point is disputed given the flexibility of some of the party's platforms (Duerr 2015; Guibernau 2004; McRoberts 2001). CDC is also the most successful political party in Catalonia, and many Catalan presidents have come from this party. Additionally, ERC also espouses a platform of pro-independence. ERC is actually the standard-bearer of the independence movement, given the founding of the party in 1931 as a supporter of independence (McRoberts 2001). ERC has gone through vicissitudes of support since democracy was reintroduced to Spain in 1978. In the 2010s, ERC has been revitalized, and, since 2015, the party joined in a coalition with CDC, and other pro-independence groups, but only at the regional level—CDC and ERC are still separate at the Spanish level. The new coalition, mainly between CDC and ERC is called Junts Pel Sí (JxSí—Together for Yes) (Duerr 2015). In the 2015 Catalan regional election, JxSí won the most seats in parliament with a plurality of 62 of the 135 seats. When aligned with CUP—a far left-wing party also in support of independence, JxSí holds a voting majority in the Catalan Parliament.

Rebuttal from the government

In a democracy, there are legitimate means through which to make change. Each government provides some level of accommodation to the people of Quebec, Scotland, and Catalonia respectively. In Canada, the UK, and Spain, each country is part of the developed world with a high standard of living, which includes: high GDP per capita, high levels of education, and high life expectancy among many other good societal indicators. All three societies are considered to be mature democracies replete with extensive rights and liberties for each citizen; Spain is perhaps an exception here in that a fascist dictator, Francisco Franco, ruled the country from the end of the Spanish Civil War in 1939 until his death in 1975. Each country devolves power to subnational levels providing some decision-making powers to more local levels.

Federalism in Canada involves specific enumerated powers for the 10 provincial governments that are outlined in the written constitution, the 1982 Charter of Rights and Freedoms. Quebec's case, at least outlined through the PQ, is to obtain special powers for the single province over and above every other province. Canadian political leaders, from both the Liberal Party and the Conservative Party, the two dominant parties in Ottawa, have resisted any intent to build a federacy structure whereby Quebec would receive more powers. Canadian leaders can sensibly argue that the province of Quebec has significant powers, and is treated with the same due respect as every other province. Moreover, on two occasions, where the PQ has won a majority in Quebec's parliament, the National Assembly, the PQ has been able to pass a bill initiating an independence referendum. In 1980 and 1995, the people of Quebec voted on whether or not to stay in Canada via convoluted plebiscites promising a different relationship between Ottawa and Quebec City. In 1980, a "sovereignty-association" was the subject of the vote; in 1995, it was a "sovereignty-partnership" with Canada. The terms of the next, future referendum will be more specific given the Clarity Act of 2000 that requires a straightforward "yes/no" answer on whether Quebec should be an independent country, rather than a negotiation on loosening the ties as in a sovereignty-partnership type agreement that is still nebulous. Again, the central point here is that the Canadian government can reasonably argue that the people of Quebec have been given opportunities to decide their own future in a democratic and peaceful way.

In the UK, the issue of "Home Rule" has been seriously discussed since the nineteenth century, especially under Prime Minister, William Gladstone. A failed devolution referendum in 1979 shuttered the idea, although the plebiscite was pegged to turnout; at least 40 percent of the population were required to support devolution. When then Prime Minister, Tony Blair, was first elected in 1997, it came with a promise of a second devolution referendum, this time not pegged to turnout. The successful votes in Scotland and Wales created a Scottish

Parliament and a Welsh Assembly (Northern Ireland's Assembly opened in 2006 with a consociational structure to share power between Roman Catholic and Protestant leaders). Although powers are limited, the UK government can reasonably argue that more powers are being devolved to the local parliaments and assemblies, and that each constituent nation can construct a unique future within a united, UK. As in Quebec, the SNP in Scotland won a majority in the Scottish Parliament and passed a bill to hold an independence referendum. In 2014, the people of Scotland voted in this independence plebiscite, which ultimately failed. The UK government, like the Canadian government, can reasonably say that the people of Scotland had a full democratic opportunity to decide their own constitutional future. In 2017, the SNP, with some parliamentary support from the Scottish Greens, voted to hold another referendum—this attempt, however, was rebuffed by Prime Minister, Theresa May, given the Brexit negotiations (and, the snap British general election of June 2017).

In Spain, the structure under the post-Franco 1978 Constitution is a system with 17 autonomous communities (ACs). Scholars debate whether this AC structure actually provides federalism, but, at the very least, there are subnational units with some powers of governance. Unlike Canada or the UK, the people of Catalonia have not been able to hold a binding, legitimate independence referendum. According to Article 155 of the Spanish Constitution, and numerous sections of the preamble, the dissolution of Spain is expressly forbidden. On several occasions, groups within Catalonia have tried to hold an independence consultation—in the Spanish Constitution, these measures have always been blocked as unconstitutional. As a sovereign country, Spain has the right to deny any independence referendum, but the Catalan people have not had the same opportunities as the people of Quebec or Scotland. This has led to a gulf in the view of Spain in comparison with the UK and Canada in the eyes of some international commentators.

Overview of major terrorist attacks carried out by the FLQ, SNLA, and TL

In comparison with the other cases studied in this volume, supporters of independence in either Quebec, Scotland, or Catalonia have carried out relatively few terrorist attacks. To briefly recap the earlier discussion, the FLQ crisis in 1970 is the most noteworthy given that the attack culminated in a murder. After a number of smaller-scale attacks throughout the 1960s, resulting in no known casualties, the FLQ increased the ferocity of their tactics. British Trade Commissioner, James Cross, was kidnapped by the FLQ, and Quebec Labour Minister, Pierre LaPorte was assassinated. After the death of LaPorte, public opinion turned dramatically against the FLQ.

The FLQ started attacking targets in March 1963 and continued throughout that year. As noted earlier, the FLQ attacked military installations, then moved to a rail line between Montreal and Quebec City in April 1963, as well as other Canadian institutions such as the RCMP headquarters and the recruitment center for the Canadian Army in Montreal. After the initial wave of attacks, the FLQ—under various splinter names—conducted attacks in 1964 and 1965 as well. The Canadian police arrested several high members of the FLQ.

On February 13, 1969, the FLQ detonated a powerful bomb on the Montreal Stock Exchange, which injured 27 people. In September 1969, the FLQ targeted the mayor of Montreal, Jean Drapeau. All of this led up to the October Crisis of 1970 with the kidnapping of two prominent members of society; thousands of students in Montreal rallied in support of the FLQ, which factored in to the government response (see the next section).

The SNLA sent a number of packages to major figures such as Princess Diana and Prime Minister, Margaret Thatcher. Fortunately, the letter to Thatcher did not explode when opened. Although the SNLA had real intent in their terrorist attacks, no fatalities were ever recorded. Some of the major players in the SNLA are now serving prison sentences for their crimes, but the deadliness of their activities were fortunately never realized.

TL also limited its force, and by comparison with ETA, was a more minimal player in Spanish politics, and Spanish counterterrorism. For TL, the goal was to commit terrorist attacks to raise the profile of Catalan secessionism, and to fight the authoritarianism of the Franco regime, but to do so without mass casualties. Of course, even a terrorist group that simply wants to raise awareness of the cause based on attacks that are not designed to kill, can ultimately still kill people when bombs are used.

In comparison with the rest of the groups studied in Chapters 2–7 of this volume, the FLQ, SNLA, and TL committed relatively few attacks, and with far fewer casualties. Yet, each group committed terrorist attacks, and, under the FLQ and TL people died—their correct labeling remains: terrorist organizations. The other major difference is that all of these organizations had relatively short periods of activity, and all laid down their arms and committed to a peaceful process of attempting to achieve their maximalist goal of independence.

Government response

The response of the Canadian government was most dramatic. During the October Crisis, the FLQ made a list of nine demands to release James Cross including the release of political prisoners, money, and the safe passage of the kidnappers to Cuba or Algeria, the Canadian government quickly denied all of these requests. After the aforementioned FLQ's terrorist attacks grew in scope and led to a mortality, the Canadian government, under Prime Minister, Pierre Trudeau, initiated emergency measures—the War Measures Act—in the streets of Ottawa (October 12, 1970) and Montreal (October 15, 1970). Effectively, the Canadian military was given the ability to send military vehicles and personnel to Ottawa and Montreal as a means of stopping the FLQ. Hundreds of people—listed formally as 465 people—connected to Quebec's independence movement were imprisoned temporarily.

Cross was detained by the FLQ, but eventually released in December 1970 after negotiations with the Canadian government. The five kidnappers secured asylum in Cuba. Even today, the response of Prime Minister Pierre Trudeau is viewed very negatively by some supporters of Quebec's independence movement according to high-profile interviews in the PQ and BQ (Duerr 2012). The aftermath of the October Crisis saw a significant loss of support for the FLQ, but also a significant rise in support for the PQ. By 1976, the newly formed political party won the provincial election, and gained a majority of the seats in parliament. The MNAs then purported a bill to hold an independence referendum, which took place in 1980. Overall, this mechanism provided the people of Quebec with a peaceful and legitimate mechanism to express their grievances, which also dis-incentivized people towards support for the FLQ as the Canadian government allowed the referendum to decide constitutional matters. Only 40.4 percent of people voted in favor of independence in 1980, so it is unknown how the Canadian government would have responded to a "yes" vote, but indications remain that some form of new agreement between Quebec and Canada would have been formed (Hébert and Lapierre 2014). Given that the referendum question purported a sovereignty-association between the two governments, some form of new relationship would likely have been formed even in the event of a referendum vote of 50.1 percent in favor of the plebiscite. In October 1995, a second independence referendum was held, this time with the concept of sovereignty-partnership; 49.4 percent of voters supported the "yes" option.

Ultimately, the emergency measures were lifted. This remains a cleavage within Canadian society. Many people in Quebec believe that the measures were draconian, and many innocent Quebecois nationalists were arbitrarily detained. In the rest of Canada, many people argue that the measures were necessary to restore order in Montreal, especially in the aftermath of a terrorist attack (Duerr 2012).

The response by the British government was more measured than the Canadian government. Given the number of attacks by the IRA (see Chapter 2 by Sutcliffe and Alchin), attacks by the SNLA were less deadly and required a less robust response. The British government, however, had tackled the IRA for some time, and thus had more practice at responding to terrorist attacks.

The response by the Spanish government was more heightened compared with that of the British government, but less virulent than that of the Canadian government. Given the terrorist actions of ETA at the time (see Chapter 4 by Cartrite), the Spanish government already mobilized. In particular, police and political coordination had already improved as a means of trying to stop Basque terrorism (Duerr 2017). As TL's attacks led to one fatality, the Spanish government took this terrorist group seriously, but, compared with the over 800 deaths related to ETA in the Basque region, TL was lower priority. Like the case of the SNLA and the UK, the experience of the Spanish government in dealing with ETA provided extra expertise with counterterrorism.

Of course, the complication for both the British and Spanish governments was deciphering between several different terrorist organizations. In Canada, the FLQ was the sole, domestic major terrorist organization, thus making it easier to understand which group conducted the attack and why. All three governments, however, have had to deal with some international terrorist threats, which, again, complicated the matter of counterterrorism.

Changes to state structure

In Canada, the Pierre Trudeau government embarked on a project to create a written constitution (to go alongside the unwritten constitution inherited from the British, Westminster-style parliament). By 1982, Canada ratified the Charter of Rights and Freedoms. The main drawback, however, being that the province of Quebec did not sign the document, and remains unreconciled. The original conception of the Canadian Confederation in 1867 built in a system of loose former colonies, which, over time, developed into a more centralized, federal model. The original four provinces: New Brunswick, Nova Scotia, Ontario, and Quebec were all very autonomous. When the rest of the provinces joined Canada in the 1870s through the early 1900s (the exception, Newfoundland, joined Canada in 1949), the country maintained the federal structure. Quebec has thus maintained specific provincial powers for 150 years. Even though Quebec did not sign the Charter of Rights and Freedoms, numerous provincial powers are enumerated in the document. Otherwise, Canada has made very few constitutional changes; Nunavut became a territory in 1999, carved out of the Northwest Territories, but there have been no other border changes.

In the UK, two referendums were held on the devolution of power to the less populated constituent countries in the union—Scotland, Wales, and Northern Ireland. After a failed referendum in 1979, the new Labour Party government under Prime Minister Tony Blair in 1997 campaigned on a second devolution referendum. The plebiscite passed granting Scotland a parliament, and Wales an assembly—both inaugurated in 1999 with an election and a legislature. Northern Ireland was also granted an assembly, but, given some historic tensions, the legislature was not opened until 2006. In the UK, the borders have remained steadfast, with no shifts occurring in the country.

In Spain, after the death of dictator Francisco Franco, Madrid transitioned to democratic governance. Albeit debated by scholars, Spain provided some level of autonomy by recognizing 17 "Autonomous Communities (ACs)" under its governance structure. Moreover, in the 1978 Constitution, historic nations like Catalonia, the Basque Country, and Galicia are recognized as distinct. Spain still possesses significant powers, and critics argue that Madrid is still more of a unitary-style government than a true federation. Both the Basque Country and Navarre—two of the ethnically Basque ACs—possess greater fiscal powers than all of the other ACs (Duerr 2017). In comparison with Canada and the UK, the creation of ACs in Spain marked a significant territorial shift from the past. New ACs were created with a sense of watering down the identity in a few areas; the Basque areas, for example, are bifurcated between the Basque Country and Navarre.

An important question to raise is whether or not additional devolved powers have satiated demands for independence, or merely whetted the appetite for more sovereignty? The academic literature is mixed on this question, noting that autonomy can serve as either glue or solvent depending on the case (Bird *et al.* 2010).

Greenland, Veneto, and Flanders

Looking more broadly beyond the three cases studied here—Quebec, Scotland, and Catalonia—regions such as Greenland, Veneto, and Flanders have experienced similar levels of terrorism, or none at all. Each of the respective countries—Denmark, Italy, and Belgium—have provided a level of autonomy similar to Canada, the UK, and Spain. In Denmark, the region of Greenland has been granted two major documents on devolution: 1979 Home Rule and 2008 Self Government (Loukacheva 2007). It is possible that the Greenlandic people will be given a viable route to independence in the future, but much depends on the economic viability of Greenland. Moreover, the population of Greenland is only 60,000, which would make it one of the smallest countries in the world. There is no history of terrorism in Greenland, which, if the Greenlandic independence movement grows, shows a difference to all of the aforementioned cases in this chapter, and in this book. In Italy, Veneto is one of the 20 regions of the country. Five of the 20 regions have special autonomy given some form of historical or ethnic distinction, but Veneto does not fall into this category. Yet, a secessionist terror organization has not developed, despite similar historic grievances and political concerns as with other cases in this volume. Veneto, for example, lost its status as an independent kingdom when Napoleon invaded in 1797. Veneto was the only kingdom not to be restored at the end of the Napoleonic Wars in 1815. This situation has caused significant concern, but no terrorist movement developed as a result. Instead, terrorism in Italy tends to fall along more radical lines along the electoral spectrum. The Red Brigades, for example, a radical leftist terrorist organization, was active in the 1970s and 1980s (Duerr 2008). In Flanders, there have been six state reforms since 1970, which have granted the Flemish much greater powers. At the subnational level, there is a powerful parliament that combines the powers of the Flemish Region with the Dutch-speaking Community. (The Walloon Region and Brussels Region also have parliaments, as well as the French-speaking Community and the German-speaking Community). The structure of Belgium's government is convoluted, but serves to pacify differing linguistic and regional differences in an arrangement that, while suboptimal structurally, maintains peaceful relations and strong economic productivity. Although one party that supports Flemish independence, Vlaams Belang, has some historical ties to Germany in World War II, the movement has been peaceful. The other major pro-independence party in Flanders, Nieuw-Vlaamse Alliantie, was founded in 2001, and won the general elections of 2010 and 2014. Never has there been a tie between a Flemish nationalist and a major terrorist attack.

In all six cases, among many others, supporters of secession have presented the case for independence without major terrorist activities. In three cases—Quebec, Scotland, and Catalonia—some terrorist activities occurred, but each group was delegitimized. Moreover, the secessionists used legitimate political means through which to lobby for independence. Both Quebec and Scotland have held legal referendums to decide the constitutional status of each region. In Catalonia, the secessionist groups and parties have been blocked from hosting a formal referendum on independence. In the other three cases—Greenland, Veneto, and Flanders—each region has been granted greater autonomy from the center. None of the regions has hosted an independence referendum, but all three regions have been governed by parties and leaders seeking independence.

ISIS/ISISL/Islamic State/Da-esh

Islamic State and its atrocious terrorist attacks on Europe provides another element to the discussion on secessionism and terrorism. Although ISIS has been largely defeated, the goal of ISIS was to seek a state in the Middle Eastern countries of Syria and Iraq, which would provide the starting point of their end goal of a caliphate. In theory, the end goal of ISIS is to take as much territory as possible, which could impede on the sovereignty of countries in Europe.

At the outset, it should be noted that ISIS has killed the greatest number of people in countries like Syria and Iraq. In addition, ISIS has also conducted frequent attacks in Egypt, Libya, Yemen, Turkey, and Pakistan with death tolls above anything in the European and Eurasian theatres. More specific to this project, ISIS, or ISIS-inspired terrorists have attacked Turkey and France with the greatest frequency. Other European countries such as Belgium and Germany are targeted with some frequency. Additionally, Denmark, the UK, Canada, Spain, and Russia have also been attacked by ISIS, or ISIS-inspired fighters, leading to casualties (Lister 2017).

Terrorists belonging to ISIS, or through ISIS-inspiration, have been responsible for a number of large-scale attacks in Europe. Causing the most carnage, the Paris, France attacks of November 2015 wherein 130 victims lost their lives. Attacks across the city increased the death toll as the Bataclan nightclub was attacked, outside the Stade de France, and several restaurants in the city. This attack was coordinated by nine different attackers who committed various types of attacks at points across the city.

Another large-scale attack on Brussels in Belgium in March 2016 carried out by ISIS killed 32 victims. The first bomb detonated at the airport in the northeastern edge of Brussels at the departure lounge. It was the most deadly component of the overall attack killing 32 people. A second bomb detonated at the Maelbeek metro station, in close proximity to the European Commission, and other EU buildings in the city.

Using the tactic of driving a lorry/18-wheel truck into a crowd, the Nice attack in southern France on Bastille Day in 2016 claimed over 80 lives. This tactic was then replicated in Berlin, Germany in the lead up to Christmas 2016, and then again on two occasions in London, UK along Westminster Bridge and London Bridge. The city of Barcelona in Spain was the next target with a truck attack on Las Ramblas through the heart of the city.

Although categorically different from the other cases studied in this volume, the case of ISIS still links terrorism and secessionism. If ISIS should gain a foothold in other parts of the world, it is theoretically possible for ISIS to expand its territory—at least, obtaining more territory is a stated goal. Coupled with the number of foreign fighters that traveled from their homes in Europe to Syria and Iraq, in some countries there are hundreds, and sometimes a few thousand ISIS fighters. This makes it at least plausible that ISIS would have some larger goal of obtaining territory in Europe. In replicating the historic caliphate, part of that territory once encompassed southern Spain, and swaths of Central and Eastern Europe all the way to the "gates of Vienna."

At the time of writing, ISIS is severely weakened in 2017, compared with its full extent in 2015 and 2016 in Syria and Iraq, and thus the likelihood of ISIS becoming a recognized state is quite low. Nonetheless, the development of a rogue "state-like entity" in Syria and Iraq threatened to occupy more territory, and possibly in other countries. Counterterrorism, in the case of ISIS looks different from the other cases because war can be taken to ISIS in Syria and Iraq. Any European country can, under the purview of the North Atlantic Treaty Organization, take the war to ISIS in the Middle East. Yet, in the greater context of a discussion on secessionist terrorism, ISIS actually fits the model. The situation is different, but ISIS sought territory in Europe through violent means. The response from NATO countries in fighting ISIS has been apt. There are dangers to losing sovereign territory if a jihadist attack is not adequately confronted. Although secession was not an obvious goal of ISIS, the desire to take and possess territory in Europe was a possible end goal as a result of the major terrorist attacks in Paris, Brussels, London, and Berlin, among other targets.

Conclusions: what are the linkages between secessionism and terrorism?

Compared with the other cases, the FLQ in Quebec, SNLA in Scotland, and TL in Catalonia all started with the same raison d'être as the groups discussed earlier in this volume. However, each organization dissipated fairly quickly by comparison. This difference presents a range of different questions. First, the death toll committed by the three organizations in Quebec, Scotland, and Catalonia is comparatively very low. Moreover, when the terrorist organizations actually killed people, any lingering public support seemed to dissipate and the groups disbanded. This point does not in any way excuse these terrorist organizations; killing innocent civilians is never tolerable. In general, the terrorist tactics used by all three organizations involved small-scale bombings including damage of property, but even this act rightly brings forth the label, terrorist, if the aforementioned definition fits.

Second, support for independence has remained very high in all three cases. In many respects, support for independence grew once each group disbanded. The linkage of the secessionist movement to terrorism seems to have had an adverse effect on the moderate center of the population in each case. Support for independence grew to a high point in Quebec in the 1980s and 1990s, in Scotland in the late 2000s and 2010s, and in Catalonia in the same late 2000s to 2010s. Independence referendums in Quebec and Scotland garnered over 40 percent of the vote on all occasions; Catalonia, should it be allowed to hold a formal vote would likely garner similar results. Tangentially, the Canadian and British examples have allowed for a "safety valve" in the sense that citizens in Quebec and Scotland have been allowed to vote on the issue of independence. The other cases in the rest of the volume have enjoyed no such liberties. Obviously, the divisibility of a given country should be based on whether it is internally acceptable, but, if the federal system is disingenuous, citizens who feel disenfranchised often rebel.

Throughout this volume, political violence resulted from perceived repression of culture, language, and/or religion. Terrorism becomes a major guerilla warfare-type tactic as a means of the asymmetric power situation that exists. Thus, terrorism almost becomes a default position for those that engage in political violence. Yet, given the cases in this chapter, terrorism is clearly not a natural position. Some subnational units engage in peaceful political actions as a means of asserting demands for greater autonomy, and possibly, independence. The cases of Greenland, Veneto, and Flanders all highlight that secessionist aspirations do not need a violent reaction through a terrorist attack. The other regions covered at length in this chapter, Quebec, Scotland, and Catalonia, all witnessed a small number of citizens engage in terrorist actions, then disband quickly once a fatality occurred.

References

Bassa, David, and Arnau Gonzàlez i Vilalta. *Terra Lliure, punt final*. Barcelona: Ara Llibres, 2007.

Behiels, Michael D. *Prelude to Quebec's Quiet Revolution: Liberalism vs Neo-Nationalism, 1945–60*. Montreal, QC: McGill-Queen's University Press, 1985.

Bird, Richard M., Francois Villancourt, and Édison Roy-César. "Is Decentralization 'Glue' or 'Solvent' for National Unity?" International Center for Public Policy Working Paper Series. Paper 103. http://scholarworks.gsu.edu/icepp/103, 2010.

Charters, David A. "The amateur revolutionaries: a reassessment of the FLQ." *Terrorism and Political Violence* 9, no. 1 (1997): 133–169.

Chilton, Lisa. "Canada and the British Empire: a review essay." *Canadian Historical Review* 89, no. 1 (2008): 89–95.

Crelinsten, Ronald D. "The internal dynamics of the FLQ during the October Crisis of 1970." *The Journal of Strategic Studies* 10, no. 4 (1987): 59–89.

Duerr, Glen. "Away from Mass Protest in Italy: Moderating the Protest Culture through the European Union and Autonomy Seeking Movements," *Carte Italiane* 4 (2008): 156–170.

Duerr, Glen. *Talking with Nationalists and Patriots: An Examination of Ethnic and Civic Approaches to Nationalism and their Outcomes in Quebec and Flanders*. Kent State University, Ph.D. dissertation, 2012.

Duerr, Glen. *Secessionism and the European Union: The Future of Flanders, Scotland, and Catalonia*. Lanham, MD: Lexington Books, 2015.

Duerr, Glen. "Independence through terrorism? The linkages between secessionism and terrorism in the Basque Country," in Romaniuk, S.N., Grice, F., Irrera, D., Webb, S. (Eds.) *The Palgrave Handbook of Global Counterterrorism Policy*. New York: Palgrave Macmillan, 2017, chapter 20.

Global Terrorism Database. Accessed on March 2, 2017.

Greer, Scott L. *Nationalism and self-government: the politics of autonomy in Scotland and Catalonia*. Albany, NY: SUNY Press, 2012.

Guibernau, Montserrat. *Catalan nationalism: Francoism, transition and democracy*. New York: Routledge, 2004.

Hébert, Chantal, and Jean Lapierre. *The Morning After/Le Matin Suivant: The 1995 Quebec Referendum and the Day that Almost was*. Toronto: Vintage Canada, 2015.

Ignatieff, Michael. *Blood and belonging: Journeys into the new nationalism*. Toronto: Penguin, 1993.

Jolly, Seth Kincaid. *The European Union and the rise of regionalist parties*. Ann Arbor: University of Michigan Press, 2015.

Keating, Michael. *Nations against the state: the new politics of nationalism in Quebec, Catalonia and Scotland*. New York: Springer, 1996.

Lister, Tim, Sanchez, Ray, Bixler, Mark, O'Key, Sean, Hogenmiller, Michael, and Tawfeeq, Mohammed. "ISIS goes global: 143 attacks in 29 countries have killed 2,043" CNN. February 13, 2017. Accessed on March 3, 2017. www.cnn.com/2015/12/17/world/mapping-isis-attacks-around-the-world/index.html

Loukacheva, Natalia. *The Arctic promise: legal and political autonomy of Greenland and Nunavut*. Toronto: University of Toronto Press, 2007.

McCrone, Gavin, and Magnus Linklater. *Scottish Independence: weighing up the economics*. Edinburgh: Birlinn, 2013.

McRoberts, Kenneth. *Catalonia: Nation building without a state*. Don Mills, ON: Oxford University Press Canada, 2001.

O'Sullivan-See, Katherine. *First World Nationalisms: Class and Ethnic Politics in Northern Ireland and Quebec*. Chicago: University of Chicago Press, 1986.

"Politicians on alert over mail scare" March 2, 2002. Accessed on October 22, 2017. http://news.bbc.co.uk/2/hi/uk_news/1850111.stm

Richler, Mordecai. *Oh Canada! Oh Quebec!: requiem for a divided country*. Toronto: Penguin Books, 1992.

Saywell, John T. *The rise of the Parti québécois, 1967–1976*. Toronto: University of Toronto Press, 1977.

Taras, Ray. *Liberal and illiberal nationalisms*. New York: Palgrave Macmillan, 2002.

Terrorism Resource & Analysis Consortium. Accessed on March 12, 2017. www.trackingterrorism.org/

9 Conclusion

Bombs, blood, and independence in Europe and Eurasia

Glen M.E. Duerr

Ethno-nationalist, or secessionist terrorism, remains a pertinent subject in counterterrorist activities and plans in Europe and Eurasia. The chapters in this volume highlight the challenge for counterterrorism in these regions of the world. Important lessons can be gleaned from victories, especially the Spanish government over ETA, as well as the British government in its actions against the IRA. Although it could reverse, the ETA ceasefire of 2011 is now a full disarmament wherein the terrorist organization has formally disbanded. The 1998 Good Friday Agreement also helped to mollify the attacks of the IRA and bring a greater sense of peace to Northern Ireland. Although imperfect, Northern Ireland is much more peaceful now than it was from the 1960s through the 1990s. In Corsica and Brittany, secessionist agitation has transitioned to the ballot box. In Kosovo, the situation is still unclear, but the region is at peace. Chechnya is also at peace, but the conflict has seemingly moved to Syria; a change in the status quo of governance in Russia or the region, will likely witness a flare-up in terrorist violence. Finally, in Turkey, the Kurdish question is still far from resolved. Like Russia, any change to the governing status quo will likely lead to another outbreak of violence.

The comparison of these cases raises two important, academic questions: What are the connections and linkages between secessionism and terrorism? How can governments best employ counterterrorism measures through policing and military measures, but also through policy changes? Throughout this volume, answers have been provided across the different situations. There is no singular best example, but there are areas of success and failure. Time is a key variable as well, because, as recalcitrant as the responses in Turkey and Russia have been from a human rights standpoint, supporters of Erdoğan and Putin will argue that their methods justified the peace that they now enjoy.

The rest of this chapter will discuss situation updates in all of the cases. Changes to political structures is another key area because, as a conclusion, this is a pivotal area where governments can make changes to reduce the likelihood of terrorism, but also the seeds through which terrorism ferments. Following the seven components of each chapter, a brief summary is provided. Next, five "core lessons," or highlights of this volume are provided as a means to help counterterrorist agencies and governments consider options to best deter terrorism. A table of comparison is provided with key variables across the cases. This provides a visual mechanism to see the differences between different countries in Europe and Eurasia. Finally, concluding points are discussed at the end of this volume.

Situation updates

In Northern Ireland, a small British province in the northeast of the island of Ireland, political contention remains. However, recent changes by the British government to allow for devolved power have helped greatly in reducing terrorism in the country. If peace is the most important metric, the governments of the UK, Northern Ireland, and the Republic of Ireland have all worked to mollify the violence in the region. In the Basque Country of Spain in the northern section of the country (which overlaps into the southwest of France), advance autonomy has been provided by the Spanish government as a key variable to deterring terrorism. The Basque Country is recognized as a historic nation within Spain, and greater devolution has been granted in this case. In fact, the Basques have been provided with special autonomy on fiscal issues, which is not even in other ACs such as Catalonia and Galicia. With peace as a major metric, this case has been successful. In Brittany, a northwestern region of France, the French government remains steadfast in promoting unitarism. Terrorism has been stifled, but the Breton language and culture have been limited, leaving open some wounds of the past. In Corsica, a French island in the Mediterranean Sea, these open wounds have begun to fester in the form of increased secessionist intensity. There are also cases where the Corsicans diverge from the rest of mainland France, which might cause challenges for the central state in the forthcoming years. For counterterrorism, the French government succeeded a long time ago. The seeds of terrorism remain, however, in Brittany with the decrease of the language and culture. In Corsica, the situation is different in that there are more institutional protections, but the unitarism of France is still dominant. In Kosovo, the status of the contested state remains a challenge for the international community. The KLA, which effectively became the Kosovar government, is now a stable actor in the international community, but not a recognized member of the UN or the EU. Serbia does not want to formally cede territory, although, some form of membership agreement with the EU might be the key to resolving the issue in the long term. The danger for the EU in not getting involved is that the underlying frictions behind the Yugoslav wars of the 1990s are not yet solved. In Turkey, increased authoritarianism under President Erdoğan is cause for concern. Turkey was a vibrant case of democracy for many decades, and a foil in the argument against western societies being most suited to democracy. Today, this is much less obvious. Violence in the eastern Kurdistan region of Turkey has waned, but the repression of the Kurds will likely cause some form of reaction in the future, which could be violent. The PKK has opted to work through existing state structures, but offshoot terrorist groups like the TAK have continued to opt for violent means. In Russia, the situation is similar to Turkey, but to a more severe degree. Under President Putin, Russia is now authoritarian again, unlike the hints of fully fledged democracy in the 1990s. Chechnya, an ethnic republic in the southwest of the country, is the site of recent civil conflicts in the 1990s and 2000s, which were started as a means of deterring terrorism (Rukhadze and Duerr 2016). The current structure, an agreement between Putin and regional governor Kadyrov, has maintained peaceful relations, but at a cost. Chechnya has, by many accounts, been rebuilt after suffering severe damage in the civil wars. Yet, separatists in Chechnya have taken the conflict to Syria, wherein the Russian government has sent forces to fight over the future of Bashar al-Assad's authoritarian government in Damascus. The seeds for terrorism remain, and could come back forcefully, especially when the presidency of Putin ends. The Russian born, American journalist, Masha Geseen, for example, argues that Russia "is not going to stay within its current borders. There is going to be some kind of redrawing of the federation" (*Time* 2017, 60). Geseen continues,

> Since Putin does not think he is going to die, there is not going to be any succession plan in place when he dies. And there is going to be a period of disarray and uncertainty. That will be the perfect opening for the final breakup of the empire.
>
> (*Time* 2017, 60)

Of course, this is the opinion of one person, but Chechnya will likely be the first place to revolt if there is a post-Putin insurrection.

Political structures

State structures also changed over time. In the UK, devolution formally occurring in 1999 changed the fabric of the society in a sense. Spain's adoption of democracy in 1978, as well as the creation of autonomous communities with some subnational powers, provided some level of subnational outlet. In France, the archetypal unitary state, and the administrative restructuring of 2016 have not really challenged the underlying causes of terrorism; however, Corsica retains a mechanism for subnational cultural autonomy because of its unique situation as an island with some institutional protections. The 2016 changes reduced the number of regions from 27 down to 18 (in both cases, five of which include overseas departments). Thus, France moved from 22 to 13 regions within the French mainland. In sum, France, historically, attempted to shed all subnational units of overt signs of difference—assimilation was the main tactic of the central government to impose Parisian French as the lingua franca of the territory and strong, centralized government from the capital city. Corsica seems to be the one exception as it remains untouched from the regional reshuffling. In Kosovo, the KLA now runs the country in a way that runs counter to the other cases in this volume. Kosovo is small so subnational units play a role mainly in the administration of the contested country; Pristina is the capital of the Kosovar unitary state. In Turkey, the government remains a unitary state, but given the size of territory some level of autonomy was provided to its provinces—in the aftermath of the 2016 coup attempt, the Erdoğan government seems much more reluctant to decrease its hold on power. Turkey's 81 regions are all relatively small, and divided in such a way as to limit any possible concentration of power for a viable secessionist movement involving the Kurds in the east of the country. In Russia, the federal asymmetric structure assigns republic status to Chechnya giving the region, on paper, measures of power. In reality, the Ramzan Kadyrov government is very closely tied to Putin revealing a warlord-type structure rather than true federalism, especially compared with advanced democratic states such as Canada, the United States, or Germany.

Recapping the seven components of each chapter

As noted in the introduction, each chapter encompassed seven parts. Given that different authors, with varying perspectives, wrote the different chapters, there are some stylistic and ideological differences; however, each author: (1) presented a general overview of the case, (2) provided a history of political grievances in the specific region as to why a secessionist movement exists including theoretical dimensions to the discussion, (3) presented a rebuttal from the viewpoint of the government; again, including theoretical dimensions, (4) provided an overview of major terrorist attacks carried out by the terrorist organization being studied, (5) explained how the government responded to these terrorist attacks, (6) described any changes that occurred with regards to the structure of the state, or any government agencies, as a means of undercutting support for secessionism, or the terrorist organization, and (7) purported conclusions.

Across the various cases, the general overview of each case, of course, gleans a range of differences. Countries such as the UK and France are mature democracies, whereas Turkey and Russia have become much more authoritarian under their respective leaders. While the differences are stark, each country has significant ethnic and regional cleavages within their respective societies.

Political grievances differ across the cases, but most revolve around language, culture, and rights from the central government, usually desired in the form of greater autonomy. There is a history of independence, or at least some level of autonomy, wherein the group in question looks back with some degree of nostalgia—whether real or imagined—for a past that provided a better situation than the present one.

Governmental rebuttals differ across the cases as different strategies have been used by these governments. In Chechnya, for example, the harsh clampdowns on separatist terrorism by the Russian government, over which two civil wars were fought, shows how a very strong response can use the military while others increase policing and other forms of state institutions to lessen the severity of terrorist actions. Chechnya also used "Ramzanization," to quote Liam Anderson in Chapter 7, as a mechanism of cauterizing dissent from the republic.

Major terrorist attacks have occurred in all of the cases studies. On the one hand, terrorism has killed a large number of people in Europe and Eurasia. Terrorism, however, has typically been more limited with cruder weapons used in four of the cases. For example, 9/11 alone killed more people than most IRA, ETA, Breton, and Corsican terrorists even over the course of decades. The case of the KLA is sui generis in many senses in that it is different from virtually every other example in the world because the group was framed as a terrorist organization by the Serb government; in reality, the KLA was as much a standing army as a terrorist group committing sporadic attacks against an enemy. The PKK/TAK in Turkey have caused significant violence, leading to far more deaths, overall, than 9/11. Violence has been widespread. In Russia, IK was responsible for hundreds of deaths, but, again, the case has its idiosyncrasies. The outbreak of two civil wars over this case presents a very different outcome to terrorism.

Government responses to terrorist attacks have been mixed. In some cases, vociferous counterterrorism changes have been made as a means of trying to form a comprehensive strategy. In other cases, police at the national, subnational, and local levels have all been granted wider purview to mollify terrorist actions. In all cases, the governments and police forces mobilized as a means to limit the violence.

As noted earlier in this chapter, political and institutional changes have been key in numerous cases. This point will be discussed further later in this chapter, but the key hinges around devolving power to subnational units. A federal structure of government, which actually provides power to subnational regions, may be the biggest key in not only decreasing violent terrorist attacks in democratic countries, but also in decreasing the conditions for terrorism by protecting language and culture. Questions remain in the literature over whether providing federalism facilitates secessionism, or merely provides enough rights to mollify the concerns of subnational groups.

Conclusions across each chapter differ, but the advance idea is to deter terrorism while simultaneously upholding human rights and undercutting the seeds of violence retaliations. In the UK, Spain, and France, democratic ideals have been maintained in the refutation of terrorism. Kosovo is not considered a democracy by various sources (Freedom House 2017), but nor is the country mired in authoritarianism. Both Turkey and Russia have changed under their respective leaders, and human rights have been eroded in exchange for peace.

Core lessons

In terms of overarching conclusions, the seven cases glean the following core lessons listed below. Creating any form of list with a number is difficult because it raises as many questions as it answers. However, over the course of this volume there are conclusions that can help to decrease terrorist attacks in a variety of situations. Scholars, students, and policymakers can take or leave any of the core lessons as it suits their own work—whether in the field or in research. Nevertheless, each of the core lessons provides insights as to what can be attempted as a means of producing effective counterterrorism.

Terrorist organizations can be defeated in the long term

In the short term, terrorism can have many brutal effects on a society. Most of these terrorist organizations emerged in the 1960s, and waged a campaign of violence lasting through the 1990s. Most noteworthy, however, is that several of these groups have disbanded, including the PIRA, which announced a ceasefire ahead of the Good Friday Agreement in 1997. ETA indicated its fourth (and last) ceasefire in 2010, before formally disarming in April 2017. The FLNC announced a ceasefire in 2014, and repeated the claim in 2016. As noted earlier, the KLA now forms much of the government in Kosovo—the group ended its militaristic element in 1999 at the end of the conflict with Serbia. The PKK, like some other terrorist groups, had previously announced a cessation of hostilities; the most recent example is from July 2015, which was promptly renounced in August 2015. As of late 2016, many supporters of IK have switched their allegiance to ISIS. The threat from IK is not over, but the conflict has seemingly morphed to Syria, and could return to Chechnya with the seemingly imminent defeat of ISIS in the Middle East.

In her 2006 book, *How al-Qaida ends*, scholar Audrey Cronin lists seven core components necessary for the cessation of a terrorist group. Cronin notes: (a) the death of the leader, (b) no succession of leadership, (c) fulfillment of aims, (d) entering into a formal political process, (e) division of the group leading to a loss of support, (f) military repression, and (g) transitioning to other forms of violence. In all of the above cases, all of which disbanded or morphed after the publication of Cronin's book, point (d) in particular—entering into a formal political process—is a key ingredient. For counterterrorist agencies and operations, the defeat of a terrorist organization is an exciting prospect. It is hard in a modern democracy to wait, especially if human rights are a goal within which the society aspires. However, terrorism can end through a formal peaceful process with enough patience. Cronin is also correct in point (f)—military repression—but the cases of the PKK and TKK in Turkish Kurdistan, as well as IK in Chechnya, could yet morph into something new, and further contest these regions.

Spillover effect?

As many of these terrorist organizations started at similar times in the 1970s, the idea of a contagion effect is an intriguing one. For example, as one group is "successful" in fighting the state, terrorist groups in other regions start similar struggles against their own governments. The idea of contagion is difficult to definitively prove, but many of these groups started at around the same time. Very few terrorist organizations started in recent years, especially post-9/11 when the view of terrorism, writ large, changed from a mix of views (the axiom of one person's terrorist is another person's freedom fighter) to widespread disdain (Pokalova 2011). However, part of the purpose of Chapter 8 is to show how secessionist terrorism may be prevalent in some cases, limited in others, and non-existent in the rest of the cases. This is a puzzle for scholars. Another puzzle is learning how terrorism may spread from one region to another—to see if a contagion effect exists? From small pieces of evidence compiled in this volume, it appears that many of the terrorist organizations started, (a) at similar periods of time, (b) with similar goals, and (c) with similar ideological factors in the background.

Political autonomy can help

As noted earlier, federalism, or devolution of power, is a potential mechanism to reduce the seeds of terrorism as many of the grievances hinge on linguistic and cultural protections. Although the academic literature is divided on the question of whether or not to provide autonomy for minority groups, given the danger of secession (Bird and Vaillancourt 2010), these cases suggest that terrorist attacks can decrease if autonomy is sensibly provided.

The decline of the SNLA and the PIRA came at a time when power was devolved to the subnational units of the UK. Initiating the Good Friday Agreement in tandem with a new parliament for Scotland, and assemblies with Wales and Northern Ireland, helped sow the seeds of peace. Obviously, the KLA disbanded formally when the war ended with Serbia, but so did claims of terrorism from Belgrade.

Other federal states in Europe and Eurasia such as Belgium, Switzerland, Austria, Germany, and Bosnia-Herzegovina, have not witnessed ethno-nationalist terrorist attacks. In the case of Quebec in Canada in Chapter 8, the FLQ lasted for a relatively short period of time. Russia is a federal state, but is not a democracy. Thus, with a qualifier of democracy, federal states do not have incidents of terrorism. Other countries with some significant devolution, but falling short of federalism, such as the UK, Italy, and Spain, have all overcome terrorist attacks. Chapters 2 and 3 in this volume show how the PIRA and ETA were ultimately defeated, especially with the incentive of peaceful political processes. In Italy, terrorist organizations like the Red Brigades—aligned more with ideology than ethno-nationalism as their central reasoning for carrying out terrorist attacks—ultimately declined as well.

Policing versus the military

Across the different cases, some governments opted to utilize the military as a component of counterterrorism. As noted in the above prompt, several governments opted to only use the police force as a means of achieving several aims. This distinction is an interesting one given that they account for different approaches to counterterrorism.

In Russia, for example, two civil wars were fought as a means of decreasing the terrorist threat from Chechnya. This constituted a serious escalation of terrorism to civil war. In Kosovo, the KLA was viewed by the Yugoslav government under Serb control as a terrorist organization—the start of the conflict also started a serious conflagration of the conflict. As Pokalova notes in Chapter 5,

"The KLA emerged from the conflict victorious. Domestically, it was celebrated as a heroic armed force. Internationally, it was legitimized as an official party to the conflict and a NATO ally." Finally, in Turkey, a military solution has also been deployed in an attempt to fully occupy the majority Kurdish southeastern portion of the country. This conflict was not as in-depth as those in Russia and Kosovo, but still constitutes a response beyond policing.

In all of the other cases, the police force has been used as the main mechanism of countering terrorism (Duerr 2017). Overall, this seems like the most commensurate use of force, one that slowly deters terrorism in tandem with other factors, over time. The number of terrorist fatalities in Turkey and Russia is in the thousands and higher than in cases in Western Europe, but the low-intensity conflict in Turkey, and the fully fledged civil wars of Russia seem to have produced changes in the short term. Of course, leadership in Ankara and Moscow heard from citizens who were deeply upset with high levels of terrorism. The question into the future is whether the hard approach—initiating conflict—will work? At the very least, the seeds of terrorism remain active in both cases, even if these situations have been pacified for the present.

Marxism/class-based discussions

In many cases, there is some form of economic grievance, which more naturally dovetails to some form of leftist or Marxist critique of the status quo. In these instances, the cases are tied to Marxist thought as an overarching reason for terrorism. Marx encouraged revolutionary actions to cause a change in governance, so the connection here should not come as a surprise. Of course, in other cases, some groups opted for leftist, but peaceful mechanisms to attain their goal of independence.

Economic grievances are purported, often in tandem with linguistic and cultural grievances, but the latter causes are subservient to the former in the view of the terrorist organization. Marxism was more popular, especially in the 1970s, suggesting links that were more apropos with the time. Contemporary links with Marxism among terrorist groups are more difficult to find, but economic grievances remain to some degree. However, many of these class-based grievances have decreased over time, partly as a result of increased economic activity across the EU. There are still disparities in wealth across regions, but much of Europe is wealthier than it was a generation ago. Marxist arguments have a hard time in this situation. Post-2008 economic recession, class-based arguments have made a comeback, but mainly in countries with severe recessions and unemployment. Yet, no recent terrorist organizations have formed with a Marx-based argument.

The next section of this chapter further investigates the cross-national approach in this volume. Table 9.1 presents a holistic comparison.

There are numerous different indicators from which a comparison can be drawn. The 10 categories listed in Table 9.1 reveal some distinctions between the cases. The first three—ideology, religion, and language—are key pillars in the existence of each movement. As noted in the previous section, Marxist-based

Table 9.1 Comparison of cases

	Northern Ireland	*Basque Country*	*Brittany and Corsica*	*Kosovo*	*Kurdistan*	*Chechnya*
Ideology	Minor	Minor	Yes	No	Yes	Islamist
Religion	Yes	No	No	Yes	No	Yes
Language	No	Yes	Yes	Yes	Yes	Yes
Government representation	Devolved power in an assembly	Autonomous community with some fiscal powers	No	N/A	NUTS	Ethnic republic
Mature democracy	Yes	Yes	Yes	No	No, recent authoritarian changes	No, recent authoritarian changes
Police/military	Both, mainly police	Police	Police	Military	Both	Military
Legislative changes	Yes	Yes	No	N/A	No	No
International involvement	Yes	Yes, Spain and France	No	Yes	No	No
U.S. involvement	Yes, mediation	No	No	Yes, NATO military action	No	No
Terrorist attacks ended	Yes	Yes	Yes	Yes	No, TAK	No, Syria

arguments are present in a number of cases. In Northern Ireland and the Basque Country, these arguments tended to be subservient to other claims. The Northern Irish case was heavily religious in nature, with some similarities to Kosovo and Chechnya. Both Kosovo and Chechnya are majority Islamic regions within a wider Orthodox Christian state; the Catholic/Protestant sectarian bifurcation remains in Northern Ireland. In the Basque Country, ethnic and linguistic concerns were at the forefront of the contestation. Linguistic concerns were also present in every other case bar Northern Ireland, where English is the most prominent language across the wider region including the UK and the Republic of Ireland.

Point number four on government representation is a discussion of federalism and devolution, points that have been developed elsewhere in this chapter. In particular, this point is further discussed in depth at the end of the chapter. On point number five, mature democracy, the first three cases of the UK, Spain, and France are all considered mature democracies. According to the Polity IV dataset, the UK and Spain were considered to be "full democracies" with a perfect score of 10 in the most recent update, 2013. France, Turkey, and Serbia are listed as "democracies," with a score between six and nine. Russia was listed as an "open anocracy" with a score between one and five (Polity IV). According to Freedom House's 2017 report on democracy, the UK, Spain, and France are all considered to be "free" countries with scores of 95, 94, and 90, respectively. Kosovo has a score of 52 and is considered a "partly free" country. Turkey is also considered a "partly free" country with a score of 38, including major authoritarian backsliding in recent years under President Erdoğan. Russia is considered "not free" with a score of 20 (Freedom House). Authoritarianism has increased significantly according to this metric under President Putin. Thus, the output of secessionist terrorism is different across the cases. Any aspiring new state that opts for violence as a means for gaining independence is unlikely to gain support within the EU, especially if the likelihood of mature democracy is low.

Point six investigates the use of police and/or military as a means of confronting terrorism. As noted earlier, some cases relied heavily on the military. In some cases, the police played the major role combatting terrorism. This was particularly evident in Spain and France where the decision was made not to escalate the conflict. The UK, by contrast, used the military at times to stave off protests, and to stop violence especially at the height of the Troubles. There is no clear conclusion here as to how best to implement counterterrorism practices.

Point seven examines legislative changes as a means of ending the terrorist threat. The big example here is Northern Ireland wherein the Good Friday Agreement dovetailed with devolution for the three major subnational groups of the UK. The Basque Country and Navarre were granted greater fiscal powers in Spain, and this move seems to have paid dividends with a more peaceful outcome. None of the other countries initiated legislative changes, at least in depth.

Points eight and nine examine international involvement, including U.S. involvement. Northern Ireland and Kosovo were both internationalized, and both sought a role from the United States. In Northern Ireland, the main thrust was negotiation. In Chapter 2, the discussion of President Clinton is particularly important in bringing the conflict to an end. From Chapter 5, the U.S. also engaged in military action in Kosovo, through NATO, as a means of ending the aggression of Serbian leader, Slobodan Milošević. Although Clinton was not inclined to get involved militarily in some regions of the world, he acted in Kosovo, helping to bring the conflict to an end. The Basque Country is also listed in the affirmative with international involvement, but this is because the region spans two different countries: Spain and France. Given this distinction, counterterrorist coordination in Madrid and Paris was necessary to help capture ETA operatives. In sum, counterterrorism works best with international cooperation.

Finally, point 10 discusses whether the terrorist group formally ended. This was discussed earlier in the chapter, with some success, especially in Northern Ireland, the Basque Country, Corsica, and Kosovo. All of these regions are much more peaceful now than in previous decades.

Discussion

Overall, secessionist terrorism, or ethno-nationalist terrorism, remains relevant today, and still fits as a category, over two decades Rapoport listed it as one of the three major types of terrorism (Rapoport 2013). Often, secessionist terrorism also has other features, especially an association with Marxist organizations. The good news, though, is that given the cases in this volume, the number of secessionist terrorist groups in Europe and Eurasia has decreased over time, especially since the 1970s and 1980s.

Several factors are responsible for this change. Over the course of time, economic improvements, at least until 2008, made terrorism more costly for all parties involved. "Rising boats" across all parts of Europe and Eurasia is a potential reason why secessionist terrorism has declined. More importantly, however, the likelihood of achieving the maximalist goal of independence is much less likely through violent means. Thus, many secessionist movements are led by political leaders with the inherent desire to achieve independence through the ballot box. In the modern EU, any violent organization is not welcome at the table. Even if a terrorist organization finagled independence, it is highly unlikely that current members of the EU would welcome a new member with a historic association with violent actions.

The lessons drawn in this volume should help to accomplish several outcomes. First, counterterrorist units and agencies across Europe and Eurasia can gain victories over terrorist organizations. Often, it takes considerable time to accomplish the goal. In exchange, however, the most useful outcome is for a genuine form of federalism to be initiated such that the grievances behind terrorism are lessened. Providing cultural and linguistic protections for minority ethnic groups is a useful mechanism to deter violent secessionism. The caveat to this point is that to maintain territorial integrity, a government should simultaneously provide autonomy while making the case that the country can provide for the needs and desires of all people within the state. This is a difficult balance to accomplish. Under the EU, it was assumed that ethno-nationalism, or secessionism, would become an ideology of the past. With high-intensity secessionist movements across the continent, the obituary of secessionist movements was clearly premature. Thus, governments should mobilize to make the case for the continuation. Providing autonomy under a genuine form of federalism is most useful because different peoples can maintain historic languages and cultures even under larger states. In the event that a secessionist movement grows and democratically agitates for a referendum, it should be verified by the state for two main reasons. First, it provides a safety valve against any form of violent terrorism because there is a mechanism to obtain the maximalist goal. Provided that the state is competent and functions well, the majority of people voting in the referendum will likely cast ballots in favor of the status quo. Second, government, especially in mature democratic states in the twenty-first century, should act for the greater good of its people. Where this is violated, people should have the right to self-determination to better hold the government to act on its behalf for good.

The terrorist attacks experienced by my parents in the 1980s and 1990s will hopefully become a thing of the past. Terrorism, however, is a long-standing tactic of weaker groups, especially in cases of relative deprivation—the sense or perception that one region is intentionally weaker, or has been subjugated, by a government, or dominant group. Terrorist attacks in central London were aimed at changing the political status quo, especially over the status of Northern Ireland. The Good Friday Agreement of 1998 has helped immensely in bringing various sides together, and violence has decreased dramatically while also bettering the government for people in Northern Ireland. In some cases, such as Turkey and Russia, there are temporary fixes to widespread terrorism. But, without genuine reform, these fixes only serve as temporary Band-Aids to stop terrorism. Grievances have not yet been solved, and thus the seeds of terrorism remain. Government must better advocate for the good of all people residing within the state.

Terrorist attacks still occur in London as evidenced by the numerous ISIS attacks on Westminster and London bridges during 2017. However, the threat from the IRA or PIRA, or any other splinter group is much less. Thus, life for many young families is more secure given the advances in negotiations to undercut grievances under which terrorism sometimes develops. Moreover, final credit must be given to police and counterterrorism forces that have tirelessly worked to stop attacks. Without diligence and intelligence-sharing, terrorism might still be an ongoing threat in many parts of Europe and Eurasia.

Federalism or devolution as a solution?

In exchange for a peaceable agreement, genuine federal arrangements are the best mechanism of providing lasting peace by enabling protections for minority languages and cultures while simultaneously making the case for the democratic and economic advantages of the status quo. Federalism does not need to occur overnight, some devolved powers are useful. Enforcing assimilation might work in the short term, but it is done with risks.

Unfortunately, none of the cases in this volume constitutes genuine federalism. Spain is the closest with a structure of 17 ACs, all of which have parliamentary assemblies and an elected president. The actual powers granted are quite limited, with the exception of the Basque Country and Navarre that have fairly extensive fiscal autonomy from the central government. The other ACs do not hold major powers in areas related to taxation, which is why Spain is not generally considered a fully federal system compared with some other countries. Moreover, with the recent initiation of Article 155 of the Spanish Constitution to revoke the governing power of the Catalan government in October 2017, any claim on genuine federalism is dubious at best. In the UK, devolved parliaments and assemblies first opened in 1999, have provided extra powers to Scotland, Wales, and Northern Ireland. The Northern Irish Assembly opened in 2006 with a consociational arrangement for including Catholics and Protestants in every government in the province. On paper, Russia is a federal state with elected space for each of its 83 subnational units in the Upper House (in addition, Russia also claims the Ukrainian territories of Crimea and Sevastopol), the Federation Council. In reality, many of the regional governors are now heavily aligned with President Vladimir Putin. Although federally structured, there is no formal power granted to subnational units without the support of United Russia, the ruling party in the country.

In contrast to the states with form of devolution above, the remaining cases all implement a unitary state system with very tight, central control. France is the archetypal case of unitarism wherein the government ostensibly tries to demand Parisian French as the lingua franca, and subservience to the central government. Regions and departments exist in France, but very little power is devolved from the center. In Kosovo, the small de facto state is also a unitary state. The seven districts in Kosovo each hold a degree of institutional power from the central government, but the powers are minimal. In Turkey, the country is divided into 81 regions, which further subdivided into 923 districts. There are further subdivisions in the countries through the EU-inspired Nomenclature of Territorial Units for Statistics (NUTS), system of counting.

In contrast with the "foil" cases in Chapter 8, federalism is used in two of the countries. Canada is a federal state with significant provincial powers to each of the 10 provinces; Quebec is one of the 10 provinces replete with an elected parliament and substantial subnational powers, including taxation. Belgium is now a federal state after undergoing six state reforms since 1970, which have created a structure of three regions and three communities in the country. Between the regional and community governments, there are significant subnational devolved powers to the point where some scholars debate as to whether the country now follows a confederal model. The final case, Spain, as mentioned above is not considered a fully fledged federal state, but some powers are devolved to the 17 ACs including Catalonia. This case is murkier now that Article 155 has been invoked; the central government in Spain called for new Catalan elections, and detained some of the democratically elected leaders.

In all of the foil cases, however, terrorism has been formally deterred by significant work by police and counterterrorism units. These cases in the UK and Canada have been successful in deterring terrorism; Spain, with some devolved powers, has also gained victory over deterring terrorist organizations in the country. Federalism is a helpful mechanism in reducing the likelihood of terrorism, especially in mature, democratic states. Although there is no statistically significant evidence, because of the limited number of cases, terrorism is more likely in unitary states than federal states. Overall, federal states such as Russia, Nigeria, and Iraq are not immune from terrorism, but countries such as the USA, Germany, and Canada, among others do not have ethno-nationalist terrorism. The challenge, however, is that the academic literature is mixed on whether devolving power facilitates or deters secessionism (Bird and Vaillancourt 2010). If a government seeks to maintain territorial integrity and deter terrorism, there are no guarantees. However, at least at the present, methodical devolutions of power can deter terrorism, while relieving the seeds of ethno-nationalist terrorism. The only question is whether these countries will hold together?

Conclusions

Across several cases in Europe and Eurasia, this volume has gleaned a lot more information and cross-national comparison on ethno-nationalist terrorism. Five core lessons are conclusions from the volume. Yet, interesting questions remain, especially on issues related to devolution. Devolving power as well as protecting cultural and linguistic minorities facilitate the end of ethno-nationalist terrorism, especially in mature, democratic countries.

Future scholars should follow up on this study by systematically investigating cases of ethno-nationalist terrorism outside of Europe and Eurasia. These studies will better provide answers on other questions related to terrorism versus more prolonged forms of violence such as civil wars. Terrorism, as discussed in the introduction, is often based on asymmetries in power; civil wars develop when a group, or multiple groups, opposed to the government feel that they have an ability to win a conflict, rather than resort to terrorist tactics. As Elena Pokalova has persuasively shown, 9/11 changed the discussion surrounding terrorism making it far less romantic as a means of national sovereignty, and much more brutal based on the widespread killing of innocent civilians. Nonetheless, terrorism remains as a tactic used by weaker groups, and will likely be used in the future. Terrorism can be deterred, and even defeated, though, but the underlying point is that policing, counterterrorism units, and multiple levels of government must all work in tandem; their maximalist goals of peace and stability can be accomplished with coordination and a lot of patience.

References

Bird, Richard, and François Vaillancourt. "Is Decentralization 'Glue' or 'Solvent' Is Decentralization Glue or Solvent for National Unity?" *Andrew Young School of Public Policy, International Studies Working Paper, Georgia State University,* 10–03 (2010): 1–41.

Cronin, Audrey Kurth. "How al-Qaida ends: The decline and demise of terrorist groups." *International Security* 31, no. 1 (2006): 7–48.

Duerr, Glen. "Independence through terrorism? The linkages between secessionism and terrorism in the Basque Country," in, Romaniuk, S.N., Grice, F., Irrera, D., Webb, S. (Eds.) *The Palgrave Handbook of Global Counterterrorism Policy*, chapter 20. New York: Palgrave Macmillan, 2017.

Freedom House. "Freedom in the World 2017" Accessed on October 25, 2017.

Polity IV dataset. Accessed on October 25, 2017.

Pokalova, Elena. *Shifting faces of terror after 9/11: Framing the terrorist threat.* Kent, Ohio: Kent State University dissertation, 2011.

Rapoport, D.C. "The four waves of modern terrorism" In Horgan, J.G. and Braddock, K. (eds.) *Terrorism Studies*, pp. 63–82. London: Routledge, 2013.

Rukhadze, Vasili, and Glen Duerr. "Sovereignty Issues in the Caucasus: Contested Ethnic and National Identities in Chechnya, Abkhazia, and South Ossetia" *Sprawe Narodowsciowe (Issues of Nationality)*, 48 (2016): 30–47.

Time. "9 Questions with Masha Gessen" October 30, 2017.

Index

Page numbers in **bold** denote tables.